Best of
Thirukkural

R. Poornalingam is a former Indian Administrative Service officer. He held many important positions both in the central and state governments. Post retirement, he is working as a consultant in the health sector for international organizations such as World Bank and UNICEF, to advise governments on improving their public procurement systems. He was also on the board of a few public limited companies.

Best of
Thirukkural

Wisdom to Enrich
Yourself and Humanity

R. POORNALINGAM

Foreword by
Gopalkrishna Gandhi

Published by
Rupa Publications India Pvt. Ltd 2025
7/16, Ansari Road, Daryaganj
New Delhi 110002

Sales centres:
Bengaluru Chennai
Hyderabad Jaipur Kathmandu
Kolkata Mumbai Prayagraj

Copyright © R. Poornalingam 2025

The views and opinions expressed in this book are the author's own and the facts are as reported by him which have been verified to the extent possible, and the publishers are not in any way liable for the same.

All rights reserved.
No part of this publication may be reproduced, transmitted,
or stored in a retrieval system, in any form or by any means, electronic,
mechanical, photocopying, recording or otherwise,
without the prior permission of the publisher.

P-ISBN: 978-93-6156-928-9
E-ISBN: 978-93-6156-419-2

First impression 2025

10 9 8 7 6 5 4 3 2 1

The moral right of the author has been asserted.

This book is sold subject to the condition that it shall not, by way of trade or otherwise, be lent, resold, hired out, or otherwise circulated, without the publisher's prior consent, in any form of binding or cover other than that in which it is published.

Contents

Foreword: Gopalkrishna Gandhi	ix
Preface	xi
Introduction	xv

Porul

1.	Qualities Expected of a Leader	3
2.	Financial Management	7
3.	Listening to Criticism	11
4.	Aim of Education	14
5.	Illiterates are Useless	17
6.	Treasure of Listening	20
7.	What is True Wisdom?	23
8.	Faults to Be Avoided by a Leader	27
9.	Guarding against the Unknown	31
10.	Seek Advice of the Wise	35
11.	Avoiding Unsuitable Company	38
12.	Importance of Planning	41
13.	Knowing One's Strength	45
14.	Waiting for an Opportune Time	49
15.	Assessment of a Person	52
16.	Delegation	55
17.	Commitment to Duty	59
18.	Just Governance	62
19.	Result of Bad Governance	65
20.	Govern with a Soft Touch	68
21.	Verifying Information	72
22.	Greatness of Human Zeal	75
23.	Zeal Essential to Growth	78
24.	Avoid Laziness	80
25.	Fruits of Perseverance	83

26.	Handling Tragedies and Obstacles	87
27.	Duties of Ministers	90
28.	Power of Cogent Speech	93
29.	Purity of Action	96
30.	Firm Mind	99
31.	Avoid Haste	104
32.	Task Completion	107
33.	How to Move with a Ruler	111
34.	Mind Reading	114
35.	Speak to Suit the Audience	117
36.	Avoiding Stage Fear	120
37.	Great Country	123
38.	Gems of a Good Country	126
39.	Power of Wealth	130
40.	Just and Fair Earning	133
41.	Pride of the Army	135
42.	Duty of True Friends	138
43.	Selecting a Good Friend	141
44.	Long-Standing Friends	144
45.	Avoid Evil Friends	146
46.	Avoid Ignorance and Self-Conceit	149
47.	Avoid Discord	152
48.	Enmity Within is Dangerous	156
49.	Listen to Men of Lofty Ideals	159
50.	Evils of Gambling	162
51.	Eat Sensibly for Good Health	165
52.	Duties of a Physician	168
53.	Nobility	172
54.	Honour	175
55.	Social Justice	178
56.	Sagely Perfection	182
57.	True Courtesy	185
58.	Citizens' Duty	188
59.	Pride of Farmers	191
60.	Poverty's Miseries	194

61.	When Begging is Justified	197
62.	Dread of Begging	199
63.	Avoid Meanness	201

Aram

1.	Praise of God	205
2.	Praise of Rain	208
3.	Praise of Great Men	212
4.	Purity of Mind	215
5.	Traits to Be Shunned	218
6.	Ideal Married Life	221
7.	Role of a Life Partner	225
8.	Joy of Children	229
9.	Parents' Duties	232
10.	Children's Duty	236
11.	Power of Love	239
12.	Always Speak Sweetly	242
13.	Gratitude	245
14.	Virtue of Impartiality	247
15.	Humility with Values	250
16.	Controlling Your Tongue	253
17.	Benefits of Ethical Conduct	255
18.	Rewards of Patience	257
19.	Envy Kills	260
20.	Avoid Slander	263
21.	Avoid Vain Speech	266
22.	Dread of Evil Deeds	269
23.	Service-Minded Individuals	272
24.	Pleasure of Giving	275
25.	Excel in Anything You Do	278
26.	Greatness of Compassion	281
27.	Reason for Lack of Abundance	285
28.	External Appearances are Unimportant	288
29.	Light of Truthfulness	290
30.	Avoid Anger	293

31. Punishment for Wrongdoers	296
32. Impermanence of Wealth	299
33. Impermanence of Life	302
34. Reduce Attachments	305
35. Finding the Truth	307
36. Reducing Desires	311
37. Power of Fate	313
Bibliography	316

Foreword
by Gopalkrishna Gandhi

The Kural's language is stunning. Is that why the work has fascinated the human mind for centuries? No.

The Kural's ideas are startling. Is that why it has gripped the human imagination unceasingly? No.

The Kural touches the reader's consciousness. It grips it like a real-life experience, like something that happens but rarely, impacting us forever. That is why it is regarded as a masterpiece. That is why it is immortal.

Scholar-administrator R. Poornalingam has captured this value of Thiruvalluvar's iconic work and has refreshed its eternal meanings for our distracted and distraught times. He tells us the couplets are of contemporary relevance. He is right. He then proceeds to show how they are contemporary through carefully selected couplets and brings out their 'today-ness', their 'immediacy', like a diamond-cutter brings out the gleam within the gem or, to be consistent with the title he has given to the book, *Best of Thirukkural: Wisdom to Enrich Yourself and Humanity*, like a pearl-diver brings up from watery depths the clasp that holds its minuscule treasure.

I have found his rendition invaluable for one novel technique—the 'Key Takeaway' that concludes the significance of each Kural. No two words can be found that are more contemporary than those. Every major essay must have, editors and publishers tell us, 'keywords'. The reader wants to know what the core of the essay is, what its inner truth is. And as to the 'takeaway', the reader must know because time is short, and the baggage already loaded, what to carry home 'for good' and what to leave behind. To find in a couplet or set of couplets that are already brief to the point of being telegraphic, another memorable brevity, another eternal verity, is no ordinary task. The diligent Kural master Poornalingam has done that meticulously.

I congratulate and thank him for having made *Thirukkural* come alive once again to our generation and future generations through his labour of a thinking heart and a feeling mind.

Gopalkrishna Gandhi
Former Governor of West Bengal

Preface

My interest in Tamil literature was kindled by a book I read during the isolation enforced by COVID-19. Seeking insight into ancient Tamil heritage, I began my journey with *Thirukkural*, often referred to as the 'holy Kural'. I was instantly captivated by its profound beauty and elegance. I had studied *Thirukkural* during my school years, but at that age I could not grasp its relevance to life, nor was it taught that way. A few Kurals (couplets) did leave a lasting impression on my mind, serving as guiding principles through my formative years. Still, I did not give much thought to *Thirukkural* or any other work of Sangam literature after my school years.

Now studying *Thirukkural* in my mid-70s, I am fascinated by its eternal wisdom. I regret not spending time on it earlier; studying it closely would have benefited me personally and officially, but more than anything, I would have been a better human being.

Reading different interpretations of *Thirukkural* by leading scholars helped me better appreciate its teachings and its relevance to the contemporary world. It was like a revelation, and I spent long hours discussing the work and its teachings with a few knowledgeable friends. After some months, they suggested that I write a book on *Thirukkural* in simple Tamil, highlighting the need for educating the Tamil people in Tamil Nadu and elsewhere about their ancient treasures. The idea was a book that would illuminate Thiruvalluvar's message, bringing out its contemporary relevance and its imperishable wisdom. It was a challenging task, and initially I was hesitant. After some persuasion and a promise of help, I took the plunge.

The outcome was a book, *Vazhvil Valampera Valluvum*, published in May 2022. I aimed to make the book different from what most others had done. Instead of giving the meaning of the Kurals in two lines, *Vazhvil Valampera Valluvam* attempts to capture the essence of *Thirukkural* through a succinct and accessible explanation of a hundred carefully selected couplets from the 108 chapters in the divisions titled 'Aram' (Virtue) and 'Porul' (Wealth). Their meaning and import have been discussed to bring out the ancient work's relevance to the world today. My attempt has been to foreground *Thirukkural's* contemporary relevance with examples from history, my personal experiences, and observations to help the reader appreciate Thiruvalluvar's teachings.

The book was well received and went into a second edition in four months. The third revised edition has just been released. Not many books in Tamil aim to bring out *Thirukkural's* contemporary relevance; that may be one reason why my book was well received. The feedback we received from readers suggests that the discussions of the selected Kurals have significantly enhanced their comprehension of *Thirukkural's* meaning and relevance to the present.

After going through the book, many friends suggested that I should translate it into English to take Thiruvalluvar's wisdom to a wider audience. I was hesitant, considering that translating into English the meaning and import of the beautiful and profound words used by Thiruvalluvar might turn out to be an even more challenging task than my original undertaking in Tamil. The final impetus came from my friend N. Ram of *The Hindu*. His unwavering conviction in the importance of spreading my book's message to a wider audience, along with his careful review of a substantial part of my initial translation, encouraged me to take on this ambitious project. The result is the English version, *Best of Thirukkural: Wisdom to Enrich Yourself and Humanity*.

I owe immensely to many great commentators and scholars of *Thirukkural* for enriching my understanding of the Kural. I have drawn extensively from their commentaries and writings while putting together this book. In particular, the in-depth commentaries of medieval scholars Manakkudavar and Parimelazhagar have been invaluable to me. Additionally, the insights provided by present-day

Tamil scholars such as Mu. Varadarajan, Thiru. V. Kalyanasundaram, Kalaignar M. Karunanidhi, T.P. Meenakshisundaram, Solomon Pappaiah, Namakkal Kavignar Ramalingam, and many others have served as my guiding light, enlightening me on the wisdom of the Kural.

Translating the Kural into English demands a special skill, and I acknowledge that my proficiency in this area is limited. Therefore, I have extensively borrowed from the translations of eminent scholars such as G.U. Pope, W.H. Drew and John Lazarus, M.S. Purnalingam Pillai, V.V.S. Iyer, Gopalkrishna Gandhi, M. Rajaram, and J. Narayanasamy, among many others. While I have edited their translations, placing a greater emphasis on conveying meaning even if it meant sacrificing rhyme, I must humbly acknowledge that my translation remains a modest substitute. *Thirukkural*'s profound depth can hardly be fully captured in any translation.

This book has thus drawn extensively from the insights and interpretations of many great scholars. With humility, I have tried to interpret the great Kural, standing on the shoulders of these distinguished scholars. I, therefore, request the reader to ignore my shortcomings and take the essence of this work, for Thiruvalluvar's teachings are so profound that no single interpretation can wholly encapsulate their depth and wisdom.

I would like to extend my heartfelt gratitude to my friends and well-wishers who consistently offered their encouragement and support for this endeavour. I must reserve my special thanks to K. Ramanujam, IPS (R), who not only generously offered his assistance but also spent considerable time to review and refine my draft. His contributions added immense value to the book, and I am profoundly grateful for his insights and expertise. I am equally grateful to N. Ram of *The Hindu*, who was the great motivating force for this venture. He kept encouraging me at every stage of the making of the book.

Finally, I thank Rupa Publications, New Delhi, particularly Kapish G. Mehra and Dibakar Ghosh, for bringing out this book in this elegant form. I am grateful to the editorial team working with Ms Sonali Rawat for their meticulous editing that has vastly improved the flow and readability of the book.

R. Poornalingam
September 2024

Introduction

Thirukkural, an ancient Tamil classic, is one of the most revered works of Tamil literature. Perhaps without parallel, it holds an equally significant place in the literary and philosophical traditions of Tamil Nadu. Translated into more than 80 languages, its reputation has spread across the world. As a sublime testament to ethical philosophy, its profound humanism resonates far beyond its linguistic boundaries. This remarkable work encompasses testable postulates and timeless wisdom without any esoteric doctrine or other-worldly speculation; these are presented in carefully chosen words and gnomic form open to multiple interpretations. Hailed as the Tamil Veda, *Thirukkural* serves as a guide for human conduct, encapsulating ideals and principles that remain relevant through the ages.

Thirukkural gained global recognition thanks to Constantino Guiseppe Beschi, popularly known by the Tamil name Veeramamunivar. He translated it into Latin in 1730, effectively sharing it with the world. This marked the beginning of its universal appeal. The first English translation, a feat accomplished by G.U. Pope in 1886, further widened its reach. M. Ariel, who translated *Thirukkural* into French (1848), described it as 'the masterpiece of Tamil literature—one of the highest and purest expressions of human thought.'[1] Nobel laureate Dr Albert Schweitzer comments: 'With sure strokes, the "Kural" draws the ideal of simple ethical humanity. On the most varied questions concerning the conduct of man to himself and to the world, its utterances are characterized by nobility and good sense. There hardly exists in the literature of the world a collection of maxims

---

[1]Munusamy, V., *Thirukkural Athikaara Vilakkam*, Vanathi Publishers, Chennai, 2021.

in which we find so much lofty wisdom.'[2]

Praise for *Thirukkural* by two great men of India needs special mention. Mahatma Gandhi called it 'a textbook of indispensable authority on moral life' and went on to say, 'The maxims of Valluvar have touched my soul. There is none who has given such a treasure of wisdom like him.'[3] Sri Aurobindo, the nationalist philosopher, characterized *Thirukkural* as 'gnomic poetry, the greatest in planned conception and force of execution ever written in this kind.'[4] Finally, the ancient Tamil poet Avvaiyar wrote about it: 'Thiruvalluvar pierced an atom and injected seven seas into it and compressed it into what we have today as Kural.'[5] No description of Thiruvalluvar's work can be more apt.

Numerous researchers have tried to ascertain *Thirukkural*'s date of composition without arriving at any definitive findings. The scholarly consensus, however, is that it belongs to the corpus of late Sangam literature, which means it is about two millennia old. Judging from its style and language, most scholars believe that it is the work of a single individual. Unfortunately, not much is known about the author, Thiruvalluvar. His real name remains a mystery, and he is primarily recognized by this name and his magnum opus, *Thirukkural*. Scanty details are available about his background and his place of residence. The stories about his life lack historical substantiation or any kind of evidence. However, what is of utmost importance is the great treatise he bequeathed humanity—*Thirukkural*.

---

[2]Sundaramurthy, E., *Kuralmutham*, Tamil Valarchi Iyakkaham, Chennai, 2000.
[3]Pillai, M.S. Purnalingam, *Thirukkural*, International Institute of Tamil Studies, Chennai, 2007.
[4]"Thirukkural Study Group", *Auroville Today*, September 2023, https://tinyurl.com/29at9rsj. Accessed on 14 September 2024.
[5]Pillai, M.S. Purnalingam, *Thirukkural*, International Institute of Tamil Studies, Chennai, 2007.

Structure of Kural

The term *kural* in Tamil means 'short'. Each Kural consists of just seven words written in the Venba metre. *Thirukkural*, a compendium of 1,330 Kurals, deals with various aspects of human life. It is divided into three major divisions—'Aram' (Virtue), 'Porul' (Wealth) and 'Inbam' (Love)—encompassing 133 chapters. Each chapter comprises ten couplets that delve into a specific subject. The chapters are grouped into subdivisions. There is, however, no consensus among scholars about this grouping. Medieval commentator Manakkudavar's grouping appears the most logical, which I have reproduced below to offer the reader a glimpse of the range of topics covered by *Thirukkural*.

Aram, 38 chapters
- Prologue, 4
- Married Life, 20
- Asceticism, 13
- Fate, 1

Porul, 70 chapters
- Polity, 25
- Ministry, 10
- Money, 5
- Friendship, 5
- Difficulties, 12
- Citizenry, 13

Inbam, 25 chapters
- Secret Love, 7
- Chaste Love, 18

Thiruvalluvar, in his timeless treatise, rarely issues instructions or commands. Instead, he presents truths and profound observations about human nature. He seldom warns against wrongdoing, choosing instead to engage with the reader—'conversing rather than proclaiming, discussing rather than prescribing.[6] His wisdom is left for individuals to absorb and act upon. Notably, Thiruvalluvar makes no gender distinctions unless necessary, addressing rulers, ministers, citizens, or individuals without bias. In my discussions, the use of male pronouns is purely for ease of reading and is not meant to prioritize any gender. Readers should understand that these pronouns include all genders.

Aram or Virtue

This division, comprising 38 chapters, starts with a prologue consisting of four introductory chapters. The first of these is in praise of God, but there is no mention of any particular God of any religion. Thiruvalluvar refers to Him as the primordial All-Knowing God, reflecting his religious neutrality. His advice is to show profound reverence to this divine entity with great humility. The second chapter underscores the significance of rain and water, a practical and timeless concern that remains vital to this day. The third chapter is about praise for those selfless public-spirited individuals who live for others. The fourth chapter in this subdivision emphasizes the importance of *aram* or virtue in a man's life. Aram represents a moral code of permanent and universal validity. This chapter contains a single commandment of this moral code: Be spotlessly pure at heart—a simple and profound definition encapsulating the essence of virtue, but difficult to follow. These introductory chapters serve as the master key that unlocks the treasures that follow.

Then comes the major subdivision dedicated to married life, offering the sage's advice for a happy and meaningful married life. Thiruvalluvar extols it so much that he equates a person leading a virtuous married life with a divine entity (50). This perspective is in contrast to many religious doctrines that place asceticism above all. At the heart of a successful married life is ethical conduct, with an abundance of love and compassion. Although women were

---

[6]Narayanasamy, J., *Thirukkural*, Sura Books (Pvt) Ltd, Chennai, 2004.

considered inferior in his days, he assigns to them a prominent role as life partners responsible for managing the household and its finances—of home minister and finance minister (51)!

The chapter 'Wealth of Children' offers insights into the joys children bring into parents' lives. It elucidates the reciprocal duties of parents towards their children and of children towards their parents. Every married couple should embrace the message of this chapter and enjoy the pleasures with the responsibilities of parenthood.

Thiruvalluvar underscores virtuous qualities such as love, compassion, generosity and truthfulness, among others, while placing significant emphasis on achieving excellence in every endeavour:

Achieve fame and glory in whatever field you enter;
Or else, better enter not. (236)

He cautions against placing undue importance on external appearances and rituals, stressing that they cannot absolve us of wrongdoing. Instead, he advises us to avoid actions that society deems unacceptable:

Tonsuring head or matted hair are of no avail, if
What world condemns is not shunned. (280)

Thiruvalluvar places a higher value on wisdom than on knowledge and education:

Whatever thing, of whatsoever kind it be,
True wisdom is to see its reality. (355)

For him, true wisdom implies nurturing a curious and inquisitive mind that questions everything, refusing to accept things at face value. This thought was far ahead of his time when unquestioning acceptance of dogmas and beliefs was the norm. As commentator Parimelazhagar points out, true wisdom, according to Thiruvalluvar, is about 'finding out the eternal truth of all after discounting the imaginations of the people of the world.[7] This outlook expresses a profound commitment to critical thinking.

Reminding us of the impermanence of wealth and life, Thiruvalluvar brings out another universal truth:

From whatever, whatever, a man gets free,
From that whatever his griefs flee. (341)

Stating an obvious but under-appreciated truth, he avoids prescribing a specific course of action and leaves the decision to us. He encourages contemplation and self-reflection by emphasizing the importance of recognizing the fleeting nature of worldly attachments and the freedom that comes from letting go.

The 'Virtue' division ends with a philosophical reflection, urging us to face life's uncertainties and events beyond our control with equanimity:

What is stronger than destiny?
It will be a step ahead of us. (380)

Porul or Wealth

This division deals with polity, encompassing leadership, governance, ministers, task execution, hard work, nobility, citizenry, and more. Although Thiruvalluvar would have been familiar only with the monarchical system, his advice, surprisingly, is relevant to the present-day polity as well, demonstrating its timeless nature. Whether one is a political leader or a leader of an organization, the insights offered in this division can provide both valuable lessons and principles for effective governance and leadership.

This division starts with the enumeration of the traits a ruler or a king must have. A worthy king must be easily accessible to all. He must not speak harsh words (386). Furthermore, he should possess the virtue of listening to criticisms of his rule, even those

---

[7]Pappaiah, Solomon, *Thirukkural*, Kavitha Publishers, Chennai, 2018.

'bitter to his ears' (389). Interestingly, the qualities outlined do not support heredity as the basis of kingship. It appears that in Thiruvalluvar's world view, anyone can be a ruler provided he is endowed with those noble qualities. Thiruvalluvar's king cannot claim sovereignty or supremacy, since he is for the citizens and the country. His duty is to be a just ruler, treating everyone as equal. Nor is Thiruvalluvar's king allowed to be tyrannical; he can, at most, be whimsical because of the pressures of his office.

Thiruvalluvar goes on to elaborate what a king must do and must not do. For example, he must always seek the advice of public-spirited men and avoid unsuitable company (448 and 455). He must find out his citizens' grievances every day and redress them. He must not be arrogant or mean (431). He must not exceed his limits and indulge in self-praise (474). There are more strictures along these lines, making it clear that Thiruvalluvar was no supporter of absolute monarchy.

Surprisingly, Thiruvalluvar underlines the importance of education not just for the elite but for all citizens. His two-millennia-old advocacy of universal education is revolutionary. Clearly, his ideas were far ahead of his time, and indeed of the times further ahead. These ideas run counter to the historical perspective of our society, where just a century ago, education was considered unnecessary for certain divisions. At the time of Independence, only one in eight Indians could read and write. Thiruvalluvar's unequivocal condemnation of illiteracy reveals his passion for education for all.

Subsequent chapters offer the ruler and his ministers valuable insights into the nuances of selection of employees and execution of tasks. Present-day managers would do well to study these chapters. Some of Thiruvalluvar's insights cover public speaking, persuasive conversation, effective listening, delegation, mind-reading, team building, and several other subjects that would be of interest to today's managers. A few chapters deal with friendship needed for both individuals and nations. Special attention is given to wealth for individuals and nations, with the all-important stricture that wealth should be earned in ethical ways. Collectively, these chapters underscore Thiruvalluvar's desire for individuals to lead a prosperous and fulfilling life while adhering to ethical and just principles.

Fully recognizing the importance of zeal and hard work for human progress, Thiruvalluvar has devoted an entire chapter to it:

Men overcome even the relentless destiny
With their ceaseless industry. (620)

His mantra is, thus, hard work and progress instead of an idle life accepting the status quo.

In a similar vein, he praises citizens who work tirelessly for the community's progress. Thus this Kural in the chapter 'Advancing Community':

Untiring efforts and profound wisdom and knowledge
combined together
With perseverance enrich society's welfare. (1022)

This highlights his profound belief in human potential and societal advancement, irrespective of social status or hierarchy. His vision portrays a dynamic society, constantly evolving and progressing.

Yet another feature of *Thirukkural* that reveals its author's progressive thinking is a distinct subdivision for citizens. He treats citizens on a par with the ruler as a vital component of the polity. This subdivision explains the duties and responsibilities of citizens for good governance and the advancement of their community and nation.

A path-breaking couplet in the chapter 'Perumai' (Honour) helps us understand and appreciate *Thirukkural*'s universality and timelessness. It makes a categorical assertion that all men are born equal, regardless of their race, religion, caste, wealth or heredity. Thiruvalluvar espouses a forward-looking and radical concept that to this day, regrettably, has not been fully accepted and practised in many parts of the world. This applies all the more to India, which is deeply divided by religion and caste. What brings pride to individuals is not their birth but their vocations and the excellence they achieve in them.

All men that live are equal in birth; only vocation and skills
Make the difference deciding their worth. (972)

We can only hope that this becomes a reality, at least in the next century.

Inbam or Love
Although this book does not discuss this division, a brief introduction is given for the reader to appreciate *Thirukkural* in its entirety. This division explores the noble and lasting love between man and woman, representing a higher form of emotional experience beyond the pleasures of lust or sex. It delves into the more elevated aspects of human love, emphasizing its enriching and noble qualities.

Many commentators have interpreted the entire division as the romantic journey of a single couple from the moment they first meet to the time they reunite after a brief separation. All but two couplets fit in with this interpretation. Yet each verse can also be viewed as describing an independent situation. The 250 couplets in this division offer a delicate analysis of the hundred different emotional states experienced by lovers.

M.S. Purnalingam Pillai's comment is noteworthy: 'A study of this division reveals that the only system practised by ancient Tamils was the post-puberty marriage arising from courtship and self-choice. It is also clear that the poet does not recognize the necessity for any religious ceremony or sanction to bind the parties in love.'[8]

Let me discuss just one couplet (1166) to highlight the beauty of this division:

Vast is the sea of joy, but
The pain of lust is far greater. (1166)

---

[8]Vasudevan, M., *Thirukkural*, 25 August 2015.

It is the soliloquy of a lady in her increasing distress which wears her down due to her lover's prolonged absence from home. She yearns for him ceaselessly and feels utterly miserable. Her misery is obviously due to *kamam* or 'lust'. The Kural's message is that the joy of the spirit or soul, represented by 'inbam', is like an ocean. However, when overwhelmed by 'kamam', her suffering far outweighs that 'inbam'.

K. Kothandapani Pillai offers an incisive technical analysis of this couplet, demonstrating why 'inbam' should not be equated with 'kamam'. He bases his interpretation on the precise arrangement of words and the use of the disjunctive *marru* or 'but' in this Kural. Pillai's conclusion is that 'inbam' is reserved for denoting a higher state of experience beyond mere sexual pleasure.

In this division, Thiruvalluvar portrays the intricate human emotions that 'love evokes in the human heart with a master stroke of elegance and charm, imaginative splendour and poetic grandeur.'[9]

In conclusion, *Thirukkural* delivers a timeless message of human equality, the significance of virtuous living, and the enduring value of arduous work—themes that have woven their way through the couplets and the chapters. Thiruvalluvar often makes it clear that what distinguish 'man from man are his learning, his wealth and his moral worth,' and crucially, he reminds us that these are not insurmountable barriers.[10] He exhorts ordinary men to become learned through systematic education, wise by questioning, advance through unflagging energy, all the while leading an ethical and happy married life with abundant love and compassion. He also advocates that every citizen should contribute to just governance as much as the ruler and his machinery, under a broad framework stipulated by him. There is little doubt that this masterpiece of Tamil literature, crafted with rare poetic artistry, will continue to serve as a guiding light for humanity for ages to come.

---

[9]Viswanatham, K.A.P., *Thirukkural Katturaikal*, Pusthak Digital Media, n.d.
[10]Vasudevan, M., *Thirukkural*, 25 August 2015.

But have the teachings of the Kural been followed in practice? Here is what Gopalkrishna Gandhi has to say about this in his book *The Tirukkural* (2015): 'Admired as literature, venerated as secular gospel, translated times without number into the world's different languages, the *Tirukkural*'s teachings have yet been ignored by generation after generation of an unwise humanity.' My book is yet another attempt to convince fellow citizens and humanity at large to follow these timeless teachings and illuminate their path to a more enlightened future.

Porul

1
Qualities Expected of a Leader

அஞ்சாமை, ஈகை, அறிவூக்கம், இந்நான்கும்
எஞ்சாமை வேந்தற் கியல்பு. (குறள் 382)

Transliteration
Anjaamai, Iikai, Arivookkam, Inhnhaankum
Enjaamai Vendhar Kiyalpu.

Translation
Fearlessness, charity, wisdom, great zeal are the four
Traits that are by nature in abundance in a king.

Meaning
Not fearing anything or anyone, a large heart that goes out to the needy, wisdom to rule, and the indomitable spirit to achieve anything are the four qualities that will naturally be in abundance in a king or ruler.

Kural Discussions
This Kural figures in the chapter called 'Iraimaatchi', meaning 'Regal Virtues', falling under polity in the 'Wealth' or 'Porul' division. In this chapter, Thiruvalluvar enunciates the important virtues, qualities and talents required of a good king.

Thiruvalluvar speaks of the king because in his age monarchy was the norm. However, because of his emphasis on fundamental human ideals, his chapters meant for the king are eminently suitable to democracy, which too emphasizes basic human virtues, freedom of thought and expression, and equality. After reading his canons for a good ruler, one cannot help but wonder about his foresight, which has such a timeless impact. The more carefully one reads his chapters on polity and governance, the more one is convinced that his advice is quite relevant to our present-day elected leaders, from the village to the national level, and equally applicable to administrative leaders. One hopes that they study these aspects thoroughly, digest their meaning, and follow his advice on good governance and betterment of the country or the organization. Let us now examine what advice Thiruvalluvar has for them.

This couplet talks of the four virtues of a good king. The first is fearlessness or courage. It covers many facets of courage: courage against the enemy, ruthlessness against criminals, bold action without fear or favour against those who commit crimes, including friends, relatives, etc. His enemies, criminals, and even friends and relatives who have committed wrongdoings should fear him. Also, he should be fearless in decision-making—to decide fearlessly in citizens' interests, even at the cost of his popularity. Furthermore, he should have the courage to decide quickly in times of crisis, but also slowly and carefully when necessary. In short, he should never fear doing the right thing. This one word—fearlessness—embodies all these aspects.

The second quality—charity—refers to the ruler's generosity, his willingness to help the needy, a heart that goes out to the poor and the needy. He should be full of compassion. Of course, this does not mean throwing away public money but refers to his readiness to spend when needed. Another Kural explains how a ruler should be vigilant while spending public money. More importantly, he should have compassion for his people that will guide him in the right direction.

The third quality is wisdom—the wisdom to rule wisely. This does not refer to mere education but the wisdom he has gained from his genuine concern for the citizens and the abundant common sense he has accumulated over the years. Tamil Nadu has seen great chief ministers with such wisdom, who governed exceptionally well. Though not highly educated, they learned the art of governance from their experiences in the real world.

The last, but not the least, requirement of a good ruler is his zeal for a public cause. The Tamil word *ookkam* means 'strong will' or 'strength of mind'. The ruler should be strong-willed to do good for his people, with passion and perseverance. He will then have the zeal and enthusiasm to execute many government tasks, big and small, fast and well. Only when the ruler is fearless and possesses a strong will, can he work with great zeal. Without zeal, he will be lazy, and so will his employees. Citizens will not benefit.

The couplet does not merely say that a ruler should have these qualities, but that he should have them in abundance. Rather, it says that he will have them naturally or inherently—they will be his innate qualities. Only then will his rule be great. The choice of words indicates that Thiruvalluvar expects good rulers to have them all in abundance and naturally. The implication is that if they do not possess them, they are not fit to rule! Ashoka the Great, emperor of Magadha, fits the standards set in this Kural.

The Greek philosopher Plato, in his monumental work *The Republic*, discussed polity in great depth. He was convinced that only a philosopher could be a good ruler and went on to explain how a utopian state could be created. His vision of an ideal state is highly impractical. But Thiruvalluvar did not discuss the nature of government or who should rule. He shared his practical wisdom on the qualities necessary for a good leader or ruler. He could be an aristocrat or a commoner; he could be rich or poor; he could be educated or uneducated. Thiruvalluvar's concept of kingship is not based on birth or heredity. Anyone can rule well if he has the qualities set forth by Thiruvalluvar. If a person possesses these qualities, his rule will be good and bring enormous benefits to the people.

Now we have a democratic government in which people have the choice to elect leaders at all levels. While exercising their franchise, people must contemplate whether the candidates have these qualities. It may turn out that no one does! The elected leaders should also ponder over the advice of Thiruvalluvar in this chapter and try to follow it. Even a passing familiarity with it may prove beneficial, for sooner or later, they may embrace the same, improving governance.

The primary role of government employees is to serve the public, and therefore, they too must possess these qualities. Those naturally endowed with them stand out in their performance, but those without them or those who do not acquire them perform poorly. If all could adopt this wisdom, the public benefit would be immense, and earn praise and admiration for the government and the leader.

KEY TAKEAWAY

A leader must have the following qualities in abundance: courage to do the right thing, compassion, wisdom to rule, and the will to complete a task.

2

Financial Management

இயற்றலும், ஈட்டலும், காத்தலும், காத்த
வகுத்தலும் வல்லது அரசு. (குறள் 385)

Transliteration
Iyatralum, Iittalum, Kaaththalum, Kaththa
Vakuththalum Vallathu Arasu.

Translation
Acquiring, enriching, safeguarding, spending wisely
Are duties of an able king.

Meaning
Developing new financial resources, improving collections, safeguarding government resources, and spending them wisely are the hallmarks of a good government or ruler.

Kural Discussions
All governments require finances to function efficiently. Financial strength is the key to the efficient functioning of a government. History is full of instances where kingdoms were lost for want of money. This Kural coming under the same chapter, 'Iraimaatchi' or 'Regal Virtues', explains how a government should handle its finances and spells out the fundamentals of preparing a budget, which is now the norm world over. What are the key components of good financial management?

The first component is finding new sources of revenue. The government should keep exploring new avenues to generate revenues. Our governments have been constantly doing that.

For example, about 70 years back, Tamil Nadu's main source of revenue was land revenue. Then came sales tax, excise income, stamp duties, motor vehicles tax, entertainment tax, etc. Land revenue became so negligible that the government abolished it. Similarly, the government of India also introduced service tax, corporate tax, securities transaction tax, and capital gains tax, among others. The word *iyatral* refers to this, which the State must do, taking care, however, not to overly burden its citizens with too much tax.

The second duty is *eettal*, which refers to the efficient collection of these taxes. The State must guard against leakages and evasion by closely monitoring and consolidating its revenues. Our governments constantly do this. Targets for collection are fixed, and the performance is constantly monitored. Tax raids are often conducted to prevent tax evasion. Nowadays, technology is effectively used to plug leakages. Although in the olden days kings did not have access to these, they must have adopted some means to perform this task, for it was their duty.

The third duty is to safeguard the resources, or *kaaththalum*. The State must guard against theft, pilferage and misappropriation by employees and others. This also includes the State's duty to prevent waste of resources. For example, our government procures food grains from farmers to protect them against price vagaries and stores the grains in large warehouses for distribution to the poor and the needy. We often read in newspapers about large quantities of food grains becoming unusable due to poor storage. This Kural expects the State to take safeguards against such waste, too; all government resources must be carefully conserved.

The last duty is to use the finances wisely, or *vakuththalum*. Obviously, the ruler must spend them for the welfare of the people and the country. Spending money wisely is not easy; it requires careful thinking and planning. To prepare a good plan, one needs to prioritize to get maximum benefit from a given resource. Implementing a plan efficiently without waste and leakage and in a timely manner also comes under this duty, or else the plan will only remain on paper. While preparing a plan, the ruler must guard against wasting resources on fancy projects that do not offer any benefit to the people.

Poor financial management causes havoc in the lives of ordinary people. Therefore, proper financial management is vital for a government and, for that matter, for everyone. Recent happenings in Sri Lanka, where people suffered without food or fuel, is an example of poor management of resources in that country, which was once prosperous. Many other countries also suffer from high inflation owing to poor financial management, making people poorer. Fortunately, financial management in India is fairly under control, though not optimal. In general, both our Central and State governments are good at developing and improving resources but are poor at spending them wisely. Since they must run for elections every five years, they tend to spend on popular throwaway schemes that are financially unsustainable—I can name many. On the other hand, without this compulsion, China has been spending wisely on human development and infrastructure projects necessary for manufacture and exports. The result is that its per capita income is five times ours, and it has become a global power, rivalling the United States of America (USA). Let us not forget, India and China had the same per capita income in the 1960s.

As a person associated with the preparation of the Tamil Nadu government's budget for a few years, I am amazed at the beauty of this Kural which aptly captures the key elements of a budget. Unfortunately, governments do not follow all the tenets of this Kural. Of the four components Thiruvalluvar has stressed, our governments are good at the first two but not so good at the other two, namely, safeguarding resources and spending wisely. I could justify my criticism with many examples, but this is not the place for it. Suffice to say, they lack in these two tenets. Realizing it, they should focus on spending resources wisely without patronage or favour or due to political considerations, but on projects that will give us a global edge. Equally important is their speedy implementation, rather than simply being satisfied with mere announcements and publicity. This couplet is a bible in financial management for our governments.

KEY TAKEAWAY

The primary duty of a good government or a ruler is to generate enough resources without causing much hardship to citizens and spend them wisely for the benefit of the people and the country, without waste or delays.

3

Listening to Criticism

செவிகைப்பச் சொற்பொறுக்கும் பண்புடை வேந்தன்
கவிகைக்கீழ்த், தங்கும் உலகு. (குறள் 389)

Transliteration
Sevikaippas Sorporukkum Panpudai Venhthan,
Kavikaikkeezhth, Thangkum Ulagu.

Translation
The world rests secure under a ruler who possesses
The virtue to bear even criticisms bitter to his ears.

Meaning
The rule of a leader will last long, if he possesses the virtue of listening patiently to differing views, unpalatable advice and even harsh criticisms of his rule.

Kural Discussions
This Kural in the same chapter 'Regal Virtues' or 'Iraimaatchi' brings out yet another important aspect of governance. The leader or ruler must listen to criticisms of his rule. What kind of criticisms? Even those that will hurt his ears, meaning unpalatable criticisms that will make him angry or sad (*sevikaippa*). These include even unjustified criticisms—those criticizing may not know the full facts. Listening to them patiently without irritation or anger is lauded as a virtue or *panbu*—a ruler must have this virtue. A tall order indeed! Normally, all of us are averse to criticism, but Thiruvalluvar expects a king to patiently listen to criticisms. In his day, kings were all-powerful; they did not have to

tolerate any criticism and could even punish their critics. Even so, Thiruvalluvar has set such a high benchmark for a king who sits on the throne!

What is the benefit of this virtue? Such a leader's rule will be long-lasting; upon seeing his citizens so happy with his rule, the entire world would be willing to live under his reign. His kingdom will thus expand and last long, for this virtue enables him to get timely advice from learned people, leading to better governance and happier citizens.

This is even more necessary for present-day rulers, particularly those elected democratically. Their rule is not permanent—today's ruler is tomorrow's citizen. And their rule is dependent on citizens' satisfaction with their leadership. Therefore, it is vital for them to listen to citizens and redress their grievances. If they are accessible and willing to listen to differing views, they will also get timely feedback and good advice, enabling them to make timely course corrections.

Elected leaders are generally eager to redress the citizens' grievances, since they are keen to continue in power. Today, they can listen to citizens through many ways: media, opinion makers, and personal interactions, among others. Forty years back, the government of Tamil Nadu thought of a novel way for administration to listen to the people. Called Manuneethi Thittam, it was named after an ancient Tamil king who was committed to justice for every citizen. Instead of one ruler listening to citizens, all responsible for administration were required to listen. It is possible that the scheme itself was an outcome of the then ruler, the chief minister, listening to good advice. Every Monday, senior managers of the district were required to be available in their offices to listen to the public and address their grievances. Since citizens could meet them repeatedly, they were compelled to act on their grievances. The government also monitored the scheme closely, which helped. As an important player in the district, I could observe that this scheme brought immense benefits to citizens, significantly improving their satisfaction. Even today, the scheme continues in Tamil Nadu, but I do not know how well it functions. Maybe it is time for an evaluation and course correction.

By and large, democratically elected leaders are good listeners. Only by listening to people have they become leaders. But once in governance, they become less receptive, especially when it comes to criticism or differing viewpoints. Since they like to be praised, they are constantly glorified by people seeking favours. As a result, they hear what they want to hear and rarely get good advice or honest feedback. Soon they lose touch with the realities faced by the common man and are, therefore, eventually rejected by the citizens. As the couplet warns, their rule becomes short-lived.

In a democracy, the opposition party can offer constructive criticism. Unfortunately, the Opposition presumes that it is their duty to oppose no matter the good that the government does, while the ruling party tends to disregard even valid criticism treating it as politically motivated. According to this Kural, the ruler should be prepared to examine the merits of the criticism rather than the motive behind it.

This advice applies equally to leaders and senior managers of organizations. By listening to employees and customers, they can get valuable feedback about their products, their services and even about their management style. While some comments might be harsh or unpalatable, they must still have the patience to listen and examine the underlying reasons behind these. Leaders with patience to listen to criticism will definitely listen to good advice too and act on it, immensely benefiting the organization. However, by and large, the habit of listening seems to be on the wane among managers and leaders for want of time or patience, so much so that many courses on effective listening are being organized!

KEY TAKEAWAY

Empathetic listening to criticisms and differing views will lead to improvement in administration or governance.

4
Aim of Education

கற்க கசடறக் கற்பவை; கற்றபின்
நிற்க அதற்குத் தக. (குறள் 391)

Transliteration
Karka Kasatarak Karpavai; Karrapin
Nhirka Atharkuth Thaka.

Translation
Learn thoroughly whatever is worthy of learning;
Then act in consonance with it.

Meaning
One must learn whatever must be learnt flawlessly without any doubt or defect, and after that, one must conduct oneself in accordance with the knowledge acquired.

Kural Discussions
This wonderful couplet figures in the chapter 'Learning' or 'Kalvi'. That it follows the chapter 'Regal Duties' or 'Iraimaatchi' reflects the importance Thiruvalluvar attaches to literacy and learning. Besides, he has allocated another chapter to 'Illiteracy' or 'Kallaamai', strongly condemning it. This is followed by yet another chapter, 'Listening' or 'Kelvi', meaning 'acquisition of knowledge through listening to the wise and the learned'. Thus, he has devoted thirty couplets to stress the importance of learning, reflecting his strong commitment to learning and knowledge. The stress here is not on learning for the king or the elite alone but for all humans. In other chapters, too, Thiruvalluvar has stressed the importance

of learning, knowledge, zeal and wisdom for individuals from all walks of life, including the king and his ministers.

With his humanistic approach, Thiruvalluvar recognizes the importance of education for all citizens and gives it a prominent place in polity. Nowhere in these three chapters has he said that education needs to be restricted to the ruler or the elite. He expects both the ruler and the ruled to be literate and educated. Looking at the way he praises learning and condemns illiteracy—in one couplet he even equates illiterates to animals—it seems that he is a strong advocate of State support for education. If that is indeed the case, he is one of the earliest pioneers of universal education, to which our State is now committed. That he was an advocate of universal education two millennia back is a matter of happiness and pride.

Let us look at what this Kural says. The first part is clear: whatever is learnt must be learnt thoroughly without doubt or defect. What must be learnt? The word used is *karpavai*, meaning 'that which needs to be learnt'. Many leading commentators have interpreted it to mean books that must be studied. A study undertaken by Google Books in 2010 revealed that 129,864,880 books have been printed since Gutenberg invented the printing press circa 1440.[1] Another estimate says eight titles are brought out every minute. These numbers do not include digital publications, which have seen phenomenal growth in recent years. Life is short while knowledge is infinite. One has limited time, and therefore, it is impossible to study all the books. Hence, one should select a few excellent books and learn them thoroughly without wasting time on others. Francis Bacon said, 'Some books are to be tasted, others to be swallowed, and some few to be chewed and digested.' The books to be studied must obviously be in the last category.

To restrict the word 'karpavai' to books appears to be a narrow interpretation, especially when the word 'book' does not figure in

---

[1] Taycher, Leonid, 'Books of the World, Stand Up and Be Counted! All 129,864,880 of You.' *Google Books Search*, 5 August 2010, https://tinyurl.com/yvdvuekj. Accessed on 17 October 2024.

the couplet. Hence, a broader interpretation given by the medieval scholar Manakkudavar seems appropriate. He says that the word does not merely refer to books but any form of learning and acquisition of knowledge. Any subject, be it literature, science or mathematics, which is chosen must be studied faultlessly without any imperfection; the study must be such as to excel in the subject.

The last part of the couplet states that after such a study, one should act in accordance with it. In our formative years, we do study about the importance of good habits, such as not getting angry or telling lies, helping others, reading good books, doing regular exercise, etc. The Kural says it is not enough to study such things; one should also put these into practice. Otherwise, there is no use in studying these. Therefore, the advice is to act according to what you studied.

Based on this interpretation, some commentators argue that the couplet is confined to general education about good conduct and not to the study of other subjects. In Thiruvalluvar's time, ethics would have been the major area of study, hence this interpretation. This appears to be a narrow interpretation, as explained by the well-known Tamil scholar Devaneya Pavanar. He says *nhitral* (living in consonance with studies) means living virtuously in accordance with general studies and excelling in your vocation according to one's special education. In short, we should strive to live virtuously, based on our general education, while excelling in our trade or occupation in the subject of our study. The advice of this couplet is thus to become a worthy human and an excellent engineer or a scientist or a doctor or a manager, or whatever one chooses to be.

From the above discussions, it is clear that whatever we study, we must study thoroughly without any doubt, and excel in our vocation while living virtuously as per our general education.

KEY TAKEAWAY

The purpose of education is to study the subject of your choice thoroughly and follow it in your life and work.

5

Illiterates are Useless

உளரென்னும் மாத்திரையர் அல்லால் பயவாக்
களரனையர், கல்லா தவர். (குறள் 406)

Transliteration
Ularennum Maaththiraiyar Allaal Payavaak
Kalaranaiyar, Kallaa Thavar.

Translation
The illiterate just exist and are nothing more than
The barren land that is useless.

Meaning
Illiterate people are nothing but the living dead; they just exist like the salt-laden barren lands that are unfit for cultivation, or for that matter, unfit for anything.

Kural Discussions
It is surprising that an entire chapter has been devoted to illiteracy, that too after stressing the importance of learning. In this, Thiruvalluvar explains the evils arising out of illiteracy and how unlettered people are a great burden to society. He has strongly condemned those who remain illiterate for whatever reason, even equating them to animals. Why is he so harsh on them? It must certainly be due to his profound yearning for all citizens to be educated, irrespective of their status or position. Undoubtedly, a visionary who had such thoughts two millennia ago! Let us not forget that in India, certain divisions of society were prohibited from learning just 100 years back, since it was considered

unnecessary. Learning was deemed a privilege limited to a select few.

This Kural in the chapter 'Illiteracy' or 'Kallaamai' considers the illiterate as the living dead; they just exist since they are of no use to anyone; they are fit for nothing. They are like salt lands which cannot be cultivated. Nothing will grow in these lands, and no one will buy them. Therefore, there is absolutely no use for these lands. So are the illiterate. Harsh words, indeed.

Do the illiterate deserve such a strong condemnation? Are such harsh words justified? Though unlettered, they may be intelligent; they may be of good character; they may be kind and considerate to others. They could also contribute through their labour. Thus, they could be useful to society in many ways. Hence, comparing them to fallow or useless lands or animals does not seem justified. The only explanation is that Thiruvalluvar must have used such harsh language out of his profound admiration for learning.

Did we listen to his exhortation? It appears we have not. Illiteracy is still so high in India that it remains a great impediment to our growth; 26 per cent of our population, namely 36 crore people, remain illiterate (2020). They cannot read or write. Seventy-four per cent are treated as literate based on a narrow definition. If you consider them capable of reading newspapers and grasping the meaning, you are mistaken. Most of the literate are counted so because they can read and sign, but their comprehension is rarely tested. Literacy should mean the ability to read and write in the local language, and to also grasp the meaning of what is read.

No doubt our governments have been trying hard to eradicate illiteracy. They have introduced compulsory education for all children from ages six to fourteen, making education up to the eighth standard a right, and free. They have poured money into this programme over the years. Has it helped? It all depends on how well these children are educated. An NGO named Annual Status of Education Report (ASER) evaluates annually the quality of teaching. As per its 2019 report, only 53 per cent of the eight-year-olds studying in the third standard could read the first-standard lessons.[2] They are thus two years behind in learning. Another evaluation done in 2018 revealed that only 73 per cent of the eighth standard students could read second-standard lessons. Fifty-six per cent could not do even simple arithmetic.[3] Even after formal education, our children are seriously lagging in learning. It is sad that enough attention is not given to learning in our country, where human capital is in abundance.

After condemning the illiterate, Thiruvalluvar has shown them ways to learn in the next chapter, 'Listening' or 'Kelvi'. Stressing the importance of knowledge acquisition through listening, he has explained how listening will help all, including the illiterate.

KEY TAKEAWAY

Realizing the evils of illiteracy, all citizens must strive to become educated, and the State must help them in every way.

---

[2] ASER, 'Annual Status of Education Report (Rural) 2019', 14 January 2020, https://tinyurl.com/3f23afrd. Accessed on 20 September 2024.
[3] ASER, 'Annual Status of Education Report (Rural) 2018', 15 January 2019, https://tinyurl.com/42a85f4z. Accessed on 20 September 2024.

6
Treasure of Listening

செல்வத்துள் செல்வம் செவிச்செல்வம்; அச்செல்வம்
செல்வத்துள் எல்லாம் தலை. (குறள் 411)

Transliteration
Selvaththul Selvam Chevichselvam; Achselvam
Selvaththul Ellam Thalai.

Translation
The most precious treasure of all treasures is the treasure of listening; that treasure
Is the crown of all kinds of treasures.

Meaning
The most precious of all treasures is the treasure of learning by listening, and it is the greatest of all treasures.

Kural Discussions
This Kural figures in the chapter 'Listening' or 'Kelvi', which deals with not just listening as such, but also acquisition of knowledge/wisdom through listening. After stressing the importance of learning and condemning illiteracy, Thiruvalluvar brings out the significance of learning by listening. In his days, when books were rare, this would have been the common mode of learning.

This couplet says that listening is the most precious of all treasures and goes on to emphasize that it is the crown of all treasures. It thus stresses the value of listening and learning, highlighting the importance Thiruvalluvar attaches to learning through listening.

Nowadays, we do not think of listening as a mode of learning, perhaps because of the abundant availability of written material. But if we ponder over what Thiruvalluvar has said, we will realize that learning by listening plays a vital role in school and college. We learn better and faster listening to lectures than by studying books on the subject. We retain what we hear in school and college better—the knowledge acquired through our ears. That is why we go to school, to listen and learn. Even after that, we continue to listen to experts and attend training programmes related to our profession, where we gain knowledge by listening. In general, our understanding through listening is better than by reading. Thus, learning by listening plays an important role even for the educated. Therefore, Thiruvalluvar is right in qualifying it as the crown of all wealth.

Yet another advantage of this mode of learning is that even those who are illiterate can acquire knowledge and become well-informed. I know of many without formal education who have accomplished great things in life through the art of listening. They have established large organizations and run them profitably by listening to the right people. Listening to the right advice is certainly an art, and many successful people have a knack for it.

Those in higher levels of administration or management should learn to listen in order to manage their organizations better. By listening, they can get more valuable feedback about their organizations than by reading voluminous reports. Those who listen and take corrective steps succeed, and those who do not, keep struggling. Listening is such a great virtue for managers that many courses on effective listening are offered now. My book, *Management by Listening* (2008), highlights its importance for effective management.

Generally, leaders are very good listeners. Perhaps they become leaders because they have cultivated the habit over time. I had occasions to observe leaders listening to differing views patiently before deciding on contentious issues. Simply by using their ears, they get to know what is happening all around them.

They understand the value of listening and employ it successfully.

Active listening is a valuable habit that will benefit us in all aspects of our lives. When we use our ears to receive information and knowledge, we open ourselves to new ideas and perspectives. This is especially true when we listen to those who are wise and knowledgeable. By cultivating relationships with people possessing these qualities, regardless of our age or level of knowledge, we can learn from them and continue to grow as individuals. Moreover, listening to wise and knowledgeable individuals can help us expand our horizons and broaden our worldview.

The above explanations make it abundantly clear that listening is a great treasure, as Thiruvalluvar has stated—a skill that merits cultivation.

KEY TAKEAWAY

Listening is essential, and all of us should add to our knowledge by continuously listening to the learned and the wise.

7

What is True Wisdom?

எப்பொருள் யார்யார்வாய்க் கேட்பினும், அப்பொருள்
மெய்ப்பொருள் காண்பது அறிவு. (குறள் 423)

Transliteration
Epporul Yaaryaarvaayk Ketpinum, Apporul
Meiypporul Kaanpathu Arivu.

Translation
Whatsoever is heard, from whomsoever,
To discern the truth of the utterance is true wisdom.

Meaning
To discern the truth in everything, whatever be the matter and whomsoever utters it, is wisdom.

Kural Discussions
This Kural is in the chapter 'Wisdom' or 'Arivudaimai'. Thiruvalluvar's view is that it is not enough that one is well educated, but one should also be wise, for wisdom is different from knowledge. He wants citizens to differentiate between wisdom and knowledge and become wise. In this chapter, he explains what wisdom is and how it can be acquired.

This is one of the couplets I cherish the most because its message is most relevant for our days, as we will see in our discussions. It says that whatever you hear from anyone, high or low, should not be accepted at face value. You should examine whether it is true or not, and only if it is determined to be true may you accept it. In our day-to-day lives, we hear many ideas and views from friends and foes, leaders and followers, the educated and the illiterate. It is not wise to accept all of them as truth and to act on them. We tend to ignore the views of unknown people but take the views of friends and leaders seriously. We tend to blindly accept whatever is said by leaders we admire; we do not attempt to examine the truth of their statements. At the same time, we ignore what is said by foes, the inconsequential or the uneducated, or by leaders whom we do not like, even if their statements are actually true. But this couplet says this is not true wisdom. True wisdom requires us to examine and discover the truth of what we hear from everyone. Blind faith in leaders and friends without verifying facts is not wisdom; discovering the truth is.

This is the most useful advice for this modern age when we are constantly bombarded with data and news in the media. Radio, television, newspapers, magazines and, in addition, social media overwhelm us with information and opinions. Most of us spend considerable time on these; for some, it is an addiction. Depending on our personal prejudices, we tend to accept what we hear at face value. Even when data from authoritative sources are pointed out, many individuals still believe what they hear on television or what the leader they like says on the subject. The message in this couplet is that this is not sensible and that it is wise to verify facts about such statements.

Taking advantage of this human weakness, political parties use social media for false propaganda. They spread false news with impunity, and their followers simply believe them and happily share such news. Even in a mature democracy like the USA, it is alleged that foreign powers used social media to swing public opinion in favour of a candidate of their choice in the presidential elections held in 2016. The same allegation was levelled in the 2020 elections. Although one does not know the extent of truth in this, there is no denying that all powers, external and internal, use media to swing public opinion in their favour. This is possible only because of our tendency to accept anything we hear without attempting to find out the facts.

If this can happen in a developed country with nearly full literacy, the situation in India, with the entrenched practice of hero worship, is worse. We have blind faith in our leaders and are ready to accept all they say. What Thiruvalluvar advises in this couplet is that independent thinking rather than blind faith should guide us. That, he says, is true wisdom.

I am reminded of what the Buddha said on the same subject: 'Believe nothing, no matter where you read it and who has said it, not even if I have said it, unless it agrees with your own reason and your own common sense.' The same message was conveyed by the Greek philosopher Socrates, who emphasized the importance of critical thinking and encouraged the youth to question everything. Many researchers of *Thirukkural* have often compared Thiruvalluvar to Socrates, since both encouraged people to question everything at a time when doing so was considered a sin.

A questioning and inquisitive mind is what has been emphasized in this couplet. Thiruvalluvar expects a wise person to question everything and accept it only after finding out the truth based on study or analysis. He even gives us the right to question his advice; it is up to us to accept or reject it, based on our reasoning. That said, I have found no occasion to disagree with him, but this couplet gives us that right.

Naturally, it is not possible to research every statement we come across to find out its veracity. We do not have the time or inclination. The least we can do is to check the veracity of messages of some importance. For example, if the government claims that the GDP of India has grown exponentially in the last five years and the Opposition disputes it, we should verify the facts in this case, as it is a matter of importance for all. That claim can easily be verified by reading reports from international organizations such as the World Bank or the International Monetary Fund (IMF) and through web searches. Still, we generally do not do this. In earlier days, print media would usually be reliable, but they too have become biased and often do not give the correct picture.

Therefore, it becomes the duty of responsible citizens to

discern the truth, at least on vital matters. The current tendency to freely spread untruths for partisan ends can be curbed only by greater vigilance on our part. The message to be remembered is that to accept everything without questioning is not true wisdom. Perhaps anticipating that society would reach this stage, Thiruvalluvar wrote this couplet long back!

KEY TAKEAWAY

Without simply believing everything people say, we should strive to find out the truth.

8

Faults to Be Avoided by a Leader

இவறலும், மாண்புஇறந்த மானமும், மாணா
உவகையும் ஏதம் இறைக்கு. (குறள் 432)

Transliteration
Ivaralum, Maanpuirandha Maanamum, Maanaa
Uvakaiyum Eedham Iraikku.

Translation
Miserliness, pride without honour, unseemly
Happiness are faults of the king.

Meaning
Not spending money for the benefit of his citizens in times of need due to his attachment to money, excessive or mean pride (ego), and unjustified happiness are faults to be avoided by a king or ruler.

Kural Discussions
This Kural comes under the chapter 'Kutram Katithal' or 'Avoiding Faults'. The word *kutram* in Tamil means many things: crime, offence, faults, mistakes, etc. The chapter heading means avoiding and eliminating serious faults. After stressing the importance of education and wisdom, Thiruvalluvar turns his attention to faults one should guard against and offers very sound advice not only to the ruler but also to the citizen. He says that everyone must avoid ego, self-praise, meanness, vengeance, wrongdoing, commission of crimes, etc. His aim is that both the ruler and the ruled must strive to be faultless, highlighting once again his democratic approach.

This couplet deals with a few serious faults or mistakes that a ruler must avoid. The words used to describe these mistakes have a profound meaning that is lost in translation. I will, however, attempt to bring out their meaning to the reader. The full import of these words became evident only after a thorough study of the commentaries of many Kural scholars. Today's governments, too, suffer from the same maladies and, therefore, have a lot to learn from this Kural. It is amazing that Thiruvalluvar's advice remains highly relevant to the present day well after two millennia! He would have arrived at his conclusions only after observing the rulers of the day. It appears that rulers have been the same since time immemorial, irrespective of the nature of government! Let us consider the three faults to be avoided by the ruler, according to this couplet.

The first is miserliness. It refers to the reluctance of a ruler to spend public money in times of societal need. This could be due to his excessive attachment to money or his desire to spend on himself or his pet projects, while being miserly when it comes to spending for the poor. Let us note that miserliness does not refer to his personal wealth but only to government money. No one expects him to be generous with his personal wealth. He is inherently miserly when it comes to spending on others.

Such miserliness is possible with a king or a dictator. Is it possible in a democratic government? I have come across such miserliness at play in modern elected governments too. I would like to recall a recent example. In March 2020, when Covid-19 struck, the Government of India imposed a stringent lockdown on the country. Most economic activities were brought to a standstill by this action. Many people lost their livelihoods and earnings. The poor suffered the most; some even committed suicide. The government, however, did not announce adequate relief even when many other governments were liberal in their assistance. Perhaps our government was more concerned with keeping the fiscal deficit in check. Similarly, many government servants too were stingy with public money, delaying relief to the public despite government approvals and adequate funds. They inherently lack generosity and fall in this category. If you look around, you will see many such instances of people being miserly without reason, even when it does not involve their personal money.

The next shortcoming to be avoided by a ruler is pride without honour. Everyone should have a sense of pride, more so a leader or ruler. But what is being referred to here is unjustified pride. Many leaders suffer from this malady. They make a decision on a whim and stick to it even though it is wrong. They refuse to change it despite the decision causing great harm to people, because of their ego or false pride. This behaviour is called pride without honour. A recent incident illustrates this point. When the central government suddenly imposed the lockdown in March 2020, millions of migrant workers were stranded far away from home. Realizing their difficulties, the government could have easily run special trains to enable them to return home. However, it chose not to do so. The result was thousands of migrant workers had to trek long distances across the country. Even the pathetic sight of them walking in the hot sun did not move the government. This is a good example of the malady referred to in this couplet.

The next failing, according to this Kural, is unseemly happiness. Happiness is highly desirable, but what is referred to here is unjustified happiness. It includes the happiness a ruler gets in harming his critics, happiness derived from petty achievements, and other similar acts. Rulers often feel exceedingly happy with their trivial achievements and tend to exaggerate their minor feats. Unseemly happiness also includes a ruler's happiness in building a palace for himself using public money, or in naming a public building after himself. Our government, too, suffers from this malady. It recently erected a statue without any popular request, spending ₹3,000 crore of public money, and rejoiced at it. Similarly, it is spending ₹13,450 crore on the Central Vista Redevelopment

Project despite no pressing need for it.[4] At the same time, it refused to spend on the much-needed Covid vaccines, leaving it to state governments to foot the bill. Fortunately, it reversed this decision later. This is a good illustration of unseemly happiness.

Another way in which this trait of unseemly happiness manifests itself is schadenfreude—delighting in the misfortune of others. The nineteenth-century German philosopher Arthur Schopenhauer had said, 'To feel envy is human, to savour schadenfreude is devilish.' To describe this emotion, the English language had to adopt the word from German as late as the nineteenth century. Imagine, Thiruvalluvar brought this out in a pithy two-word phrase two millennia ago.

These examples clearly reflect the true meaning of this couplet. That the ruler or government should avoid these lapses at any cost is the import of this couplet. Present-day rulers should carefully study this couplet, understand its full meaning, and follow its advice in governance for the welfare of the people. They will then earn the people's respect and admiration.

KEY TAKEAWAY

Rulers must guard against the maladies of miserliness at times of public need, unjustified pride, and unseemly happiness at their petty achievements. The public should be wary of leaders with these maladies.

---

[4]IANS, 'Govt spent Rs 3,000 cr on Patel statue, Rs 2.64 cr more in advertising it', 16 January 2019, https://tinyurl.com/4yrzvts5. Accessed on 27 November 2024. Wikipedia, 'Central Vista Redevelopment Project', https://tinyurl.com/3xptdrkc. Accessed on 27 November 2024.

9

Guarding against the Unknown

*வருமுன்னர்க் காவாதான் வாழ்க்கை எரிமுன்னர்
வைத்தூறு போலக் கெடும்.* (குறள் 435)

Transliteration
Varumunnark Kaavaathaan Vaazhkkai Erimunnar
Vaiththooru Polak Ketum.

Translation
Life of one not guarding against the unforeseen
Is like the stack of straw near fire.

Meaning
The life of someone who has taken no precautions against unforeseen events and eventualities is like that of a stack of straw kept near fire; it will be destroyed anytime.

Kural Discussions
This Kural figures in the chapter 'Avoiding Faults' or 'Kutram Katithal'. The advice in the chapter pertains to how an individual or a ruler must be conscious of their own mistakes and guard against them, and how they must avoid these, at least when pointed out. Since people tend not to recognize their faults and do not easily accept them even when they are pointed out, Thiruvalluvar has devoted a chapter to it. Although it pertains essentially to rulers or those responsible for governance, all individuals will benefit from his advice.

This couplet talks about taking precautions against unexpected or unforeseen events and eventualities. It stresses that this quality is vital in life. If it is missing, one's life will be destroyed like a stack of straw kept near a fire. Thiruvalluvar is quite adept at using easily understandable similes to explain his points. After harvest, people in Tamil Nadu store their rice straw in stacks for use as animal fodder. Straw is highly flammable, so farmers take care to ensure that fire is never brought near it. Despite this precaution, stacks are often destroyed by a spark from firecrackers during festive seasons, or other careless acts. People are well aware of this danger and do take precautions. Thus, he compares the life of one who does not take precautions to that of a rice stack near fire, so that everyone can easily understand the meaning.

This couplet does not specifically mention against what eventualities precautions must be taken. Inferring from the chapter title, many commentators have said that it is against faults (kutram). A wider interpretation is given by the Tamil scholar Manakkudavar. He says that not taking precautions itself is a fault. Thus, this couplet covers not taking precautions against faults, difficulties, failures, miseries, etc. The message is simply that one must take precautions against all eventualities.

Another word used in this couplet is 'life' or *vaazhkkai*. The couplet says life will be destroyed without precautions. According to leading commentators, the word 'life' also includes wealth. Individuals may thus lose their life or wealth if they commit this mistake. Governments or organizations will primarily lose wealth, but could also vanish by not taking precautions against change—this has happened in a few cases.

For the larger part of the twentieth century, Kodak was the market leader in photographic equipment and film, so much so that Kodak was synonymous with photography. But it failed to take safeguards against the threat posed by digital photography. As a result, it vanished, like the stack of straw destroyed by fire.[5]

---

[5]'Case Study: Kodak's Downfall—A Lesson in Failed Digital Transformation and Missed Opportunities', *The CDO TIMES*, https://tinyurl.com/57f32483. Accessed on 27 November 2024. Mui, Chunka, 'How Kodak Failed', *Forbes*, 14 July 2020, https://tinyurl.com/48nvddpe. Accessed on 27 November 2024.

Similarly, IBM, the leading computer firm, failed to take steps against the threat posed by the creation and adoption of personal computers and lost heavily. Fortunately, it reinvented itself in time.[6] Failure to take precautions against change cost one company its existence and the other a significant loss of wealth. Many such examples can be quoted. To guard against such eventualities, courses on anticipatory management are now offered, and risk mitigation is part of corporate governance.

Similarly, individuals should also take precautions. Adhering to a healthy lifestyle and a healthy diet guards against many diseases; a healthy mind keeps us happy, for example. Those who ignore these norms live like the stack of straw near the fire—they can vanish suddenly. So is the case with personal finances. Those who spend beyond their means without any savings end up in misery. Thus, the couplet applies to organizations and individuals. Taking precautions is, therefore, vital for both individuals and organizations.

I recall a step I took as chairman of the Tamil Nadu Electricity Board (TNEB) to safeguard its finances. Soon after being appointed chairman, a proposal was brought before the board to add 6,000 assessors to the existing 10,000. This proposal was based on detailed negotiations with the unions, as authorized by the board. The additional staff proposed would increase the annual expenditure of the TNEB by ₹60 crore, which was unaffordable. On my suggestion, the proposal was not approved, but deferred to examine other cost-effective options.

As I anticipated, the unions vehemently opposed this move. Claiming that the workload of their members was far too heavy, they started defaulting on meter readings, leading to public complaints. Senior officials of the board advised me to concede to their demands since they had held the board to ransom in an earlier agitation. Concerned with the complaints, the electricity

---

[6]IEEE.ORG, 'IBM's Fall from World Dominance', https://tinyurl.com/3zpw3ekb. Accessed on 27 November 2024.

minister also advised me to compromise, pointing out that the meter had not been read even at the chief minister's house.

Explaining the precarious financial position we faced, I suggested to the unions that, as an alternative, we could implement a scheme whereby meters would be read once every four months instead of the current frequency of every two months. That way, the existing staff could not only handle the current meter readings, but because of the surplus in capacity we would realize, it could even take care of future increases. As anticipated, the unions refused to accept this suggestion and continued their agitation.

From the available data, I could see that the revenue from domestic services accounted for just 20 per cent, with the remaining 80 per cent coming from a few industrial and commercial customers, for which the reading was done differently. If the unions held the board to ransom earlier, it was because of mere panic, without looking into this data. As a warning to the unions, I introduced self-assessment in two units on a pilot basis, following the model of the income tax assessment. It was successfully implemented, with a 10 per cent increase in revenue. I hinted that this scheme could easily be expanded to other units, possibly costing them their jobs. Sensing the risk, they quickly fell in line and dropped their agitation. This savings was possible only because all the threats were anticipated and handled effectively with innovative ideas. It is a practical example of safeguarding an organization's wealth erosion by anticipating threats and planning in advance.

KEY TAKEAWAY

Always take precautions against the unexpected.

10

Seek Advice of the Wise

இடிப்பாரை இல்லாத ஏமரா மன்னன்
கெடுப்பார் இலானும் கெடும். (குறள் 448)

Transliteration
Idippaarai Illaatha Eemaraa Mannan
Keduppaar Ilaanum Kedum.

Translation
The king none to censure him, bereft of safeguards all,
Though none to ruin, shall surely fall.

Meaning
A king without the assistance of wise and knowledgeable men, who can correct him by boldly pointing out his mistakes, is with no safeguards, and he will face ruin even without enemies.

Kural Discussions
This Kural figures in the chapter 'Seeking Advice of the Wise' or 'Periyaaraith Thunaikkotal'. It stresses the importance of the king seeking the advice of the wise and knowledgeable, and of men of virtue and greatness. Although the advice is essentially for kings, others too can benefit by it.

This couplet stresses the need for a king to have in his court great and wise men capable of boldly pointing out his mistakes and correcting him, which itself is a great safeguard for him and his reign. Failure to do so will bring him ruin even without enemies. In those days, kingdoms usually fell because of enemy invasions. But a king who does not associate himself with such wise and bold men need not have enemies for his ruin. This advice applies equally to present-day rulers—many have indeed lost their position by ignoring this advice.

Normally, a ruler's advisors will be hesitant to advise him against his wishes. In those days, the king was sovereign. Therefore, his advisors, even though knowledgeable and wise, would be reluctant to advise him against his thinking. But the king, in his own interest, must seek the company of public-spirited men who are bold enough to give him timely and correct advice and correct him. Such men are committed to public causes. With no personal agenda, they do not curry favour and, therefore, can be bold and fearless. They are likely to be few, but the king must seek them out, have them among his advisors, and listen to them.

If this is the advice to kings, it is even more pertinent to present-day democratic rulers. In a democracy, the Opposition and media are expected to perform this duty, but what really happens is disappointing. The lies of the ruling party are matched by an equal measure of falsehoods from the Opposition. Media is run by industrialists for their personal interests and is often biased, therefore failing to perform its duty. As a result, honest and true criticism essential for good governance is missing. Even so, nothing prevents leaders from seeking advice from public-spirited individuals. Are they doing that? Generally not, but they tend to surround themselves with yes-men; rarely do they seek out advisors who will give them honest and frank advice. Their rule is then like an elephant running amuck without a mahout, as the scholar Parimelazhagar put it.

History is full of instances of regimes ending for want of sound advice to rulers. One such instance is Adolf Hitler's fall. Among his many mistakes, this one was fatal. When World War II was raging, the USA declared war against Japan following its attack on Pearl Harbour, but at that time, it had no intention of declaring war against Germany. On hearing this news, Hitler returned immediately to Berlin and, in three days, declared war against the USA, without any consultations. He was aware that his troops were on the retreat in Russia, and that the USA had five times the armament production capacity compared to Germany. This forced the USA to join the war against Germany and led to his and his country's destruction. If only he had kept wise advisors and had listened to them, this disaster would not have happened. In any event, it is unlikely that Hitler would have sought wise counsel.

In recent times, Donald Trump, former president of the United States, committed many mistakes because of his reluctance to listen to sound advice. Denying the existence of the coronavirus, he refused to heed expert advice to control its spread. Even after the deaths of tens of thousands of citizens, he kept calling it a hoax spread by the Opposition, and his followers believed him. His advisors and cabinet were subservient and did not have the courage to tell him the truth and correct him. Further, prominent leaders in his party did not speak out, likely for selfish reasons. That such a thing could happen in a mature democracy that prides itself on open debates and freedom of speech is a matter of concern. Bold voices were missing in Trump's immediate circle. As a result, the USA suffered the highest number of deaths due to the pandemic.[7] Trump lost his presidency in the 2020 election.

Many such examples can be cited from India—the reader also could easily recall some. The lesson is that leaders must associate themselves with men of stature who value the country's interest above theirs, and listen to their advice for their own sake and for the welfare of their country.

KEY TAKEAWAY

Rulers must listen to the counsel of public-spirited advisors for their and the country's benefit.

---

[7]Worldometer, 'Coronavirus Statistics', 13 April 2024 https://tinyurl.com/27x4ssru. Accessed on 27 November 2024.

11
Avoiding Unsuitable Company

மனத்தூய்மை செய்வினை தூய்மை இரண்டும்,
இனந்தூய்மை தூவா வரும். (குறள் 455)

Transliteration
Manaththooymai Seyvinai Thooymai Irandum,
Inanhthooymai Thoovaa Varum.

Translation
Both purity of mind and purity of action depend
On the purity of a man's company.

Meaning
A man's purity of mind and purity of action depend essentially on the purity of the company he keeps.

Kural Discussions
This Kural figures in the chapter 'Avoiding Wrong Company' or Sirrinam Seraamai'. After advising the ruler to associate himself with and listen to wise people, Thiruvalluvar cautions him against associating with people of small and petty minds. He advises him to avoid them, listing the ills of such associations and the benefits of disassociation. He describes how bad company affects one's thoughts, words, deeds, habits, good name, etc. Who are these individuals the ruler should avoid? Ancient scholar Parimelazhagar, defines them as those 'who deny the benefits of virtuous deeds and the evils of bad deeds'[8]—an excellent definition of evil association.

---

[8]Parimelazhagar, *Thirukkural Moolamum Uraiyum*, Aruna Publishers, Chennai, 2016.

This couplet merely says that the purity of a ruler's mind and action depends on the purity of the company he keeps. It does not explicitly advise him against bad company. The implied message is clear: Since purity of mind and action is essential for the ruler, he should not associate himself with evil-minded individuals or groups. Any wrong association will affect his rule and the welfare of his people. Although this advice is meant for a ruler, it applies to all. In other words, one's purity depends on the purity of one's associates. Therefore, one should choose one's company carefully.

Purity of action refers to the ruler's good deeds, which give him a good name and ensure the well-being and happiness of his people. This in itself is not enough; in addition, he should act with a pure mind. Why is a pure mind important? Throughout his rendition, Thiruvalluvar has consistently underscored the importance of virtue, whatever be the action. He is not merely satisfied with the ends but wants the means also to be proper. For him, the end does not justify the means. Hence, the stress on pure mind or noble thought. Good deeds without good intentions, say for publicity or self-aggrandizement, are not acceptable to him. He, therefore, stresses both purity of mind and action. A tall order indeed! To achieve this the ruler should avoid evil company, is his advice. But this rarely happens in our polity. Many of our representatives have criminal records; despite that, our leaders select them, and we elect them.

The more deeply one thinks of the import of this couplet, the more convinced one is that it applies to all. Take government employees. They often get into bad ways because of undesirable company. Even some senior government employees fail to carefully choose their company and commit many irregularities, spoiling their reputation. Bad company slowly but steadily expands over time, eventually leading to their downfall. I have had occasions to observe my colleagues going astray because of the bad company they kept. Such is also the case with private sector employees.

Even individuals will benefit from this advice. Children who keep undesirable company from an early age often get spoiled and end up leading a wasteful life, becoming a burden on their families and society. Many parents are, therefore, watchful of the company their children keep. We frequently come across news of crimes committed by individuals due to undesirable associations. Those who avoid evil company do lead a better life. One should, therefore, choose one's company carefully to lead a meaningful and happy life.

In today's modern age, online groups on platforms such as Twitter, Facebook, and WhatsApp too have the potential for bad influence. Many groups propagating falsehood, hatred, superstition, enmity, etc., have sprung up. Many of them act as echo chambers where prejudice is reinforced by continual repetition. Subscribers may end up being brainwashed and lose their ability to think dispassionately. Associating with them is not good for our thinking and mental health. They can affect our purity of mind and influence our thinking. Therefore, we should be careful in our choice of groups.

'Bad company is a bad investment. Nothing will come of it,' said a learned man. Another equated it with an infectious disease. This couplet, too, advises us to avoid bad company like the plague since it can affect our purity of mind.

KEY TAKEAWAY

To do good with a pure mind, we should avoid the company of evil people.

12

Importance of Planning

எண்ணித் துணிக கருமம்; துணிந்தபின்
எண்ணுவம் என்பது இழுக்கு. (குறள் 467)

Transliteration
Ennith Thunika Karumam; Thuninthapin
Ennuvam Enbathu Izhukku.

Translation
Think carefully before undertaking a task. To undertake,
Thinking we can think later is a disgrace.

Meaning
Before starting a task, a project, or a reform, or for that matter anything important, one should examine its pros and cons, the difficulties and the obstacles on the way ahead, and plan well in advance how to handle them to complete it in time. An approach to simply start without thinking and think later as we go along is not proper. In fact, it is a disgrace.

Kural Discussions
This Kural figures in the chapter 'Acting After Careful Consideration' or 'Therinhthu Seyalvakai'. After advising the ruler on various aspects of governance, Thiruvalluvar turns his attention to the implementation of government tasks. In this chapter, he highlights the importance of detailed planning for tasks or projects, big or small. Some pieces of advice are: The undertaking should be beneficial to the country or citizens, otherwise it should not be undertaken; minute planning for managing obstacles and

timely implementation is vital; experts should be associated in its planning and implementation; long-time perspective should be kept in view.

This couplet says that the pros and cons of a task should be examined first, and only if found beneficial should it be undertaken. Detailed planning is the next step. Ways to overcome obstacles, difficulties, possible opposition, etc., should also be thought through. Only then can the task be completed on time and within budget. This is the meaning of the first two words of the couplet. Think of all eventualities in advance and then decide firmly, is his advice. What most do is the opposite. They start a task or project with little thinking, sometimes even without funds, and get stuck in the middle. It is because of over-confidence that they think they can tackle issues that may arise as they go along.

The second part of the couplet condemns thinking after starting as a disgrace. It is not just improper but also a disgrace! So much thinking should go into planning before starting that no more thinking will be necessary afterwards. I have often come across individuals regretting midway through a task, wondering why they started it in the first place. Some keep changing the project components so often that the sight of the original objective is lost.

Although meant for a ruler, this guidance applies equally to ordinary people like us. I have seen individuals taking up projects with little thinking and getting into difficulties. I recall a friend who decided to build a house for himself—a good objective. He planned well to limit the cost to ₹50 lakh based on his resources. After all the approvals, he started the construction. During construction, he kept adding and deleting many elements based on gratuitous advice from his friends. He even demolished structures built at a huge cost, merely on someone's advice. He knew that the cost would go up but assumed that he would somehow manage. In the end, he was forced to borrow at an exorbitant interest to complete it at double the cost, that too after a delay of two years. The project ruined him financially, and he suffered for a long time.

This is a typical example of ignoring the advice of this couplet. You can easily observe many such instances if you look around. Those who follow the advice will stick to the original plan and complete the house within the estimate and in time because they would have planned the minutest detail carefully even before starting and would not deviate from it.

Even governments are prone to this malady. With little thinking, they initiate many projects, and halfway through, they face insurmountable difficulties and abandon the project at a huge cost to the public exchequer. Or they complete it with a huge cost escalation.

However, if a government takes a decision in the public interest after careful analysis, people will benefit immensely. I recall one such important decision of great public benefit in my official career. When I was health secretary in the government of Tamil Nadu, the government decided to improve drug distribution in the public sector by setting up an autonomous corporation. We anticipated many difficulties and stiff opposition to this reform from many vested interests. At the outset, we brought them to the notice of the health minister and got his assurance of full support. This was an important first step for the success of the project. Without it, it would have been derailed anytime.

After this, we made a meticulous plan as to how to implement the project. We worked out a careful strategy to handle the opposition from those who benefited from the prevailing system, namely the drug companies and the procurement bureaucracy. As anticipated, we faced stiff opposition and false propaganda during implementation. Thanks to our well-thought-out plan, they could not succeed.

We associated experts in procurement, supply chain management, information technology, drug standards and quality assurance right from the beginning to design efficient processes and systems. The procurement process was simplified with total transparency; the distribution mechanism was streamlined; IT was used for effective management control and timely procurement decisions; quality standards were upgraded; and a team of motivated managers was brought in to implement the new system.

At the end of one year, the corporation was up and running successfully; drug shortage in public health facilities was eliminated throughout Tamil Nadu; a saving of 36 per cent in the drug budget could be achieved thanks to transparent procurement and elimination of wastage. The government was immensely happy with this achievement of great public benefit.

Soon, this corporation became a model for drug procurement and distribution, with all states in India adopting it. This is a good example of the successful implementation of a difficult project, following the advice of this couplet. Its success was possible only because of the minute planning of every step of its implementation well in advance.

However, many projects in both the government and the private sectors are started without much thinking and abandoned midway. Modern management teaches the importance of detailed planning for successful implementation of projects. Somehow, this remains in theory. The Japanese are well known for their detailed planning; they start a project only after considering all aspects, as advised in this couplet. They are, therefore, known for their prompt project implementation.

KEY TAKEAWAY

Before starting any project or task, think through the details carefully and prepare a detailed implementation plan to complete it successfully in time. This is essential for the success of any project.

13

Knowing One's Strength

அமைந்தாங்கு ஒழுகான், அளவறியான், தன்னை
வியந்தான் விரைந்து கெடும். (குறள் 474)

Transliteration
Amainhthaangu Ozhukaan, Alavariyaan, Thannai
Viyanthaan Virainthu Ketum.

Translation
He who agrees not with those around, knows not his limitations,
And is full of self-conceit, will have a swift end.

Meaning
Those who do not move amicably with people around them and do not give them due respect, and those who do not know their as well as their enemy's strength, and those who think highly of themselves, are doomed for a swift end.

Kural Discussions
This Kural figures in the chapter 'Assessing Strength' or 'Valiyarithal'. It is meant for the king to assess his strength before waging a war. Thiruvalluvar has dealt with wars in three chapters, namely 'Assessing Strength' or 'Valiyarithal', 'Choosing the Right Time' or 'Kaalamarithal', and 'Choosing the Right Place' or 'Idanarithal'. Although these thirty couplets may have been written with war in mind, they apply to any major activity of the government. Most make no reference to war—only six couplets mention war specifically. A careful study of these chapters reveals that they are applicable not only to governments but also

to organizations. When a major initiative is undertaken, every organization should assess its strength, and find a good time and place to implement it. Those in management positions should study these couplets in order to succeed and excel.

This couplet mentions that a ruler who cannot move amicably with his team and his neighbours, who does not know his strength, and who thinks too much of himself will face a swift end. By implication, the ruler should avoid these faults.

The first reference is about moving amicably with the people around, which refers to the ruler keeping good relationships with other rulers, his cabinet ministers, and all those working with him. He should be able to carry them along in an amicable way. In today's management parlance, it is called team building, which is vital for organizational success.

The next reference is to his strength; he should know his strength and that of his enemies. One should not overestimate one's strength. Undertaking an enterprise based on a false notion of one's strength will lead to disaster. Senior managers in business, too, should know their strengths and those of their competitors to succeed in business. In fact, they commission studies to assess this. Some even resort to espionage, as governments often do.

The third trait to be avoided is self-conceit. The ruler thinks too much of himself, which firstly arises out of his pre-eminent position and is fuelled by the coterie around him. He is always full of self-admiration. Corporate bosses, too, often suffer from this malady. *Good to Great* (2001), James C. Collins's popular book on management based on an empirical study, comes to the conclusion that the humility of the top boss is one of the hallmarks of great companies.

Why are amicable behaviour and self-conceit mentioned in a couplet dealing with knowing one's strength? A person lacking in amicable behaviour is not likely to attract the company of learned and upright individuals. Consequently, he will miss out on receiving valuable feedback regarding his true strengths and weaknesses. Furthermore, he will always be surrounded by yes-men, eager to reinforce his false belief in his invincibility. He will thus continue to admire himself without knowing the reality. These traits are impediments to a ruler knowing his true strength. Hence, they figure in this couplet.

The couplet's message is that a ruler with these traits will fail or face ruin, and hence should guard against these. Leaders in key positions should, therefore, move with their team amicably, avoid boasting, and carefully assess their true strengths to meet any challenge in order to succeed in their objectives.

A recent incident illustrates the meaning of this couplet. In May 2021, Covid-19 ravaged India, causing great havoc, one reason being that the government was not aware of its weakness. Our public health facilities were grossly inadequate. Beds and essential supplies were in short supply. In addition, the government underestimated the strength of the enemy, the virus, because it was cleverly changing its strategy through mutation. Without knowing our strength (or weakness) and the strength of the virus, the government had to struggle, while thousands of citizens lost their lives. Self-conceit also played a role in this tragedy. The government was in a self-congratulatory mode, claiming that the country was the best in handling the first wave. Lulled by this self-praise, it perhaps did not anticipate the onslaught of the second wave and was caught off guard.

Yet another example is the US government. Its leader was underplaying the virus, calling it a hoax, and failed to take precautions. He, too, failed to carry his team, did not listen to experts, indulged in self-praise, and failed to appreciate the strength of the virus. The result was that the country suffered the highest per capita deaths in the world despite being the richest. These two examples highlight the importance of governments assessing their strengths.

Strength, weakness, opportunities and threats (SWOT) analysis is a strategic management technique used nowadays to help an organization handle business competition and in project planning. It evaluates internal strengths and weaknesses and external opportunities and threats in an organization's environment to formulate strategic decisions. This is the principle stressed in this couplet while highlighting the traits to be avoided by a ruler or king.

KEY TAKEAWAY

A leader must govern, carrying his team with him, without thinking too much of himself, and with full knowledge of his strength and that of his competitors.

14

Waiting for an Opportune Time

கொக்கொக்க கூம்பும் பருவத்து; மற்றதன்
குத்தொக்க சீர்த்த இடத்து. (குறள் 490)

Transliteration
Kokkokka Koombum Paruvaththu; Marrathan
Kuththokka Seerththa Itaththu.

Translation
As crane stands with folded wings, so wait in waiting hour;
As crane snaps its prey, when fortune smiles, put forth your power.

Meaning
One should wait for an opportune time to act like a crane waiting patiently for its prey. Once the right time comes, one should move swiftly and finish the task without fail, like the crane snapping its prey.

Kural Discussions
This Kural figures in the chapter 'Knowing the Opportune Time' or 'Kaalamarithal', containing advice on the necessity to choose the right time for a task. As we saw in the previous chapter, this too was written with war in mind but has universal application. While stressing the importance of choosing the right time, Thiruvalluvar has given no specific advice on the right time. He is not, of course, referring to any auspicious time fixed by an astrologer. It is left to the ruler or task implementor to choose the right time, based on his knowledge, experience, skill, intelligence, etc. History speaks of great rulers choosing the right time and succeeding in their campaigns.

This couplet explains how one should wait patiently for an opportune moment through an easily understandable simile. The patience should be like that of a crane. A crane stands still in a pond, waiting for its prey. It refrains from making any movement at all so that its prey concludes that it is sleeping and keeps moving about unconcerned. Once the prey is in sight, the crane springs to life and strikes at it with its long beak, leaving no room for the prey to escape from this sudden onslaught. Most people would have witnessed this sight. The technique resembles an ambush. The couplet says that one should wait patiently, like a crane, for the opportune time. One should not show anxiety or haste; one should not worry about others' teasing because of inaction. But at the right moment, one should move fast and finish the task like the crane. No hesitation should be shown when the right time arrives. In this example, the right time is decided by the crane. Similarly, the ruler should decide the right time—he should be as sharp as the crane.

Obviously, this advice does not apply to minor tasks. Perhaps swift action is required in such cases. But this is useful for major tasks or programmes. I recall one such programme. In 1995, the government decided to launch the massive Pulse Polio campaign to eradicate polio from India. Besides procurement and distribution of polio vaccines, a massive campaign to educate mothers to bring all eligible children for vaccination was also launched. The timing of the campaign was carefully chosen, taking into account the convenience and ability of mothers to attend the vaccination camps. Ample time was allocated for creating awareness, and consideration was given to avoiding the agriculture and rainy seasons. The decision on the timing was made through extensive consultations between the centre and the states. This turned out to be a major reason for its success. Polio was eradicated from India after many years of similar campaigns.

Similarly, when the government wants to introduce a major reform, it should first assess the mood of the public. If it is adverse, the first step is to change the mood through a campaign and wait for the right time. Rushing a reform without consensus will backfire. If the government wants to increase taxes, the opportune time is when the country is prosperous. Governments are aware of this principle, but sometimes they make mistakes and are forced to backtrack. Even companies look for an opportune time to introduce new products—they choose the festive season. Individuals, too, look for a good time to achieve their goals. When a subordinate wants something from his boss, he makes the move when his boss is happy—he waits for that good moment. Even with a spouse, one looks for the right time to get what one wants. Looking for the right time for personal ends seems to be in our blood. Thiruvalluvar's advice is to hone this skill and use it for major organizational tasks benefiting the country and organizations.

KEY TAKEAWAY

One should patiently wait for the right time to successfully complete a task, and once the moment arrives, one should act swiftly.

15

Assessment of a Person

குணம்நாடிக், குற்றமும் நாடி, அவற்றுள்
மிகைநாடி, மிக்க கொளல். (குறள் 504)

Transliteration
Kunamnhaadik, Kutramum Nhadi, Avarrul
Mihainhaadi, Mikka Kolal.

Translation
Weigh a man's virtues and faults, and
Choose him by virtues that prevail.

Meaning
Before coming to a conclusion about someone, we should carefully consider his virtues and faults, and then assess which are in excess and take a view based on those in excess.

Kural Discussions
This Kural figures in the chapter 'Test and Trust' or 'Therinhthu Thelithal'. A ruler cannot carry out all tasks himself, and, therefore, needs the support of trusted employees. This chapter advises him on how to choose them. He should carefully consider their skills, talents, trustworthiness, experience, etc., before selection. Once selected, he should trust them fully without constantly doubting them, for that would be counterproductive. Hence the chapter 'Test and Trust'. It explains how people should be chosen for senior positions like that of a minister and others. Those who do not hesitate to do wrong and are not virtuous should not be selected; biased selection should be avoided; all selections should be on

the principle of test and trust—the test should be such that those selected would be trustworthy forever.

This couplet talks of first examining one's virtues and faults; the next step is to assess which is in excess. The decision to select a person should be based on this assessment. Virtue here means skills and ability to execute government tasks, not moral virtue. It recognizes the reality that no one is perfect—all have good and bad attributes. Merely because someone has faults, he should not be rejected, because he may have the skills for the job in question. Therefore, faults should be compared with virtues and then a considered view taken on his suitability.

The couplet talks of decisions being taken based on what is in excess, *mihai* in Tamil. Tamil scholar Manakkudavar says this refers to excess both in quality and quantity. Hence, proper weightage should be given to quality or quantity depending on the nature of the job. For example, a job that involves handling money requires integrity more than knowledge of accountancy. Another interpretation of the word 'excess' is as follows: 'A person may have many bad qualities; at the same time, he may have an important quality needed for the task at hand. In this case, excess refers to this exceptional quality. He should be chosen, ignoring his many bad qualities.'

This advice is relevant to the private sector too, which operates through a human resources (HR) wing for recruitment. It should assess the job applicant's skills and compare them to his faults before deciding. Faults alone should not be grounds for rejection. For example, an engineer may be good in his subject but poor in communication. Instead of rejecting him, he may be considered for the design or R&D wing, where poor communication skills do not matter. On the other hand, if the person is good in communication but inadequate in technical knowledge, he may be good as a project head with his ability to build a team and execute tasks well. The excess should be assessed, considering one's strengths and weaknesses in relation to the job, and a decision taken. A careful study of this chapter may benefit the HR wing.

This message is useful to individuals too. While grumbling about the faults of friends and colleagues, we should also consider their virtues. We will then change our assessment and stop grumbling, which will improve our relationship with them, enhancing our happiness. A well-known Tamil proverb says: 'You will lose friends and relations by harping on their faults.' Surprisingly, it is human nature to exaggerate faults, ignoring virtues.

KEY TAKEAWAY

Everyone has some faults. Hence, both the good and bad qualities of a person should be weighed together while considering them for employment or even for personal association.

16

Delegation

இதனை, இதனால், இவன்முடிக்கும் என்றாய்ந்து
அதனை, அவன்கண் விடல். (குறள் 517)

Transliteration
Ithanai, Ithanaal, Ivanmutikkum Enraaynhthu
Athanai, Avankan Vidal.

Translation
This task, by these means, if this man can complete,
Test him thoroughly; if convinced, leave it to him.

Meaning
Before entrusting a task to an employee, evaluate whether he is capable of executing it, and whether he has the resources to implement it, and after entrusting, leave it to him.

Kural Discussions
This Kural figures in the chapter 'Evaluate and Entrust' or 'Therinhthu Vinaiyaadal'. After advising the king on how to choose his key employees, Thiruvalluvar, in this chapter, turns his attention to getting work out of them. Choosing the right man for the right job is the primary task of the ruler. Even after a careful choice, the employee may turn out to be a misfit. Therefore, monitoring his performance is necessary, which is also the ruler's responsibility. This chapter gives many nuggets of administrative wisdom to the ruler as to how to extract work from his workers. Since execution is hard, those responsible for execution should study this chapter thoroughly.

This couplet deals with the art of delegation. The ruler should, in the first place, find out whether his employees, including the minister or senior administrator, are capable of executing the task. This he can do based on his own judgement or feedback from others. He should then find out how he proposes to complete the task. What are the skills or means he will employ? After that, the ruler should decide whether the chosen person is capable of executing the job. Only after that must the ruler entrust it to him. Having done that, the ruler should forget it.

A key word in this couplet is *ithanaal*, meaning 'ways of executing the task'. The leader should be satisfied that the ways proposed are right. It implies that he himself should know the execution methodology; or even if he does not, he should find it out from the chosen person and satisfy himself that it is right. It also implies that the leader could contribute to the means while assessing the execution of the task because he is equally interested in the task.

Another key word is *vidal*, meaning 'leave it' or 'forget about it'. How can the leader forget about a task? After all, the ultimate responsibility is his. If his assessment is right, he will not lose by forgetting. On the other hand, if his choice is wrong and the task is not implemented in time or well, he will get a bad name. This word, however, does not preclude him from keeping an eye on the task and intervening when necessary. Another couplet says that the king should keep a careful watch on all that is going on in his country. Hence, the leader should review the progress; the frequency of such reviews will depend on the employee's motivation and progress.

I recall a personal experience that illustrates the principles of this couplet. The ruling party lost the parliamentary elections in 1989. The defeat was attributed to the abysmal performance of the public distribution system (PDS). I was brought in as food secretary with a new team and was told that I had been handpicked to set the PDS right. However, the means were not discussed, as the couplet says! Normally, this is not the practice in government postings. The government, however, followed the advice 'vidal' and left things to me. It was getting regular feedback from the public and elected representatives on the PDS. With the encouraging feedback, it did not intervene till the end of my tenure. As administrative head of many organizations, I adopted this principle by leaving tasks to the right persons, which vastly enhanced my productivity in addition to improving organizational efficiency.

This principle is thus vital not only for the leader but also for managers at all levels. They do entrust a task after assessing the competence of the task manager and discussing ways of implementing it. But what happens afterwards differs. Some will not leave it to them, as the couplet says, but continue to micromanage the task, affecting the task manager's morale and efficiency. Their time is wasted, leading to neglect of other vital tasks, affecting organizational efficiency. They are unable to assess the correct level of monitoring needed to improve the overall efficiency.

A leader's primary task is to get things done in his organization. He cannot execute all tasks by himself, and therefore, he should delegate them. If he delegates to the right person with high motivation, he needs to monitor lightly, say once a month. Suppose the task manager is found somewhat inadequate—the leader can monitor more often, coach him, and assist him. Of course, if an unworthy manager has been wrongly chosen, no amount of monitoring will help. Also, the leader's efficiency will be affected. The solution is to change the manager, admitting an error in selection. These are fundamental principles of delegation, which I have explained in simple terms in my book *Your 27 Hour Day* (2010).

Leaders are of different types. Some delegate everything and forget about it; others struggle to delegate and get submerged in detail; many delegate but continue to micromanage; only a few know the art of delegation enunciated in this couplet. And they are highly productive. All leaders should, therefore, learn the art of delegation to improve productivity in their organizations.

KEY TAKEAWAY

After entrusting a task to a competent employee, and having thoroughly examined the means of execution, the leader should leave it to the employee to execute it, and focus on other important tasks.

17

Commitment to Duty

இழுக்காமை யார்மாட்டும் என்றும் வழுக்காமை
வாயின், அதுஒப்பது இல். (குறள் 536)

Transliteration
Izhukkaamai Yaarmaattum Enrum Vazhukkaamai
Vaayin, Athuoppathu Ill.

Translation
To never relax in vigilance, ever watchful
Where this is found, there is no greater gain.

Meaning
If the trait of not forgetting one's duty either due to forgetfulness or other reasons is present without fail, there is no other greater gain than that.

Kural Discussions
This Kural features in the chapter 'Pochchaavaamai,' which means 'Not Forgetting Duty', which is the opposite of *pocchaamai*, an ancient Tamil word meaning 'forgetfulness'. Learned Kural commentators have interpreted it as not forgetting one's duty or not being indifferent to one's duty because of forgetfulness or other reasons. This chapter contains advice for the king's employees on how to be vigilant and watchful in whatever they do and remain committed to their duty. Ancient scholar Manakkudavar's explanation is worth quoting: "'Pochchaavaamai' means "not

being forgetful."[9] It also refers to not paying attention to others' mistakes and misdemeanours due to laziness. This chapter condemns non-performance of duty due to forgetfulness, laziness, or complacency.

This couplet says that if one has the habit of not forgetting one's duty, nothing is equal to that virtue. Doing one's duty faithfully is considered a great virtue. The ability to complete tasks efficiently and faithfully is a valuable trait, making individuals with this skill highly sought after. In addition to earning the respect of their employers, they will also be respected by their colleagues for their dependability and productivity. For an individual, it is a great virtue and nothing else can equal it—it is the greatest gain for him. This is one interpretation. The message is that if one does not have this quality, one should strive to acquire it.

There is yet another interpretation: If all persons possess this virtue, nothing is equal to that. The benefit to society will be immense. Obviously, this advice applies to the king as well. If he is forgetful and neglects his duty, his subordinates cannot be expected to be diligent.

I have often observed forgetfulness leading to neglect of tasks. The normal excuse for the non-execution of a task is forgetting it! It is understandable if it happens once or twice, but if it happens persistently, it is mainly due to indifference or complacency. I am sure this is the experience of many managers. Lazy people forget their duties because of a lack of focus and forgetfulness. I also tend to neglect some tasks due to forgetfulness. Therefore, I keep a to-do list to remind me of the tasks, thereby improving my productivity, and advising others to do so. This couplet's key advice is that employees should be vigilant in their duties without any room for complacency.

This advice is quite relevant to present-day government employees. Due to job security, they often become complacent

---

[9]Mankkudavar, *Thirukkural Moolamum Uraiyum*, Poompuhar Publishers, Chennai, 2015.

and forget that their primary duty is public service. All are selected through a competitive examination that can be cleared only by hard work. However, once recruited, they become complacent, leading to neglect of duty. Even All India Service officers are no exception. Only hard work and commitment can get them through the tough competitive examination, but these traits may vanish over the years. Complacency sets in owing to ego, self-praise, forgetfulness, enjoyment, security, etc., affecting public service delivery.

History has recorded many kings losing their kingdoms owing to neglect of duty. One such figure is the Roman emperor Nero. He was believed to be playing a musical instrument while Rome was burning. His primary duty was to wage a war against the fire. Instead, he gave in to his pleasure, forgetting his duty. This is an example of *pochchaappu* or 'forgetfulness'.

KEY TAKEAWAY

Employees should steer clear of forgetfulness, indifference and complacency to contribute significantly to the organization's success.

18

Just Governance

குடிபுறம் காத்து, ஓம்பிக் குற்றம் கடிதல்
வடுவன்று; வேந்தன் தொழில். (குறள் 549)

Transliteration
Kutipuram Kaaththu, Ompik Kutram Katithal
Vaduvanru; Venthan Thozhil.

Translation
Guard, tend, punish, brings
No reproach; it is the duty of a king.

Meaning
Protecting citizens from external and internal harassment, caring for their welfare, and punishing crimes are not faults of a king; they are his duties.

Kural Discussions
This Kural figures in the chapter 'Just Governance' or 'Sengkonmai'. In this chapter, Thiruvalluvar describes what a king should do to give his citizens a just and fair government. This is followed by another chapter, 'Bad Governance or Cruel Rule' or 'Kotungkonmai'. He has thus devoted twenty couplets to guiding the king on just and proper governance. He is as interested in good governance as he is in universal education, for which too he has devoted two chapters. Just governance means an impartial and fair rule, a reign based on virtues, a rule in which all are equal before the law. The rule is for the benefit of citizens and not for the benefit of the king or his friends.

This couplet talks of the duties of a good king. His first duty is to protect citizens from external enemies and criminals from within. A few commentators have mentioned that this includes protection from the king too. He should not harass them, nor should his agents. His citizens should be able to lead a peaceful life without fear of anyone. In today's parlance, this refers to the role of the ruler in ensuring the country's defence and maintaining law and order. The king should do both well.

His next duty is to take care of his citizens' welfare. He should find out what they need to lead a happy life. In an agricultural society, the king should think of schemes to increase agricultural production, such as building tanks, dams, taking up drought mitigation measures, etc. He should also encourage trade and commerce to improve the country's prosperity.

The third duty is to act firmly against crimes. Only then will crimes come down. Crime-free governance is his important duty. In another couplet, Thiruvalluvar's advice is to forgive and forget the mistakes and crimes of others, but it was meant for an individual in his private life. Here he stresses it is the public duty of a king to punish those committing crimes, in a fair and just manner.

There is a mention that these are not faults. How can such acts be considered faults? Many commentators have interpreted this to mean that the king should not worry about his name being tarnished by his stringent actions. Without going soft on crimes, he should take deterrent action without fear or favour, even against friends and relatives committing crimes. Only then is his rule just. The mention of 'not a fault' is to stress his duty to curb crimes without favouring anyone, including known friends.

This advice is quite relevant to present-day rulers also. We often see them going soft on crimes to favour their friends, relatives and party workers, but they do not spare members of the Opposition. The same law is used in different ways. This is not the just government envisaged by Thiruvalluvar. He expects the ruler to treat his partymen and members of the Opposition equitably and punish them severely for crimes. We also see the government itself slapping cases against citizens criticizing it. A government that needs to protect its citizens itself harasses them!

The foundation of democracy is the rule of law, implying that all are equal before the law. This is the principle enunciated in this couplet: 'Guard, Tend and Punish' in an impartial and just manner. Long before democracy was thought of in this way, Thiruvalluvar had the foresight to lay down its principles because of his humanist approach. Will we absorb and follow them scrupulously to enrich our polity?

KEY TAKEAWAY

The duty of the ruler is to protect his citizens without any discrimination and to care for their welfare.

19

Result of Bad Governance

நாள்தொறும் நாடி முறைசெய்யா மன்னவன்,
நாள்தொறும் நாடு கெடும். (குறள் 553)

Transliteration
Nhaalthorum Nhaati Muraiseyyaa Mannavan,
Nhaalthorum Nhatu Ketum.

Translation
He who makes no daily search for citizens' grievances, nor redresses them, that king
Does day by day his realm to ruin bring.

Meaning
The king should examine the shortcomings and deficiencies of his rule and take remedial steps daily; otherwise, his rule will deteriorate day by day, eventually bringing ruin to his kingdom.

Kural Discussions
This Kural figures in the chapter 'Cruel Rule' or 'Kotungkonmai', which describes the disasters that will result from a cruel or tyrannical rule and warns the king against it. Thiruvalluvar is against a rule that strikes terror in the minds of the people, and many couplets in this chapter highlight this. Although a sovereign king can afford to be cruel, can a democratically elected leader be cruel or tyrannical? We do see that in many countries. Once elected, leaders resort to tyrannical methods to consolidate their powers without any concern for just governance. Hence, this couplet is as relevant today as it was in the age of monarchy.

Since just governance is fundamental to the welfare of citizens, Thiruvalluvar has devoted twenty couplets to stress its importance.

This couplet deals with another aspect of just governance, namely the welfare of citizens. It points out the dangers of a rule that does not address its ills or shortcomings. It says that the king should examine the ills or shortcomings of his rule every day, find out the reasons behind these, and eliminate these. If he does not do so, his rule will deteriorate day by day, and his kingdom will be ruined soon. What is demanded of a king is quick action to remedy the ills, which essentially means the grievances of his citizens, that too each day. A tall order indeed!

This was a difficult task for a king of those days, since he had no modern means to get feedback on the ills. He could get information only through his spies or ministers, who might not have been that reliable or that well-informed. To expect him to go around finding out the ills was difficult, that too on a daily basis. Even so, Thiruvalluvar expects him to do it. We have heard of kings going around their kingdom incognito to find out the difficulties of their citizens. According to Tamil legend, a king named Manu Neethi Cholan had a gong installed outside his palace. Anyone demanding justice could sound it and get an audience with him.

It is not enough to listen to the grievances; the king should address them immediately. If he does not do so, Thiruvalluvar warns, he will lose his kingdom soon. With a strong condemnation of the *muraiseyyaa* king—one who fails to render justice—Thiruvalluvar highlights the importance he attaches to just governance. The key point is that even a king cannot afford to ignore his citizens' grievances but should address them quickly.

The contemporary relevance of this couplet is unmistakable. Addressing citizens' grievances is even more important for elected leaders. They now have the wherewithal to get feedback on their governance. Media and the internet give them instant feedback. In addition, they get feedback from the official and party machinery. Do they remedy the ills? Not always. Those who do so get re-elected and get another mandate to rule. However, some leaders consider any feedback not to their liking a conspiracy by either a foreign power or the Opposition, and remain blind to the ills of their governance. They do not want to hear anything bad about their rule. Thiruvalluvar calls such a rule cruel! We consider it a bad rule, for which a price must be paid in the subsequent elections.

Although many examples of cruel rule can be cited from our democratic governments, one example of misrule under the British comes to mind. Three million people lost their lives in the Bengal Famine in 1943 because of British misrule. Agricultural production was badly affected in Bengal because of severe drought. The Bengal government did not announce any famine relief; in addition, it continued to deny the existence of the famine, although it was evident to any observer. Newspaper reports were ignored, and the government continued to be in denial mode. To make matters worse, the central government banned the movement of food grains between the states and permitted exports to meet the needs of the British people. Refusing to accept any responsibility for the famine, Winston Churchill, the then prime minister of the United Kingdom, made a ridiculous claim that the famine in Bengal was because 'Indians breed like rabbits'. This shows that leaders can be blind to the sufferings of the people and also get away with making false claims.

Fortunately, India faced no famine after Independence, thanks to responsive governments. Amartya Sen has claimed that death due to hunger was eliminated in India because of the major role played by the media, giving timely feedback that could not be ignored by an elected government. However, hunger and malnutrition remain a major concern, with successive governments largely ignoring both. When will we get a government to address these issues?

KEY TAKEAWAY

A good government's primary responsibility is to assess the ills or shortcomings of its governance and take immediate remedial action.

20

Govern with a Soft Touch

கடிதோச்சி மெல்ல எறிக, நெடிதுஆக்கம்
நீங்காமை வேண்டு பவர். (குறள் 562)

Transliteration
Katithochchi Mella Erika, Nhetithuaakkam
Nheegngaamai Vendu Pavar.

Translation
To reprimand firmly and punish lightly is the way
For lasting name and fame of the ruler.

Meaning
A ruler who wishes to improve his governance and be remembered forever should reprimand his citizens and workers strongly for their mistakes or faults but punish them lightly.

Kural Discussions
This Kural figures in the chapter 'Not to Terrorize' or 'Veruvanhtha Seyyaamai'. Some rulers conduct themselves in a manner that creates fear among their subordinates and citizens. In this chapter, Thiruvalluvar advises them to govern without terrorizing anyone. He envisions citizens living peacefully without any fear of the ruler, and government employees performing their duties without unnecessary apprehension. This differs from the tyrannical rule condemned in the previous chapter. In a democracy, it is unthinkable to terrorize citizens, making Thiruvalluvar's advice on governing without fear more relevant for government employees. Occasionally, a few elected leaders do terrorize people, but they are

often thrown out in subsequent elections.

This couplet advises a leader how to govern. When he notices mistakes by employees of the State or citizens, he should reprimand them harshly. But he should be soft while punishing them. This should be done by those wanting long-lasting improvement in governance. The word used in the couplet is *nhetithuaakkam*, meaning 'long-lasting improvement', which includes administrative improvements and long-lasting name and fame for the leader. Simply put, the leader should adopt this strategy for long-term improvement in governance and for his everlasting good name and fame.

How will such behaviour ensure a good name? Harsh reprimand will prevent people from committing mistakes—they will remember it, and will not commit mistakes again. Moreover, they will naturally expect harsh punishment from such a person. When, however, they end up with a lenient punishment rather unexpectedly, they will be happy and try to be more diligent in future. After all, the ruler's aim is to correct mistakes; if there is an improvement, there is no need for punishment. Therefore, the strategy of harsh reprimand and light punishment will improve the morale and productivity of employees while ensuring admiration for the leader.

Some of my schoolteachers followed this principle while punishing us. In those days when the maxim 'spare the rod and spoil the child' was taken seriously, they would raise the cane as if to strike a painful blow, but the blow would be a gentle touch. The fear was good enough for us to improve our behaviour. I remember those schoolteachers even today because their intention was good—to correct us but not to punish us harshly. But schoolteachers who mete out punishments mercilessly are soon forgotten.

This advice applies to present-day administrators and managers. They should aim to correct their subordinates instead of punishing them. When punishment is needed, it should be light. Those whose bark is worse than their bite may make better bosses.

Strong punishment should be reserved only for the incorrigible. Elected leaders are generally soft on punishments and resort to harsh punishments only when unavoidable. But administrative heads are of different types. Some mete out harsh punishments for light mistakes, whereas others punish even without mistakes, out of sheer whim or anger. Yet others neither reprimand nor punish, in order to earn a good name, leading to overall administrative decline. Those who know the balance advocated in this couplet are highly successful and bring about major administrative improvements, with everlasting good name.

Justice should be tempered with mercy. In this context, a story about Napoleon Bonaparte, a French military officer and statesman, is worth recalling. Known to be a stern leader, Napoleon understood the importance of swift justice in order to maintain the morale of his troops. Any deserter or runaway would be summarily executed if caught. On one occasion, a poor old woman presented herself before the general, pleading for mercy for her son, who was to be executed the next day for the offence of desertion. Napoleon told the mother, 'Your son does not deserve mercy.' The mother replied, 'I did not ask for justice. I asked for mercy, which is not something that is deserved.' The emperor pardoned the deserter.

I drew some inspiration from this couplet when I was in service. For a long time, I was convinced that meting out punishment appropriate to the offence was proper governance. My decisions were, therefore, in line with this principle. An incident changed this forever. After about ten years of service, I was heading an organization with 3,000 employees. One day, a proposal to decide the punishment of an employee was put up to me. He had misappropriated ₹5,000. Since it was a serious offence, I ordered his removal from service. After that, I forgot about it.

About ten days later, I received a letter from his wife, describing her miserable condition in graphic detail—she and her three children had been going without food for days. This distressed me. I did not realize this other dimension while deciding the ex-employee's case. Clearly it was not humane, though legally correct. I wondered whether I had committed a mistake and what I could do to correct it.

At that time, this couplet came to mind. After studying it, I was convinced that my punishment had been harsh. Therefore, I decided to review it. Giving him a lighter but appropriate punishment, I reinstated him, after which I really felt good. When his family met me later, I advised him not to waste money on horse racing and to take care of his family—I hope he did. This couplet gave him a second chance!

After this incident, I followed this advice right through my career. Since employees were unaware of my policy, they took my reprimands seriously and were always vigilant, giving me little occasion to punish. Reprimanding firmly without punishing got me their willing cooperation to improve organizational output and bring about major reforms. This technique of pretending to be harsh while being kind at heart to get things done is an art to be learned by successful administrators.

KEY TAKEAWAY

Managers who reprimand firmly and punish lightly will deliver better and earn a good name.

21

Verifying Information

ஒற்றொற்றித் தந்த பொருளையும், மற்றுமோர்
ஒற்றினால் ஒற்றிக் கொளல். (குறள் 588)

Transliteration
Orrorrith Thantha Porulaiyum, Marrumor
Orrinaal Orrik Kolal.

Translation
Confirm not merely on one intelligence report;
But verify it through another's report.

Meaning
The information brought by one spy should be verified independently through another spy.

Kural Discussions
Spying is an important function of the State. Therefore, Thiruvalluvar has devoted a chapter to 'Espionage' or 'Orraadal', the art of spying. Six couplets deal with how spies should function, and four on how the king should handle them. In the olden days, kings used espionage mainly to safeguard the country against enemy invasions.

This Kural advises the king that he should verify the information brought by one spy through another. He should act only after that, on the assumption that the information received could be wrong.

Spies are well-trained in their art and quite reliable. Therefore, where is the need for verification? Although well-trained, they could commit mistakes or could even double-cross. Suppose the king acts without verification and starts a war or embarks on a wrongful course; the consequences will be disastrous. Hence this advice. In fact, another couplet advises the king to verify facts through two spies. Perhaps this applies to more serious decisions like starting a war. Corroboration is always essential.

Also, a king should know what is happening in his kingdom. He should know what his friends, enemies, and other nations, both friends and foes, are doing in order to govern well. He can get this information also through spies but verify it himself or through another spy. In ancient times, such intelligence was gathered only through humans, but today, technology plays an important role in espionage. Countries compete to modernize their technology for espionage and keep spying on each other. Also, terrorism and other threats to our peaceful existence have added to the need for effective spying.

Many wings of our Central Government are engaged in espionage. External intelligence is gathered by the Research and Analysis Wing (RAW) and military intelligence, and internal intelligence by the Intelligence Bureau, which collects information on terrorism and other anti-national activities. This helps the State to take timely preventive steps. State governments, too, have an intelligence wing that collects information on local terrorism and anti-state activities. These are manned by well-trained spies, ensuring our internal and external security. Seasoned leaders do check the information collected by one source through another before acting on it.

A recent failure to follow this principle led to the disastrous Iraq War. The US government simply accepted its intelligence wing's report that Iraq was manufacturing weapons of mass destruction (WMD). However, after the war, the US could find no evidence of Iraq manufacturing WMD. The war was apparently started on false intelligence, and if the US government had reverified the report or checked it through another intelligence agency, the war could have been prevented, and many lives spared. It is, however, alleged that the US government deliberately used this false intelligence as a pretext to wage war for its geopolitical objectives.

This advice to verify information is useful to the ruler in other ways too. In his official capacity, he meets many people every day, who constantly pass on information to him. Instead of simply believing them and acting, he should verify the information through other sources. Some leaders fail to do this, act in haste and suffer. Even senior managers should follow this principle: Verify all information through another source.

Recently, newspapers reported an incident of a prominent leader condoling the death of a national leader, and regretting later because the prominent leader had acted on wrong information. Therefore, individuals too should not trust one source of information and check it through another source to avoid mistakes and misunderstandings.

KEY TAKEAWAY

Information received from one person should be verified through another before one acts on it.

22

Greatness of Human Zeal

உடையர் எனப்படுவது ஊக்கம்; அஃதிலார்
உடையது உடையரோ மற்று? (குறள் 591)

Transliteration
Udaiyar Enappatuvathu Ookkam; Ahthilaar
Udaiyathu Udaiyro Marru?

Translation
The rich are those who have zeal; who do not have it
Own nothing, whatever else they possess.

Meaning
Only those having zeal are considered wealthy; can we consider those not having it wealthy, though they are very rich? No, they cannot be considered so.

Kural Discussions
This Kural figures in the chapter 'Ookkam Udaimai' or 'Zeal'. An exact translation of the word *ookkam* is difficult, as it refers to many human qualities such as zeal, enthusiasm, determination, great energy, strong will, etc. The word also implies 'positive outlook'. Those who have it pursue their goal vigorously and achieve it. After advising the king on many aspects of governance, Thiruvalluvar turns his attention to citizens and emphasizes the importance of zeal for their progress and their country's betterment. No doubt the king should have it too.

This couplet says that only those with zeal are wealthy, and those without it cannot be considered wealthy. Normally, we associate wealth with a person's material possessions or bank balance. In earlier days, those possessing large tracts of land were admired and respected as landlords. Nowadays, we hear about billionaires and unicorns. Every day, we read about a new unicorn or another Indian joining the billionaires' club. It looks as though wealthy people are competing for prominent positions in the wealth possessed—for instance, the wealth of the shares in companies owned by them. This couplet says that such people are not wealthy, but only those with zeal are!

How can this be accepted when everyone goes after material wealth? What can anyone do with just zeal but without money? Thiruvalluvar himself has emphasized the importance of wealth in another chapter. Why, then, this statement? Consider a person born into enormous wealth. If he lacks zeal, his wealth will quickly dissipate owing to his mismanagement and indifference. History is full of such cases. On the other hand, those with zeal and enthusiasm—in other words, 'ookkam'—can acquire wealth, excel in education, become talented and accomplish anything they desire. That is why 'ookkam' is considered the greatest wealth; through it, one can acquire any other wealth. Those admired as billionaires have attained such status mainly because of their zeal.

The message is: irrespective of position or status in society, one can come up in life if one has zeal. The illiterate can become educated; the poor can become rich; the ordinary can become extraordinary; the rich can become richer; the ruler can govern better. Thus, there is no limit to what one can achieve with this great wealth of zeal! This message is intended for all humanity, as zeal is the foundation of human progress. Thiruvalluvar wants citizens and rulers to embrace this message and live a life of zeal and enthusiasm for all-round prosperity.

All of us would have come across ordinary people achieving great heights thanks to this wealth. One such example is Jack Ma, among the richest people in Asia. Born poor, he struggled to come up. In his youth, he faced innumerable failures that would have put off anyone. He failed the university entrance examination twice. He applied for thirty jobs and was rejected from them all. Harvard University rejected him ten times. Still, he did not lose his enthusiasm. Utilizing the opportunity offered by the internet, he set up many companies and worked with great zeal to become a very wealthy man. Undeterred by his failures, he persevered and succeeded, thanks to his wealth of zeal. Many such real-life examples abound. The reader would know at least one such person who succeeded in life just by zeal. Let us, therefore, lead a life of great zeal and enthusiasm.

KEY TAKEAWAY

The foundation for human progress is laid by zeal and enthusiasm.

23
Zeal Essential to Growth

வெள்ளத்து அனைய மலர் நீட்டம், மாந்தர்தம்
உள்ளத்து அனையது உயர்வு. (குறள் 595)

Transliteration
Vellaththu Anaiya Malar Nheettam, Maanhthartham
Ullaththu Anaiyathu Uyarvu.

Translation
The deeper the water, the longer the stem of lotus;
The greater the men's zeal, the higher they rise.

Meaning
The length of the lotus's stem depends on the depth of the water in the pond; likewise, a man's growth depends on his zeal.

Kural Discussions
This Kural has remained my guiding spirit from the day I studied it in school. Whenever I had the occasion to address the youth, I used to quote it, explaining its in-depth meaning to encourage them to always aim high.

It figures in the same chapter 'Ookkam Udaimai'—we discussed the meaning of the word 'ookkam' in the previous couplet—and states that a man's progress or growth depends on his zeal. If a person has it, he can become whatever he wants to—a great doctor, scientist or engineer, or excel in any other field. Furthermore, zeal encourages him to aim high, gives him the energy to work hard and the doggedness to achieve his aim. Therefore, a person's achievements are closely linked to the intensity of his zeal.

The couplet explains it through a simple simile. It likens the rise of a person to the length of the lotus's stem, which depends on the depth of the water in the pond. The deeper the water, the longer the stem. Similarly, a man's rise depends on his 'ookkam'. Zeal is compared to the depth of the water and the length of the stem to the rise of the person. This simile provides an easily understandable analogy, especially for youngsters.

We often come across stories of ordinary individuals achieving remarkable success solely due to their unwavering zeal. One such notable example is A.P.J. Abdul Kalam, former president of India. Despite being born into a modest family in a small village near Rameswaram and attending ordinary schools, he possessed immense zeal that propelled him to the prestigious position of president of India. Abdul Kalam himself was a staunch advocate of 'ookkam' and consistently encouraged our youth to set their aspirations high. 'Have an aim in life, continuously acquire knowledge, work hard, and have perseverance to realize the great life,' he told them, stressing the pivotal role of zeal in achieving greatness.

This couplet and the previous one should be read together. The previous one highlights how zeal is the greatest wealth, whereas this one emphasizes that our growth depends on our zeal—the more of it we have, the higher we grow. Thiruvalluvar's passion for zeal is quite evident because he himself had it in abundance. Humanity still benefits from reading *Thirukkural* and finding new and relevant meanings to enrich our lives.

KEY TAKEAWAY

Our growth essentially depends on our zeal.

24

Avoid Laziness

நெடுநீர், மறவி, மடி,துயில் நான்கும்
கெடுநீரார் காமக் கலன். (குறள் 605)

Transliteration
Nhedunheer, Maravi, Madi, Thuyil Nhaangum
Keduneeraar Kaamak Kalan.

Translation
Procrastination, forgetfulness, indolence and sleep
Are the pleasure boat of those doomed to ruin.

Meaning
Continuously delaying tasks, forgetting to do them, just being lazy without executing them, and sleeping over them are the four habits comparable to a pleasure boat doomed to sink.

Kural Discussions
This Kural comes under the chapter 'Avoiding Indolence' or 'Madi Inmai'. Although meant primarily for the king's employees, it applies equally to citizens. It is astonishing that Thiruvalluvar is as concerned about citizens' laziness as my parents, who used to constantly urge me to not be lazy in my younger days. Indolence is a major concern in our country. Almost a disease. One can see people whiling away time in front of tea shops or under a tree. Lazy people cannot progress in life. Hence, Thiruvalluvar has condemned laziness in this chapter, after praising zeal. While zeal is a must for growth, indolence must be avoided at all costs.

This couplet talks about four traits to be avoided by employees and citizens. What are they?

The first trait is procrastination. It means postponing the task to tomorrow. 'You cannot escape the responsibility of tomorrow by evading it today,' said Abraham Lincoln, former president of the United States. Procrastinators delay tasks endlessly. They allow procrastination to take over their life without realizing that it is the enemy of productivity and efficiency.

The second trait is forgetfulness, which refers to forgetting to do a task in time. This, too, affects our productivity. Most of us suffer from this malady. Management books advise us to keep a to-do list to overcome it, since we cannot keep everything in our memory.

The third trait is laziness or indolence. It is also quite common. Many indulge in indolence and while away their time in frivolous activities. They do not realize that they are wasting precious time.

The last trait is sleep, which refers to the tendency to sleep over an issue. Not being alert on the job is also referred to as sleeping. It is another form of indolence. All should be alert on their job.

This couplet does not explicitly say that these undesirable traits should be avoided. Instead, it says that they are like a pleasure boat doomed to ruin. Imagine a pleasure boat that is in bad shape. When it goes to sea, it is doomed to sink. Those with these traits are ill-equipped, like the pleasure boat destined to sink. The word used to describe the boat, *kaamak kalan*, implies that such people willingly get into the boat. For the sake of the pleasures of a laid-back life, they ruin their life, that too willingly! This couplet is a stern warning against leading a life of indolence.

Why are procrastination, forgetfulness and sleep mentioned in a couplet on indolence? For these traits invariably go together, one supporting the other. Lazy people normally procrastinate, are forgetful and not alert, and therefore, are not good employees.

I recall a popular song in a Tamil blockbuster of the late 1950s. It cautions youngsters against getting branded as idlers, pointing out that one who sleeps in class misses out on education; one who is not alert in business loses his capital, while one who naps on his job loses his reputation. Hence, there is no point blaming Dame Fortune for the consequences of one's own inertia.

Avoiding these self-destructive habits, government employees should work with zeal for the betterment of the country and their own personal growth. Otherwise, they will be ruined like the pleasure boat. Similarly, citizens too should refrain from such habits, and work with zeal for their progress and for the betterment of the country.

KEY TAKEAWAY

Everyone should avoid procrastination, forgetfulness and laziness, and be always alert in order to achieve all-round progress.

25

Fruits of Perseverance

தெய்வத்தான் ஆகாது எனினும், முயற்சிதன்
மெய்வருத்தக் கூலி தரும். (குறள் 619)

Transliteration
Theyvaththaan Aahaathu Eninum, Muyarsidhan
Meyvaruththak Kooli Tharum.

Translation
Though destiny be against, yet hard work
Will pay to the extent of the hard work.

Meaning
Even if God wills that something cannot be achieved, hard work and perseverance will certainly bear fruit to the extent of the hard work.

Kural Discussions
This Kural figures in the chapter 'Aal Vinaiyutaimai', meaning 'persistent hard work'. *Aal* in Tamil means 'govern' and *vinai* means 'task'. Therefore, the chapter title literally means 'governing a task'. The great commentator Parimelazhagar explains, 'This chapter stresses the need for everyone acquiring the habit of persistent hard work.'[10] All couplets in this chapter stress the importance of non-stop effort in the performance of a task, so much so that the Tamil scholar Solomon Pappaiah has rightly renamed it

---

[10]Pappaiah, Solomon, *Thirukkural*, Kavitha Publishers, Chennai, 2018.

'Ceaseless Effort'. After praising zeal and condemning indolence, Thiruvalluvar emphasizes hard work in this chapter.

This is my favourite couplet in this chapter. Whenever I failed a task, I used to recall it. Wondering whether my effort was not good enough, I would double it. I succeeded many times, but not always. What is referred to as God is what we commonly reckon as fate or destiny. Most of us believe in fate. Thiruvalluvar himself believes in it and has composed a chapter on it, in which he has stated that nothing can be more powerful than fate (380). But here, he says that persistent effort will bear fruit despite the all-powerful fate. How much fruit? It depends on the intensity of the hard work. The more you strain, the greater your effort, the more will be your gain. In sum, our persistent effort will certainly bear fruit despite the powerful fate lined up against us.

What this couplet hints at is that ceaseless effort can beat the all-powerful fate. Is this correct? Is there not a contradiction with another couplet (380) that claims that nothing is more powerful than fate?

Let us look at the words used in this couplet. Nowhere is there a word that explicitly states that fate can be defeated. What is said is that the fruit will depend on your effort, on its quantity and quality. Although you may not reach your goal, you will still get some benefit to the extent of your effort. The couplet does not specifically say that you will win over fate. Does it mean that fate is undefeatable? Are we to accept that fate is invincible? Is this Thiruvalluvar's view? Fortunately, Kural 620 throws clear light on this. It categorically states that one can defeat it. However, not everyone can; only a limited few can. Who? Those who work very hard—those who work ceaselessly, tirelessly, without ever losing heart. In short, those who are driven can reach their goals despite fate willing otherwise. A similar view has been expressed in this couplet as well, but in a slightly different manner—the message here is that our reward depends on our effort. If it is intense, we will win, but if it is inadequate, we may not. Perhaps we need the blessings of fate to put in the required effort!

A person known to me was keen to join the Indian Administrative Service (IAS) and worked very hard towards his goal. He wrote the examination seven times and was called for the interview thrice but did not succeed. Since he had already spent seven long years, I advised him not to waste further time on this (because I thought his fate was against him) and look for other jobs. But he persisted and worked harder with double the energy and passed the examination in his eighth attempt. He finally got the benefit of his persistent effort. Perhaps even fate took pity on him and changed its course! This is one example of persistent effort scoring over powerful fate. When you look around, you will see many such instances of hard work succeeding, even accomplishing impossible feats. History is full of such success stories.

Still, why do we believe in fate or destiny? Since it offers us some comfort to move on with life's tribulations. When something unexpected happens in life despite our efforts or the precautions we take, we take it as fate and carry on. Anyway, we have no other option. On the contrary, a few consider fate as inevitable and neglect hard work and effort. The weak and lazy find it easy to blame everything on fate. Thiruvalluvar is totally against this. After strongly condemning laziness in the previous chapter, he eulogizes the virtues of hard work in this chapter. As a counter to those who use fate as an excuse for laziness, this couplet implies that fate can be overcome through diligent effort. The quantum and quality of the required effort will vary from task to task and occasion to occasion.

Faced with failures in my official career, I put in additional efforts on many occasions and succeeded. More hard work and detailed planning converted failures into successes. Not that I succeeded on all occasions. The right approach in such cases was to accept with humility that my effort was not up to the mark, instead of blaming fate. This is the message of this great Kural.

Human progress has been possible only through the great efforts of countless individuals over millennia. Hunger was mitigated by the hard work of peasants; health was improved dramatically thanks to the toil of a great many doctors; inventions were the result of the tireless efforts of numerous scientists. The tireless efforts of millions have improved our standard of living, and the ceaseless efforts of just a few make a disproportionate impact on our lives—a testament to the power of hard work and determination. Thiruvalluvar has, therefore, rightly stressed the importance of hard work and the will to succeed despite unfavourable circumstances or destiny. If our youth heed his advice and work hard with dedication and commitment, India will soon become a great country like China or Japan, which are renowned for hard work.

While discussing hard work and fate, the following quote by Thomas Jefferson, the former president of the United States, is pertinent: 'I am a great believer in luck, and I find the harder I work, the more I have of it.' He seemed to have grasped the essence of this couplet. It is hard to beat a person who never gives up. Even fate cannot!

KEY TAKEAWAY

Hard work is essential to perform our tasks well and to progress in life. Blaming fate for failures is incorrect.

26

Handling Tragedies and Obstacles

வெள்ளத்து அனைய இடும்பை, அறிவுடையான்
உள்ளத்தின் உள்ளக் கெடும். (குறள் 622)

Transliteration
Vellaththu Anaiya Itumbai, Arivudaiyaan
Ullaththin Ullak Ketum.

Translation
Though sorrow, like a flood, comes rolling on,
When wise men's minds regard it, it is gone.

Meaning
A great sorrow that comes like a flood faced by a wise man will vanish the moment he thinks of it, on how to handle it with courage and determination.

Kural Discussions
This Kural figures in the chapter 'Idukkan Azhiyaamai' or 'Fortitude in Distress'. The word *idukkan* means 'obstacles and sorrows of life'. After praising zeal and perseverance, Thiruvalluvar describes ways to handle obstacles in task execution and the sorrows of life in this chapter. When such things happen, one should not be devastated but should handle them with fortitude. The obstacles should be met with courage and determination, and the ups and downs of life with equanimity. The key message is: One should not break down or be overwhelmed by the hurdles and tragedies of life but should develop a mindset to cope with them with fortitude.

This couplet talks of a great sorrow or tragedy that comes like a flood. A deluge comes suddenly and causes great havoc. Unusually heavy rains in Chennai in 2015 flooded the entire city and many homes, leading to huge loss of lives and property. This sorrow is like such a flood. How does one handle it? The solution suggested is simple. If one has the right frame of mind and just thinks about it, it will vanish! This is what the couplet says.

Two key words of the couplet are difficult to translate, but grasping their meaning is important to appreciate its message. The person who can ably cope with such great sorrow is called *arivudaiyaan*, which means 'wise man'. In another chapter, Thiruvalluvar describes the characteristics of a wise person, but the wisdom here takes on a different meaning. It refers to the ability to navigate through challenges, and overcoming the sorrows and obstacles of life. This individual has the wisdom to understand that pleasures and sorrows come in cycles, and sorrows are unavoidable. Aware of the Buddha's teachings that sufferings are inevitable, he can take them in his stride. Or, he has the fortitude to deal with them calmly. He has this wisdom. One need not be a saint to possess this wisdom; anyone can acquire it by developing this mindset.

Another phrase, *ullaththin ulla*, literally means 'thinking in the mind'. The wise man just thinks of the sorrow, and that is enough for it to vanish! How can it vanish just by thinking, however wise he may be? What is referred to is his attitude or approach to sorrow. He may take it as his fate; or, he may consider it insignificant; or, he may look at it philosophically and take it as normal; or, he may simply not consider it sorrow at all; or, he may handle it with great determination to get over it. A man facing a significant calamity may become paralyzed, and uncertain about the appropriate course of action. However, if he is wise, he will employ his reasoning powers, comprehend the nature of the calamity, devise strategies to address it, and act accordingly, instead of remaining in a state of bewilderment, overwhelmed by the enormity of the problem.

It is all in the way a man thinks of sorrow or obstacles. We have often seen different people handling the same difficulty in a distinctly different manner. For some, it is a great tragedy; for others, it is nothing. I have observed people losing their cool over a flight delay of just half an hour, but some celebrate the extra time with coffee. It is all in the mind.

We all face obstacles and sorrows in life. We can overcome obstacles with perseverance and determination, but some succumb and run away from them. When faced with business losses, those with fortitude fight back and revive the business successfully, but those without courage are distraught, and some even commit suicide.

Then there are personal sorrows. The loss of loved ones causes great pain and sorrow, like a flood. But wise people handle it calmly and recover quickly. They are aware of what the Roman stoic philosopher Seneca said: 'Great grief does not itself put an end to itself.' I am reminded of Benjamin Disraeli, former prime minister of the United Kingdom, who said, 'Grief is the agony of an instant; the indulgence of grief the blunder of life.' The wise man referred to in this couplet is aware of this principle. Hence, he knows how to handle great sorrow.

Many other obstacles in life, such as loss of a job, failure of a business, failure in a task or exam, etc., can be handled with courage and wisdom. Unlike the loss of loved ones, these can be overcome with fortitude. Where there is a will, there is a way. We have already read Thiruvalluvar's advice that we can change even destiny through hard work. Remember theoretical physicist Albert Einstein's statement: 'In the middle of every difficulty lies opportunity.' We should have the wisdom to see the opportunity.

KEY TAKEAWAY

We should develop the mental skills necessary to handle any tragedy or obstacle in our life calmly.

27

Duties of Ministers

தெரிதலும், தேர்ந்து செயலும், ஒருதலையாச்
சொல்லலும், வல்லது அமைச்சு. (குறள் 634)

Transliteration
Therithalum, Thernhthu Seyalum, Oruthalaiyaach
Sollalum, Vallathu Amaichchu.

Translation
Making the right choice, planned execution, doubtless
Expression of opinions are a minister's hallmark.

Meaning
Choosing the right priorities for the regime; identifying the tasks to achieve them; executing them expeditiously, and boldly giving the right advice to the king on any issue, particularly delicate and contentious issues, are the talents required of a good minister.

Kural Discussions
Thiruvalluvar now moves on to the 'Ministry' or 'Amaichhiyal' sub-division. It has ten chapters describing the qualities expected of a minister, such as eloquence, honesty, task execution capability, and ability to carry his team, including the king, with him. We will discuss these in the coming chapters.

This Kural comes under the first chapter, 'Minister' or 'Amaichchu'. Back then, the king was assisted by a council of ministers, as in the present day. As his first level of support, ministers should be competent. Otherwise he cannot perform well. A chapter has, therefore, been earmarked for ministers like the one for kings (*see* Regal Duties), describing the traits of a good minister and his duties and responsibilities. While it is an excellent guide to a minister, it is also useful to the ruler in the selection of ministers.

This couplet describes the talents expected of a minister. It mentions three. The first is setting priorities, which means that the minister should be fully aware of the country's needs and choose the right priorities, keeping in mind its limited resources. Only then can the country and its citizens get maximum benefit. Also, he should be able to convince his colleagues and the ruler of his choice, which will not be possible unless his priorities are right. A minister should, therefore, possess the ability to choose the right priorities, since wrong ones will drain resources, yielding little benefit to citizens. For example, the right priority in May 2021 was Covid vaccination. Fortunately, the government chose it, launched an excellent media campaign, made vaccines available in all centres across the country, and also monitored the vaccination programme through an excellent software. This choice of the right priority prevented many deaths.

The second talent is timely execution of tasks. This calls for excellent planning, anticipating obstacles and ways to tackle them, building a motivated team, giving them freedom and guidance for proper execution, regular monitoring and course correction, among other things. This is what is expected of a talented manager or a CEO today. The king's minister should have this talent! Only then will government tasks be implemented well and in time.

The third talent is the minister's ability to give clear and bold advice to the cabinet and the ruler. He should be able to justify his advice with facts and figures—not just give an opinion. He should enjoy the trust of his colleagues and the ruler. The ruler often faces controversial issues where decisions are not that clear-cut. He will be in two minds. This couplet expects the minister to give bold and categorical advice even to the ruler; it should not be tailored to the ruler's liking. Independent advice in the interest of the country and citizens is what is expected of him. Even democratically elected ministers often hesitate to express their views to the head of the government, but Thiruvalluvar expects appointed ministers to boldly advise a king!

Without a doubt, these traits are required for present-day ministers and government executives in key policy formulation and implementation roles. They should learn the art of setting priorities and programme implementation. However, many government employees in high positions consider file disposal more important than task execution. In my book *Your 27 Hour Day*, I have explained in detail how priority setting is important and how execution can be sped up.

Equally important for them is the third talent—the ability to give independent advice. Over the years, it has diminished. Senior administrators tend to give the advice liked by the political executive. Often, they desist from giving any advice, leaving the decision to the political masters. They have forgotten their fundamental duty to give free and frank advice on governance, which results in many wrong and improper decisions. They should ponder over this Kural and follow it to improve governance. The prime minister and chief ministers too should choose people with these talents for ministerial and top government positions.

KEY TAKEAWAY

Ministers and top officials should have the skill to prioritize, to execute tasks well, and to give bold and frank advice on crucial issues.

28

Power of Cogent Speech

விரைந்து தொழில்கேட்கும் ஞாலம், நிரந்தினிது
சொல்லுதல் வல்லார்ப் பெறின். (குறள் 648)

Transliteration
Virainthu Thozhilketkum Gnaalam, Nhiranhthinithu
Solluthal Vallaarp Perin.

Translation
The world will act fast at the will and command of one with
Well-ordered and cogent speech in persuasive language.

Meaning
If there are persons who can speak cogently and sweetly, people will immediately implement the tasks commanded by them and ask them yet again what more needs to be done.

Kural Discussions
This Kural figures in the chapter 'Eloquence' or 'Solvanmai'. It stresses the power of oratory and contains advice on how to be eloquent. One should speak in such a manner that listeners like the speech; long-winded or meaningless talk should be avoided; the speech should be crisp and clear; it should be sweet and not hurt anyone. Since the subdivision deals with ministers, many commentators have held that the advice is meant for them. Since none of the couplets mentions ministers, we can take it that they are applicable to everyone, especially politicians and senior executives. Realizing the importance of eloquence, many courses on effective public speaking are now run for senior managers.

We can all benefit by learning the art of eloquence advocated in this chapter. If only we could focus on speaking sweetly, our lives would be enriched with greater happiness and harmony!

This couplet says that the entire world will listen to people with eloquence! What kind of eloquence? The speech should be cogent, convincing and without inherent contradictions. And, on top of that, sweet. Only those with such eloquence will command the respect of the world. Some can speak cogently and convincingly but not sweetly; their speech will not command that much respect. Sweetness in speech is, therefore, as important as cogency, if not more. A minister with such eloquence will easily be trusted and respected by his colleagues and the ruler.

What is the outcome of such eloquence? Not only will the world, namely the people of the country, immediately carry out the tasks assigned by such a speaker, but they will also rush back to ask him about their next task. That is the power of eloquence!

The couplet merely says if there are people with such eloquence, citizens will implicitly obey. It does not specify where they should be. Obviously in the cabinet. They will be able to carry the citizens with them with ease. The king should keep such persons in his cabinet to make his job easier. If he himself has this talent, it is even better.

One may wonder whether eloquence has such power. I recall Mark Antony's famous speech in Shakespeare's *Julius Caesar*. Fearing that Julius Caesar, the ruler of Rome, would declare himself king, the conspirators assassinated him in the Senate. Hailing Brutus, a noble man, as the liberator and the new leader, they projected the assassination as the liberation of Rome from a tyrant. Welcoming it, the people of Rome, too, hailed Brutus as liberator. Mark Antony, a friend of Caesar, sought permission to pay a eulogy to Caesar, which was given on the condition that he only praise Caesar but not say anything against the conspirators. When he finished his oration, it moved the crowd so much that it rose against the conspirators and chased them away from Rome, denouncing them for murdering Caesar. Such was his eloquence even in a dire situation.

By and large, our politicians have this ability to a varying degree. Our towering leader Anna (C.N. Annadurai) was credited with great eloquence. Our prime minister (Narendra Modi) has this power, such that citizens are willing to do whatever he asks of them. There are many such examples of great speakers influencing public opinion. I have observed eloquent ministers easily gaining approval for their proposals through their speaking skills. The same is true of senior executives—those with eloquence can get things done with ease.

Even individuals benefit from this talent, particularly by speaking sweetly. If they can express their point of view cogently and sweetly, it will carry greater conviction. They will be loved and respected by their friends and relatives. Eloquence can thus contribute to happiness also.

Is not Thiruvalluvar himself an excellent example of great eloquence? He has succinctly laid down life's universal laws in couplets of just seven words. We study, research their meaning, and attempt to follow his advice, even after two thousand years! Most great men are inspiring during their lifetime, but what sets Thiruvalluvar apart is his ability to continue inspiring us with his eloquent writing.

KEY TAKEAWAY

If we can speak cogently and sweetly, not only will everyone listen to us, they will also happily do whatever we ask them to do.

29
Purity of Action

இடுக்கண் படினும் இளிவந்த செய்யார்,
நடுக்கற்ற காட்சி யவர். (குறள் 654)

Transliteration
Idukkan Patinum Ilivanhtha Seyyaar,
Nhadukkarra Kaatchi Yavar.

Translation
Though fallen on evil days, no demeaning deed they do
Those with a clear and unwavering mind.

Meaning
Whatever may be the magnitude of the fall or troubles one faces in life, those with a clear and unwavering mind will not resort to anything demeaning to overcome the situation.

Kural Discussions
After highlighting the importance of eloquence, Thiruvalluvar deals with integrity in the chapter 'Purity in Action' or 'Vinaith Thooymai'. In it, he stresses the importance of integrity for high officials. Their actions should extend beyond mere popularity so as to benefit citizens. They should refrain from any actions that wise men would disapprove of, and their motivations should never be driven by personal gains. Instead, all their deeds should align with principles of virtue and ethics.

As before, there is no mention of ministers in any couplet in the chapter, but many commentators have held that these couplets are meant for them. Given that their decisions have a significant impact on a large population, it is only natural that the highest level of integrity is expected of them. How relevant is this advice for the present-day ministers and administrators!

This couplet has a simple yet profound message: One should never do anything demeaning to get out of a difficult situation. Refusal to deviate from ethical principles under any circumstances, even in the face of adversity, is the hallmark of integrity. People with integrity normally do nothing dishonourable, but even they may start wavering when in serious trouble and end up doing something dishonourable. I have observed honest men committing folly when they or a member of their family get into a tight situation—they invent some justification to do so. This couplet asserts that those with a clear and unwavering mind will never do any such wrong. The message is clear: High officials and ministers should maintain integrity under any situation, even when their job is at stake. A high benchmark for them!

What is happening today is really distressing. Lack of integrity and corruption are rampant at all levels. It appears some ministers want the position just to make money. Decisions are often taken ignoring public interest but for personal gains. Their defence is that they need money to win elections. Although this has an element of truth, it does not justify corruption. However, high officials cannot use this excuse, since they are paid well and enjoy a long and secure tenure. Still, some of them lack integrity and help politicians make money and help themselves too in the process. Newspapers often report unimaginable wealth amassed illegally by senior officials. Despite sustained efforts by the government, there are no visible signs of a decrease in corruption. Corruption at the higher level encourages corruption at the lower level, making it endemic.

That Thiruvalluvar has allocated an entire chapter to the purity of action shows that corruption was prevalent even in his days. It seems corruption is a disease born with humans! History records the prevalence of corruption in the Roman Empire 2,000 years back. Corruption is an upshot of unchecked power.

Transparency International, the global alliance against corruption, is striving to create a corruption-free world. It assesses the corruption perceptions index (CPI) every year; a CPI of 100 reflects a corruption-free nation, whereas 0 reflects the most corrupt nation. As per its 2023 survey, Denmark occupies the first position of 176 countries with a score of 90. More than two-thirds of the countries score below 50, reflecting that the world has a long way to go in eradicating corruption. India, with a score of 39, just below the average of 43, stands at 93rd position in the company of 'more corrupt countries'. Although tighter laws and strict enforcement are helping, a dramatic improvement will be possible only if government employees genuinely believe that honesty is essential for the public good. Also, leaders and ministers should show genuine concern about the lack of integrity and set an example for others to follow.

KEY TAKEAWAY

We should discharge our duties with the highest integrity, even in the face of great personal hardship.

30

Firm Mind

எண்ணிய எண்ணியாங்கு எய்துப, எண்ணியர்
திண்ணியர் ஆகப் பெறின். (குறள் 666)

Transliteration
Enniya Enniyaangu Eiythupa, Enniyaar
Thinniyar Aakap Perin.

Translation
What they will, men achieve in the way they will,
If they will with a firm mind.

Meaning
Those with a firm mind will achieve whatever they will, in the manner they willed.

Kural Discussions
In the following three chapters, Thiruvalluvar focuses on the execution of tasks, which is crucial for ministers. This Kural figures in the chapter 'Firmness in Action' or 'Vinaiththitpam'. After stressing the need for zeal, hard work and integrity, he now highlights the importance of firmness. Many government decisions usually face opposition and obstacles. Weak-minded ministers abandon them at the slightest resistance. Hence the need for firmness to implement government tasks. This chapter contains plenty of practical advice on how to execute them efficiently. All those responsible for execution will benefit from studying it.

This couplet has a simple message: those with a firm mind will always achieve whatever they will, the way they willed. It thus simply stresses the importance of a firm mind in getting a job done. Firm-minded executives will not be deterred by any opposition or impediment. They will go ahead with determination and complete the task in the way it was originally envisaged. Firmness of mind is, therefore, a prerequisite for the successful execution of tasks.

The word *thinniyar* means 'one who possesses a fired-up human will'—in other words, firmness of mind or determination to complete a task or achieve a goal. If a minister possesses this trait, the king can leave any task to him with the confidence that he will execute it competently. Those without it will abandon it midway or even modify it so much that it is not what was originally envisaged. The king with multifarious responsibilities needs many 'thinniyars' to lighten his burden. He should, therefore, choose individuals with this trait as ministers. Timely completion of tasks without leaving room for corruption will bring him a good name, in addition to huge benefits to citizens.

Obviously, this principle applies not only to ministers but to everyone. Those with a firm mind invariably achieve great things. We read about Olympic players—all of them work hard, undergo rigorous training, participate in many international events, and constantly excel in their performance, benchmarking it with Olympic records. A lot of money is poured into their efforts, with countries competing for medals. Yet, only three people win medals in each game. They are the 'thinniyars' referred to in this couplet. They do not rest until their goal is achieved and go after it with great determination and unparalleled commitment. The message for ordinary individuals like us is that if we have the will, nothing is beyond our reach.

I recall one such accomplishment when I was the administrator of the Corporation of Madras. The corporation was in financial distress since the property tax had not been revised for 20 years. All those years, it was under an administrator without an elected body. Revision of tax would be tough even for an elected body, and certainly more difficult for an administrative regime. We thought through the pros and cons. Since the lack of funds badly affected our performance, raising taxes was the only way to improve civic amenities. We knew it would be resisted but looked at ways to overcome it. Considering all the hurdles and despite advice from colleagues to leave it to the elected council, we were confident that it could be successfully completed.

As a first step, we got the in-principle clearance of the chief minister and the municipal administration minister, after which we also got the cabinet's approval. This was the essential first step for our success.

We were a little more ambitious and decided to improve the system of assessment along with the revision since the tax regime was riddled with corruption. Those who paid off assessors got a lower assessment. As a result, the tax of similar houses in the same locality differed by even ten times, reflecting the level of corruption. We, therefore, decided to bring about equity in assessment while revising taxes, which would naturally be resisted by assessors. We also anticipated objections to the revision by the public and the media. We, therefore, chalked out detailed plans to handle these obstacles.

To minimize the role of assessors, we decided to levy property tax based on the plinth area of the property. We decided to get the required data from property owners themselves instead of through assessors, to eliminate malpractices. We even issued orders that they should not interact with owners. Owners were requested to file a return containing details of their properties. While this was going on, we had to face an unexpected hurdle. A public interest litigation (PIL) petition was filed in the Madras High Court that our method of assessment was illegal on the grounds that the assessment should be based on property value and not on the plinth area. A stay by the court would have derailed our reform. We effectively argued our case, employing senior advocates, and got the petition dismissed.

Simultaneously, we took up and completed many civic works speedily, meeting long-pending demands of citizens. The works and the improvements were perceptible. We could sense the feeling of satisfaction among citizens. All the while, we kept harping on the lack of funds as a major constraint. The media was briefed on the justification for and the benefits of the revision. Although softening the public mood would help, any loud public protest could lead to political intervention at any time, resulting in the cancellation of the revision. We kept this possibility in mind but were confident we could sail through, thanks to our detailed planning.

Even after receiving returns from property owners, assessors were not given a role—they were hoping to get an opportunity to verify them. We simply decided to rely on the returns received from the owners. To assess the property value, we arrived at a standard square-foot rate for each residential area based on consensus; we deliberately fixed it less than the market rate. With these rates, property value and tax were calculated by the IT system, leaving no discretion to anyone.

After revision, some owners faced an increase up to ten times, while others had no increase at all. This merely reflected the prevailing inequality in assessment due to corruption. But this time, our assessment was fair and equitable. Still, as anticipated, the sharp increases led to protests from the public and criticism from the media, despite our media campaign.

We addressed this problem by providing for an appeal and encouraging the owners to appeal; the media was used to convey our message that speedy relief could be obtained through an appeal. The appeals were disposed of in record time—many got relief. We also eliminated discretion in appeals through standardizing the quantum of relief by linking it to the increase. All this mollified most houseowners. The protests subsided; the government did not intervene, and the tax revision could be accomplished in an administrative regime!

Thanks to this revision, property tax revenues went up by three times, enabling the corporation to perform better. All this was possible only because the top administration of the corporation had a firm mind, as suggested in this Kural.

KEY TAKEAWAY

If you have the will, there is nothing that you cannot accomplish!

31
Avoid Haste

தூங்குக தூங்கிச் செயற்பால; தூங்கற்க
தூங்காது செய்யும் வினை. (குறள் 672)

Transliteration
Thoongkuha Thoongkis Seyarpaala; Thoongkarka
Thoongkaathu Seyyum Vinai.

Translation
Delay deeds that merit delay; delay not
Deeds that demand prompt action.

Meaning
Deeds that call for leisurely execution without hurry should be implemented leisurely, whereas those requiring prompt action should not be delayed.

Kural Discussions
This Kural figures in the chapter 'Task Execution' or 'Vinai Seyalvakai' dealing with task execution. Such is the importance Thiruvalluvar has attached to timely and proper execution of tasks. He has also explained ways of achieving it.

This couplet has excellent advice for those responsible for the execution, particularly those in management positions. The poetic usage of words in the couplet is completely lost in translation.

Some tasks require careful analysis and detailed discussion for proper implementation. One should not hurry them through but execute them leisurely because any undue hurry will spoil them. Others, however, require quick action, and therefore should be executed quickly without any delay. The couplet does not explain which tasks call for leisurely execution and which need prompt implementation. That judgement is left to the one executing the task. It only offers him the advice not to hurry all tasks, but to reflect on them carefully, and choose the appropriate course of action.

The ruler and senior government officials implement numerous tasks as part of their jobs. To delay a task or not is a decision based on the particular circumstances. Some tasks will face stiff opposition, in which case a delay for dialogue with opponents may help. Delay itself will sometimes blunt the opposition. Others brook no delay at all. For example, when people are faced with severe floods, prompt action is necessary. The ruler and the ministers should then act swiftly, cutting red tape and bureaucracy. To categorize tasks this way is left to the ruler and his ministers. They should have the skill for it.

For example, our government introduced three farm laws in 2020, which were opposed by farmers. Their agitation continued for more than a year, but the government stood firm. Many supporters of these laws claimed that they would usher in an agricultural revolution in India. The opponents, of course, alleged that these would destroy the livelihoods of farmers. Finally, the government was forced to repeal these laws in the face of stiff opposition. Enacting such laws required widespread consultations with state governments, farmer groups and other interested stakeholders, but the government failed to do that. It acted in a hurry. What needed to be done slowly was hastened up, with the result that the much-needed reform got derailed.

An example of speedy action by the government was when Covid-19 struck. The lockdown was introduced promptly to contain the virus despite causing huge sufferings to ordinary people. In addition, a massive vaccination campaign was launched to vaccinate the population against the virus. This is an example of prompt action.

The government and senior officials often act swiftly when it is not needed but sometimes fail to act promptly when needed, perhaps because of an inability to make the correct assessment. They should develop this skill. Only then can they act correctly and deliver better public services. The 'one size fits all' approach does not work in most circumstances.

The couplet has lessons for individuals too. Many of us tend to act hastily without much thought. However, there are times when delaying action can actually benefit us, as hasty actions can lead to costly mistakes. As the well-known proverb says, 'Haste makes waste.' We should, therefore, develop the skill to know when to act and when not to act. If we look around, we can identify many successful people who have honed this skill. We should emulate them.

KEY TAKEAWAY

We should act promptly on some occasions but leisurely on others, and should develop the skill to differentiate between the two.

32

Task Completion

முடிவும், இடையூறும், முற்றியாங்கு எய்தும்
படுபயனும், பார்த்துச் செயல். (குறள் 676)

Transliteration
Mutivum, Idaiyoorum, Murriyaangu Eiythum
Patupayanum, Paarthus Seyal.

Translation
Judge well the mode of completion, hurdles and
benefits on completion, before venturing on a task.

Meaning
Before starting a task, examine carefully the ways of completing it, the obstacles that will arise on the way, and the great benefits that will accrue on its completion.

Kural Discussions
This is another Kural in the chapter 'Task Execution' or 'Vinai Seyalvakai'. It explains three aspects to be taken into account by those responsible for execution. The first is to focus on the timely completion of the task. Even before starting it, one should carefully examine whether it will be possible to complete it as planned and as scheduled. There is no point in starting and abandoning a task midway or delaying it endlessly. The second aspect is to anticipate the obstacles that may arise during execution. Any major task invariably faces some hurdles, more so government tasks, because of conflicting interests and pulls and pressures. Anticipating these and working out a strategy to handle them is necessary. Only then

can the task be successfully implemented. The last is to examine the benefits that will accrue on its completion. The word used, *patupayan*, means 'great benefits', implying that government tasks or projects should bring great benefits to the public. The king's ministers should examine all these aspects before taking up a project.

Present-day governments should follow this advice too. Often, projects are started with mere announcements but without examining the cost-benefit. Schemes with little benefit to the public are also taken up but with ulterior motives. One can only hope that our ministers will keep this sound advice of Thiruvalluvar in mind and take up schemes of at least some, if not great, benefit to the public.

This advice is applicable to the private sector as well. In fact, firms do follow it. Before embarking on a project, they examine whether it is welcomed by the people living in the project area and the government, and whether any objections from regulatory agencies, among others, may be raised. Only after concluding that they will be able to overcome the hurdles and objections do they start the project. They do examine benefits as suggested. They calculate the return on investment, and only if found to be attractive do they invest in the project. Despite all these precautions, some projects are abandoned midway or even after completion, owing to some erroneous assumptions or unforeseen circumstances. Government projects, too, face a similar fate. Despite the extra caution as advocated by the couplet, a few failures do take place mainly because of inaccurate assumptions or faulty management.

A good example of a task that was executed well as per the tenets of this couplet comes to mind. Despite all efforts over the years, the maternal mortality ratio (MMR) and the infant mortality rate (IMR) in Tamil Nadu did not come down below certain levels. An expert committee that investigated the reasons for this recommended establishing first referral units (FRU) at taluk or sub-district hospitals. Accepting this, the government decided to implement it.

But it was not an easy task. Upgrading facilities at taluk hospitals to the district level would cost about ₹20 crore compared to our normal annual allocation of ₹2 crore for all our schemes. Finding that kind of money would, therefore, not be easy. Another major hurdle was getting specialists to work in taluk hospitals when it was difficult to get enough to work even in the district hospitals. We were, however, determined to overcome these hurdles and implement the project because of the huge benefits to the state. The health minister was also very keen and was willing to support any initiative we took.

An FRU requires a team of specialists consisting of a gynaecologist, an anaesthetist and a paediatrician in addition to diagnostic equipment and a good operation theatre. We needed all this in 200 taluk hospitals. Fortunately, there were enough vacancies for doctors, but the recruitment rules permitted the recruitment of only a generalist, not a specialist. We, therefore, amended the rules to facilitate the recruitment of specialists. Moreover, recruitment can be done only through the Tamil Nadu Public Service Commission, which normally takes about two years. Unwilling to wait that long, we initiated a dialogue with them to simplify and quicken the recruitment process. Appreciating the great benefit to society, they readily cooperated with us, simplified the process and completed the recruitment in nine months. Yet another problem surfaced: we were still short of anaesthetists. We solved this issue by training generalist doctors in anaesthesia, with the skills to handle the work in the FRUs.

Funds for upgrading the facilities were the next hurdle. Fortunately, a World Bank project for population control under implementation in Chennai had surplus funds. We approached the bank officials to permit us to use these for our project, as this, too, would lead to population control. Accepting our logic, they agreed. We were able to get ₹25 crore, more than we had hoped for. We then focused on spending the money wisely, which required considerable effort.

We pursued our task at multiple levels and closely monitored the progress throughout implementation. Finally, in about two years, the task was successfully completed, taking the number of functioning FRUs in Tamil Nadu from 100 to 300! This dramatic improvement in maternal and child health (MCH) services led to a secular decline in MMR and IMR in the state. As the couplet advises, the government was convinced about the huge benefit of the project. Thereafter, it first examined ways to successfully complete it, anticipated potential obstacles, and devised ways to handle these before embarking on the project. This resulted in lasting benefits to the public.

KEY TAKEAWAY

The government should prioritize tasks that yield lasting benefits to the public, proactively anticipating and overcoming obstacles to ensure their successful completion.

33

How to Move with a Ruler

அகலாது அணுகாது தீக்காய்வார் போல்க,
இகல்வேந்தர்ச் சேர்ந்தொழுகு வார். (குறள் 691)

Transliteration
Akalaathu Anukaathu Theekkaayvaar Polka,
Ikalvenhthars Sernhthozhuku Vaar.

Translation
Neither be too close nor too far from fire;
Thus let them act, they who move with a mercurial king.

Meaning
While moving with a mercurial king, one should be like those enjoying the warmth of fire on a cold day—neither too close, nor too far.

Kural Discussions
This Kural figures in the chapter 'Conduct with the Ruler' or 'Mannarais Sernhthu Ozhukal'. It is surprising that Thiruvalluvar thought of a chapter about one's conduct with the king. The advice primarily applies to high officials, ministers and close friends who have regular interaction with the king. The chapter highlights their responsibilities to support him in his rule and provides guidance on how to interact with him, offer advice, and avoid misusing their proximity to him.

Through a simile, this couplet explains how one should move with a king. We all enjoy the warmth of fire on a wintry night. To enjoy it, we should be neither far from it nor too close. We should position ourselves at the right distance to get the best out of the fire. Our body tells us how far we should be from it. So should we be with the king; we should not get too close to him nor too far from him. If we get too close, we may irritate him and get hurt. At the same time, if we keep too far away from him, our effectiveness may come down, which naturally depends on the common perception of our closeness to the king. Those moving with the king should always remember the fire simile to keep the right distance.

Why is such caution needed? Kings are mercurial. The word used in the couplet is *ikal*, which has many meanings: differing views, complicated, argumentative, mercurial, easily provoked, etc. The mood of a ruler varies dramatically because of his heavy responsibilities. He is kind one moment, and angry the next moment; similarly, he changes his views and decisions suddenly. He suffers from such mood swings because of his sovereign powers and responsibilities. That those moving with him should be prepared for these mood swings and learn to move with him carefully is the message. They cannot afford to take him for granted.

Although the couplet talks about the mercurial nature of ancient kings, our elected leaders, too, are similar. Therefore, those moving with them closely will benefit from this advice. I have observed some trying to get too close, which often backfires; they are thrown out suddenly and fall out of favour. Also, too much close association with the ruler generates envy among his other aides, which, too, creates problems. Only those who maintain the right distance can retain a long-term association with him. They know exactly how far away they should be from the fire!

Human behaviour seems to have remained the same through time. Thiruvalluvar has admirably captured that in this couplet. All those moving with the present-day ruler should remember that getting too close to him can hurt them in the long run, but keeping the right distance will help them in effective governance.

KEY TAKEAWAY

Those who work for the leader should move with him carefully to be effective.

34

Mind Reading

குறிப்பிற் குறிப்புணர் வாரை, உறுப்பினுள்
யாது கொடுத்தும் கொளல். (குறள் 703)

Transliteration
Kuripir Kurippunar Vaarai, Uruppinul
Yaathu Kotuththum Kolal.

Translation
He who reads others' minds just by a look,
Secure him whatever part he wants.

Meaning
Employ in your government someone who can quickly read the mind of another person just by looking at him, by offering him whatever part he wants.

Kural Discussions
This Kural figures in the chapter 'Judging by Looks' or 'Kuripparithal'. Judging another person's capability just by looking at him is an art that is essential for task execution—a rare trait that only a few possess. The king will benefit immensely by employing people with this trait in his court, thanks to their capability to execute tasks promptly and efficiently. Management studies neglect this aspect even today. Surprisingly, Thiruvalluvar has devoted a full chapter to it. As one who has personally witnessed its benefits in task execution, I cannot help but admire his insight into this important management aspect. Not only ministers and senior officials need to develop this trait, but even the ruler will benefit if

he can read the faces of those working with him.

This couplet advises the ruler to employ in his court persons capable of reading faces. With this rare skill, they can execute tasks efficiently. He should, therefore, employ them, giving them anything they want. They may demand a particular position, or independence in action, or anything else they value. The king should agree to it and employ them in his court. Since they are so capable, they will get his priorities executed fast just by reading his face. Not only that—with this unique ability, they will be able to read the faces of their team members and direct them properly. Such people are so valuable that they should be brought on board at any cost!

Getting them at any cost implies two things: Such persons are rare, and they are good at job execution. I observed this on many occasions. Among those working closely with me, a few had this trait; they would quickly read my face and know that there was something amiss, find out the issue and help me to resolve it with alacrity. Others would not notice anything. As the head of many organizations, I remember the timely help of many such officers in resolving organizational crises even without my asking—my face was good enough for them to come forward and help. They were indeed invaluable. If even small organizations could benefit from such individuals, imagine the benefits to governments and rulers!

Similarly, the ruler also needs to hone this skill. He could then read assent or dissent to his views just from the faces of his aides. In case he senses dissent, he gets an opportunity to correct himself, for, most of the time, his aides may be reluctant to openly express dissent for fear of upsetting him.

I recount one such incident to illustrate the importance of face reading. Kalaignar M. Karunanidhi, former chief minister of Tamil Nadu, was discussing the law-and-order situation in the state with senior police officials. The chief secretary and I, as home secretary, were also present. A senior police officer raised an issue concerning a transgression committed by a senior Opposition leader. He did it for publicity and to embarrass the government.

It was punishable under law, and therefore, the senior police officer asked the chief minister whether he could be taken into custody. Perturbed by the deliberate violation of law, he immediately gave his consent. I was silent all the while, thinking of the repercussions of this decision. The senior Opposition leader would raise it in Parliament to capture media attention and to embarrass the state government further. It was one of his political games to which we should not fall prey. But I did not offer my opinion because it was not asked for.

The chief minister must have read my face and my thoughts. After a few minutes, he asked me what I thought of his decision. I explained my thinking and suggested an alternative. We could register a case, investigate, and file a chargesheet in a court of law, avoiding the arrest, and thereby denying the leader the sensationalism associated with it. On hearing me out, he immediately reversed his decision. His ability to read my face in a group of 20 officers reflected his rare talent as a face reader. This unique skill afforded the ruler an opportunity to avoid potential embarrassment.

Besides leaders and senior administrators, even individuals will benefit immensely from this skill. Their personal interactions with family and friends will improve, making them highly popular and likeable.

KEY TAKEAWAY

Reading faces is an important skill for effective management and congenial living.

35
Speak to Suit the Audience

*அவையறிந்து, ஆராய்ந்து சொல்லுக, சொல்லின்
தொகையறிந்த தூய்மை யவர்.* (குறள் 711)

Transliteration
Avaiyarinhthu, Aaraaynhthu Solluka, Sollin
Thokaiyarinhtha Thooymai Yavar.

Translation
Those pure in thoughts and well versed in words
and their shade of sense,
Study well their audience and suit their speech to it.

Meaning
Those who know well the power of words and their effectiveness when used cogently will first study their audience and only then address them.

Kural Discussions
This Kural figures in the chapter 'Judging the Audience' or 'Avai Arithal' and highlights the need to know the audience and speak to suit it. It follows chapters on the importance of eloquence and the ability to read the face. As commentator Manakkudavar explains, 'Even though the minister has read the king's face, he should still speak only after judging the audience.'[11] Naturally, speaking hastily without judging the court could be counterproductive.

---

[11]Varadarajan, Mu, *Thiruvallvar Allathu Vaazhkai Vilakkam*, Paari Nilayam, Chennai, 2019.

Even eloquent speakers should speak only after judging the audience. The chapter has many pieces of advice for speakers: the speech should be easily understood; it should be interesting and captivating; choice of words is important, etc. Although the advice is meant for ministers, all public speakers will benefit greatly from studying this chapter.

This couplet highlights two important aspects of public speaking. The first is that the speech should suit the audience. For a learned audience, it should be erudite with facts and figures to support the argument. The speaker should be fully prepared to meet searching questions from the audience. Only then will it make an impact and be remembered. If the audience is a group of students, the speech should be simple and clear enough for them to understand the subject. One meant for a learned audience will not suit them. On the other hand, if it is for the public, it should be even simpler. Even complicated concepts should be put in simple terms to enable them to understand. I have often observed good speakers adjusting their style to suit their audience. This couplet stresses this important aspect of speech-making.

The second aspect deals with the speaker's knowledge of words. The word *thokaiyarinhtha* used in the couplet encompasses the precise and skilful usage of words, incorporating rhymes, employing rhetorical speech, and using these cleverly with full knowledge of their power. Some speakers with a good grasp of the subtle differences in word meanings are skilled in their usage.

Thus, the message in this couplet is that ministers should use words in their speech with full knowledge of their intricacies. With this talent, they will be able to convince the ruler, the cabinet and the public with ease and thereby be an asset to the government. Thiruvalluvar himself is an example of this. His choice of words is so brilliant, conveying profound wisdom in just seven words. *Thirukkural* researchers are still struggling to completely unravel his wisdom.

Our leaders generally possess this talent. With their ability to choose the right words for any audience, they are able to carry their colleagues and the public with them. This talent is somewhat missing in executive leadership, though it is equally important for them. They too should, therefore, cultivate this skill to be more successful. One way to develop it is to listen to TED Talks, since most TED talkers have this skill.

KEY TAKEAWAY

Before delivering a speech, it is important to carefully consider both the audience and the nuanced meanings of words.

36
Avoiding Stage Fear

கற்றாருள் கற்றார் எனப்படுவர், கற்றார்முன்
கற்ற செலச்சொல்லு வார். (குறள் 722)

Transliteration
Karraarul Karraar Enappatuvar, Karraarmun
Karra Selassollu Vaar.

Translation
Learned among the learned are those who can
Convince a congregation of the learned.

Meaning
Those who are capable of speaking convincingly what they have learned to an audience of the learned are considered learned among the learned.

Kural Discussions
After highlighting the importance of eloquence and judging the audience, Thiruvalluvar, in this chapter titled 'Confidence before an Audience' or 'Avai Anchaamai', emphasizes the need to overcome stage fear in public speaking. He expects a minister to be eloquent, judge his audience, and speak confidently and appropriately. Most of us have stage fear, especially when speaking in public for the first time. Unless we get over it, we cannot make a good speech. Stage fear arises because of our lack of clarity on the subject and the worry that some among the audience may be more knowledgeable and, therefore, think poorly of our speech. Thiruvalluvar's view is that we should build the confidence to

face even a learned audience, not just the ordinary. This calls for thorough knowledge of the subject. He even considers learning as wasteful unless the learned are good at public speaking. His message is: public speaking is so important that all educated persons should be good at it. Nowadays, we consider it only as an added advantage, but it is essential for some professions.

This Kural talks of a person giving a speech to a group of learned people on a subject of his study and learning, convincingly, fluently and without any stage fear. The audience is completely taken in by his speech. The key phrase of this couplet, *selassollu vaar*, means the ability to speak in a manner not only to convince the audience but also to make them wholeheartedly accept what is said. Such a person is considered learned among the learned, deserving the praise of all. The message is: those who can speak confidently and convincingly before a learned audience are worthy of great praise. All should develop this skill, particularly ministers.

Public speaking remains an ordeal for many. Addressing a common audience is challenging in itself, but delivering a speech to a learned audience, especially on a specific topic, can be even more demanding, given the potential presence of individuals with extensive knowledge on the subject. As a public servant, I frequently gave speeches. Even so, I used to prepare my speech every time, as otherwise it would be dull and uninspiring. Before an address to experts, I would prepare for days. Even after that, the speech should be delivered cogently and convincingly, with correct modulation to capture the audience's attention. Otherwise, the response would be lukewarm. No doubt, those who deliver a convincing speech to the learned deserve the highest honour, as highlighted in this couplet.

Public speaking skills are vital for ministers, administrators and managers. Those who are not good at it struggle to succeed. Ministers and political leaders are invariably good at public speaking. They have no stage fear and can speak convincingly to a lay audience since they have become leaders mainly through speaking. They, too, prepare thoroughly for important speeches.

Those in senior management positions too need this skill. Senior government officials should be able to speak clearly to a group of ministers, other officials, and the public. Managers in private organizations, too, need this skill. Those with this skill definitely have an edge, and those without it need to acquire it.

Recognizing the importance of public speaking, many courses and training programmes are organized for managers nowadays. Management guru Dale Carnegie was among the first to write a book on the importance of public speaking—*The Art of Public Speaking* (1915) is still popular, having gone into many editions and having been translated into many languages. An institute started by him is still offering courses and training programmes on public speaking. Innumerable institutions have sprung up to improve the public speaking skills of managers. I saw one even for students! The message of all these programmes is the same recommended in this couplet: Acquire the skill to speak boldly and convincingly.

KEY TAKEAWAY

The acquisition of public speaking skills is essential for success in any management position.

37

Great Country

தள்ளா விளையுளும், தக்காரும், தாழ்விலாச்
செல்வரும், சேர்வது நாடு. (குறள் 731)

Transliteration
Thallaa Vilaiyulum, Thakkaarum, Thaazhvilaas
Selvarum, Servathu Nhaadu.

Translation
Unfailing yields, men of virtue, honest men of wealth
Combine to make a great country.

Meaning
A combination of abundant harvest, impartial and fair-minded people, and wealthy people who have earned their wealth in a fair and just manner make a great country.

Kural Discussions
This Kural figures in the chapter 'Country' or 'Nhaadu' in which Thiruvalluvar discusses the characteristics of a good or great country. After discussing the wisdom required for the king, ministers, government employees and citizens, he proceeds to define a great country in this chapter. Is it because he expects good governance based on his advice to make the country great, or because he wants the king and his ministers to keep this as their goal? Whatever his intention, this chapter describes the key elements of a great country, a country of choice for humankind.

Nhaadu in Tamil means 'desire' in addition to 'country', the implication being that a country should be one people desire to live in, a sought-after country. People wish to live in a place of abundance and peace. This is one reason for the migration of the skilled from India. History tells us that humankind was constantly on the move for thousands of years in search of a better place, till the concept of nationhood took root. Thiruvalluvar's idea is that a ruler, by his good governance, can make his country the most desired.

This couplet lists three key requirements for a great country. The first is *thallaa vilaiyul*, meaning 'abundant harvest'. The word 'thallaa' means 'without laziness'. The land should yield without laziness! This is possible only with fertile land, proper irrigation or sufficient rainfall, and diligent peasants. Only then will the land yield bountiful crops without laziness year after year, and no citizen will go hungry. Thus, plenty of food to meet citizens' fundamental needs is the first requirement. Surprisingly, even today, food for all continues to remain a distant dream.

The second is the presence of *thakkaar*, which refers to people with a just and fair mind. They are never after personal gains but stand for justice and fair play. A great country should have plenty of such people; they should have a say in the polity or public affairs, and the king should listen to them.

The third requirement is the presence of wealthy men, but their earnings should be from *thaazhvilaa* acts, meaning that they should not have done anything mean or demeaning to earn their wealth, nor harmed anyone to acquire it. They should have earned it through fair and virtuous means. Furthermore, they should spend it wisely on good causes. All these are implied in this one word. Some commentators have also interpreted it to mean tireless merchants who earn their wealth through foreign and domestic trade in a fair manner. This couplet thus recognizes the need for wealthy people in a country to support art and culture. It is well documented that one of the major causes of the European Renaissance was the wealth created by the merchants of Florence.

The couplet says that all three components are vital for a great country.

A bountiful harvest is a must for any country. Even in this twenty-first century, most countries aim for self-sufficiency in food, because they do not want to rely on others for food. At the time of Independence, our position was quite bad. Millions suffered from hunger and malnutrition. We did not produce enough food and had to import. But after the green revolution in the 1980s, we became self-sufficient in food production. It is a matter of pride that we are now in a position to export food grains. Yet, hunger has not vanished; millions are underfed and malnourished. Perhaps we do not have enough fair-minded people. The prevailing mindset is to somehow earn money with no concern for the means, even at the cost of the poor. Although governments have been taking many measures to eliminate hunger, it is still widespread, with the rich becoming richer and the poor becoming poorer. Being just and fair-minded seem rare qualities. Those in governance are not fair-minded either, with leaders focusing on election victory rather than eliminating hunger. Let us hope that we will get great and thoughtful leaders who will make India a great country desired by all.

KEY TAKEAWAY

Abundant food grains, fair-minded citizens and wealthy people make a country great.

38
Gems of a Good Country

பிணியின்மை, செல்வம், விளைவு,இன்பம், ஏமம்
அணியென்ப நாட்டிற்கு இவ்வைந்து. (குறள் 738)

Transliteration
Piniinmai, Selvam, Vilaivu, Inbam, Eemam
Aniyenpa Nhaattirku Ivvainhthu.

Translation
Unfailing health, wealth, bountiful yields, joy and safety,
These five are the ornaments of a country.

Meaning
Absence of diseases, sufficient wealth, bountiful harvest, joy and absolute safety are the five factors that are considered ornaments of a good country.

Kural Discussions
This is another interesting Kural in the chapter 'Country' or 'Nhaadu'. It amplifies the previous one on a great country. While the previous one describes the requirements of a great country, this one focuses on the outcomes of good governance, namely benefits to citizens. The couplet lists five factors as ornaments of a good country, adding to its glory. What are these?

The first ornament is good health and freedom from diseases. All citizens should be able to lead healthy, disease-free lives, for which they should have access to nutritious food. Food should be available not only in plenty, but within everyone's reach, which presupposes adequate earnings for all. Measures for disease prevention and cure should also be in place. A strong public health system to help citizens lead a disease-free life is implied. This is an outcome of good governance.

The next ornament is wealth. This refers to a country's wealth as well as the wealth of individuals. A country should be endowed with agricultural, marine, mineral, forest and other natural wealth in addition to the wealth of human resources. Furthermore, citizens should be talented and spirited to create wealth, for which access to good education and skill development is required. Also, equitable distribution of private wealth thanks to equal access to education is implied. Japan, with few natural resources, could make immense progress thanks to its hard-working and skilled citizens.

Another ornament is bountiful yields so that no one goes hungry. The previous couplet too mentions this. It is again highlighted here as one of the five ornaments.

The fourth ornament is happiness and joy. Citizens should be able to lead a happy and joyous life. In a good country, they can afford to spend their leisure time on arts, sports, drama, music, etc. If their daily life is a struggle, they will have little time for leisure or entertainment. This is not the hallmark of a good country. While citizens should work hard, they should also have the time and means to enjoy life. In a good country, a good work–life balance should be widespread.

The last ornament is the safety of citizens. They should be able to live without any fear for their life or property. The threat to safety could come from outside the country or from within. The government or the ruler is primarily responsible for safeguarding citizens against this threat. In another couplet, Thiruvalluvar has stressed it as a vital aspect of good governance. The rapid growth of countries that ensured the safety of their citizens has been a notable trend throughout history. In contrast, look at the sufferings of the people of Ukraine owing to external aggression. The safety of a nation and its citizens is, therefore, paramount.

The couplet concludes that these five are the ornaments of a country. While citizens too have a responsibility, the government has the major responsibility of creating these. Is it possible to create such a Utopian country or is it just Thiruvalluvar's dream? In any case, he has set it as a goal for rulers to create a country with these ornaments. How far are we from this goal?

The World Bank assesses annually the human capital index for countries, reflecting the capability of their citizens. It is calculated based on people's knowledge, skills and health. As per its 2020 report, India ranks 116th out of 174 countries, reflecting a poor picture. Singapore, which stood first, had a score of 0.88, whereas India's was just 0.49, indicating that we have a long way to go.[12] Similarly, the United Nations Development Programme (UNDP) assesses the Human Development Index (HDI) every year. In this, India's position was 134 out of 193 (2023).[13]

Another international agency, Sustainable Development Solutions Network, assesses the happiness level of citizens. As per its 2023 report,[14] India fares poorly, occupying the 126th position out of 137 countries, indicating a high level of unhappiness. Lack of employment opportunities, low income, poor health, anxiety about the future, etc., should be the causes.

Fortunately, India is self-sufficient in food production. As a result, we have largely eliminated deaths due to hunger, but hunger is still widespread due to inequalities in income, leading to malnutrition and stunted growth in children. Welthungerhilfe, an international organization, assesses the prevalence of hunger in a country and comes out with a Global Hunger Index. India's ranking in the Global Hunger Index (2024) is 105 out of 127

---

[12]World Bank Group, *The Human Capital Index: 2020 Update*, 2021, https://tinyurl.com/bd56f6mu. Accessed on 17 October 2024.

[13]UNDP, Human Development Insights, https://tinyurl.com/3fs793v8. Accessed on 27 November 2024.

[14]World Happiness Report, https://tinyurl.com/mrx6b9tk. Accessed on 27 November 2024.

countries,[15] reflecting the need for greater efforts to eliminate hunger.

Similar data on citizens' safety indicates that this also needs improvement. From these, it is evident that India is lagging in all the ornaments mentioned in this couplet. Poor governance, which deviates from Thiruvalluvar's vision, is the main reason. If those responsible for governance could only follow his advice, India's position would improve vastly, and it could become the dreamland envisaged in this couplet.

KEY TAKEAWAY

The duty of a ruler or leader is to make his country fit for good living, attracting global citizens.

---

[15]Global Hunger Index, India, https://tinyurl.com/2jrh8w5v. Accessed on 27 November 2024.

39

Power of Wealth

பொருளல் லவரைப் பொருளாகச் செய்யும்
பொருளல்லது இல்லை பொருள். (குறள் 751)

Transliteration
Porullal Lavaraip Porulaakas Seyyum
Porullallathu Illai Porul.

Translation
Nothing exists like wealth that can
Change a man of no consequence to a man of worth.

Meaning
Wealth has the unique ability to elevate a person considered worthless to worthiness, unlike anything else.

Kural Discussions
This Kural figures in the chapter 'Earning Wealth' or 'Porul Seyalvakai'. We have already read Thiruvalluvar's view that wealthy citizens are needed for a good nation. In this chapter, he stresses the importance of wealth for individuals. He wants everyone to aspire to wealth. We may wonder why a sage like him gives so much importance to wealth. It only brings out his practical wisdom. Fully aware that wealth is essential for a virtuous life, he advises all citizens to strive to be wealthy. Amplifying this point, Tamil scholar Mu. Varadarajan says, 'To understand Valluvar, one should have the mindset to treat wealth earned through labour as real wealth; otherwise, he can be misunderstood to accept that wealth accumulated by any means is respectable. One may be surprised

why Thiruvalluvar, who stands for virtuous life all through, has given importance to wealth, unless one appreciates that he talks of the wealth obtained through hard labour and virtuous means.'[16] We should also remember that no religion is against wealth but only against the use of unfair means to acquire it.

This couplet says that even those who do not deserve any respect will be respected if they have wealth. It is merely an observation of human conduct to highlight the importance of wealth. If such people could command respect just because of wealth, those with virtues would naturally get even more respect if they were wealthy. Therefore, individuals should strive to create wealth. The couplet uses words beautifully, but the beauty is lost in translation.

One may question this statement, perhaps rightly. After all, a person gets respect for his good character or behaviour, education, position and achievements, among other things. How can someone without any of these be respected just because he is wealthy? The couplet does not say that they should be respected but merely says that they will get respect. That is what we see in real life. It simply highlights normal human behaviour that has existed for two millennia! It is highlighted just to bring out the importance of wealth creation, in the right ways of course.

Another couplet in this chapter emphasizes virtuous means to earn money. It conveys that wealth acquired through unethical means should be rejected, and the respect given to those who accumulate such wealth is false. Additionally, when their unlawful means are exposed, and the wrongdoer is punished, all respect is lost. Thiruvalluvar emphasizes the importance of wealth creation through fair means, as it enables individuals to lead an honourable and virtuous life.

This is true even for nations. The respect for a nation depends on its wealth. Among the top economies in the world today are the

---

[16]Ramalingam, Namkkal Kavignar, *Thirukkural*, T.D.V. Publishers, Chennai, 2021.

USA, China and India. Due to their wealth, most nations are eager to trade with them and try to be on their right side. Thus, wealthy nations are respected for the opportunities they offer. Another way of looking at a country's wealth is its per capita income. On this basis, the USA ranks 6th, China 68th and India 135th (2023)[17]. This shows that though these countries are wealthy, individuals are not that wealthy. Countries with lower per capita income do not command that much respect. If citizens work hard and boost their income, the country's per capita income will go up in addition to its total wealth. Individuals' standard of living will go up in addition to respect for the country.

KEY TAKEAWAY

Citizens should work hard and generate wealth in a fair manner, while governments should create enough opportunities for such wealth creation. Individuals and the country will then become wealthy, commanding the respect of others.

---

[17] TheGlobalEconomy.com, 'GDP per capita, current dollars—Country rankings', https://tinyurl.com/yesr9mkx. Accessed on 30 November 2024.

40

Just and Fair Earning

*அறன்ஈனும், இன்பமும் ஈனும்; திறனறிந்து
தீதின்றி வந்த பொருள்.* (குறள் 754)

Transliteration
Araniinum, Inbamum Iinum; Thiranarinhthu
Theethinri Vanhtha Porul.

Translation
Wealth earned by one's skills and through fair means
Is a source of virtue and great delight.

Meaning
Wealth created by one's skills and hard work and earned in a fair and virtuous manner without causing any harm to anyone will help one live virtuously and joyously.

Kural Discussions
The previous Kural brought out the importance of wealth, whereas this Kural from the same chapter explains how it should be earned. It should be earned without any blemish or dishonour and by fair means regardless of the profession or trade. And it should not be earned by cheating or harming someone or depriving anyone of his rights. Accumulating wealth through illegal means, such as corruption, is clearly prohibited.

This Kural stipulates one more condition. Wealth should be created by *thiranarinhthu*, which means 'knowing one's skills'. This implies that wealth should be earned using one's talents and abilities with diligence and hard work. Also, this stipulation excludes wealth acquired through methods such as lottery or gambling, as well as inherited wealth.

The couplet goes on to explain the benefits of such wealth: it will lead to a virtuous and joyous life. Only a person with untainted wealth will be able to live virtuously and joyously. Virtuously, because his mind will be pure, inspiring him to lead an honourable life, helping others and the community in ways envisaged by Thiruvalluvar. Joyously, because he will be able to afford to spend on leisure, sports and entertainment, art and culture, and good education only with money. Only wealth earned by one's skills through fair means will give such pleasures of life, while also helping him lead a virtuous life.

Without understanding this primary truth, many run after money and earn it by dubious means and ultimately suffer. Newspapers often report about senior officials amassing huge wealth through illegal means, which cannot bring them real happiness. They spend their entire life worrying about safeguarding their ill-gotten wealth. When caught, their life becomes miserable. They can neither be happy nor lead a virtuous life.

The fate of Ferdinand Marcos, former president of the Philippines, is an example of miseries wrought by ill-gotten wealth. He amassed a fortune through unfair means during his 20-year rule. His wealth was said to be between 5 and 10 billion dollars. Finally, when opposition to his rule mounted, he was forced to flee his country and spend the rest of his life as a refugee in Hawaii. During this time, he had to face many investigations and court cases. He lost all respect and dignity. Unable to return to his country, he died as a refugee in a foreign country. His ill-gotten wealth could not help him in any way or bring him any happiness.

KEY TAKEAWAY

Earn money through honest means, for only such wealth will bring you true happiness and enable you to lead a virtuous life.

41

Pride of the Army

கைவேல் களிற்றொடு போக்கி வருபவன்,
மெய்வேல் பறியா நகும். (குறள் 774)

Transliteration
Kaivel Kalirrotu Pokki Varupavan,
Meivel Pariyaa Nhahum.

Translation
The warrior returning after losing his spear attacking an elephant
Plucks another from his chest and laughs.

Meaning
The warrior returning to the battle after losing his spear while fighting an attacking elephant discovers another in his chest, plucks it and laughs.

Kural Discussions
A nation requires a robust military to deter external aggression, necessitating that a deep sense of pride be instilled in the armed forces. Hence, Thiruvalluvar has devoted a chapter to 'Pride of Warriors' or 'Pataich Cherukku', in which he talks of proud and brave warriors. Soldiers should fight for the country with pride; they should never fear enemies. At the same time, they should be generous and help the distressed among enemies, and they should be willing to lay down their lives for the country. Although modern-day warfare is vastly different, it has in no way diminished the need for pride among soldiers. That is why we honour soldiers sacrificing their lives in the defence of our nation. We mourn their

deaths and confer many honours on them, in addition to erecting memorials in recognition of their sacrifices. Only an army with pride can defend a country well and win wars.

This Kural just describes the courage exhibited by a warrior in a battle. He is on the battlefield, fighting with his spear. An elephant tries to attack him, and without fear, he attacks it with his spear. Seeing his ferocious attack, the elephant runs away or falls to the ground. As a result, the warrior loses his spear. After finishing with the elephant, he looks up and sees that the battle is still raging. He quickly returns to the battlefield to resume fighting, for which he needs a spear. He, therefore, desperately looks for one and is happy to find one thrust into his chest, which he plucks out to continue his fight. As he does so, he laughs, happy that he could quickly discover another spear to fight the enemy, oblivious to the injury. What courage and what dedication! This is how the couplet describes his valour—he was chasing the elephant even without realizing that an enemy had thrust a spear into his chest!

Admiring the beauty of the couplet, leading Tamil scholar K.A.P. Viswanatham gives his poetic interpretation of the word *nhahum*, which means 'laughs'. Why does the soldier laugh? Viswanatham gives possible reasons:

- Is it because he got another spear quickly without having to look for one?
- Or is it because it was so easy for him to remove the spear from his chest?
- Or did he laugh at the usefulness of the worthless spear that did not even pierce his chest while his own downed an elephant?
- Or did he laugh sadly that such cowards exist in the Tamil country because he did not see the enemy attacking him from the front?
- Or did he laugh happily thinking about his unconcern for his chest injury, whereas the elephant ran away in fear of his attack?

- Or did he laugh fiercely at the enemy inviting him for a fight without worrying about his injury?

With such astute imagination, he lists many such possibilities to bring out the beauty of the word 'nhahum', used in this couplet. According to him, every word used by Thiruvalluvar has a deep meaning, and we can appreciate it only if we grasp its full meaning. We should, therefore, develop the sense to appreciate the beauty and richness of the words used in *Thirukkural*. He adds that we should feel proud of such courage exhibited by our Tamil ancestors without disregarding it as old-fashioned valour, for there are lessons to be learnt from old valour and pride.

Pride of warriors is relevant even today. Instead of spears and arrows, they fight with guns and cannons and even more dangerous weapons. Many have often exhibited courage similar to the kind brought out in this couplet. We salute them for their acts of valour and honour them. Pride of soldiers and the army is essential for the defence of our country and for our safety.

KEY TAKEAWAY

Pride of the army is a must for the safety of a country.

42

Duty of True Friends

நகுதற் பொருட்டன்று நட்டல்; மிகுதிக்கண்
மேற்சென்று இடித்தற் பொருட்டு. (குறள் 784)

Transliteration
Nahuthar Poruttanru Nhattal; Mikuthikkan
Mersenru Itiththar Poruttu.

Translation
True friendship is not merely for merrymaking,
But for sharp reprove to correct when one goes astray.

Meaning
True friendship is not merely to make merry in the company of a friend but to castigate him when he makes mistakes and to prevent him from committing further mistakes.

Kural Discussions
After dealing with the defence of the country, Thiruvalluvar turns his attention to friendship and has devoted five chapters to it. The first chapter, 'Friendship' or 'Nhatpu', is on good friendship. Although it is meant for kings and rulers, it is relevant for all. For the safety of his citizens, a ruler should maintain cordial relations with other rulers. This will reduce the burden of his defence expenditure. In addition, he can get the support of friendly nations in times of need. This is true even today. All nations try their best to maintain friendly relations with each other. India wants to maintain peaceful relations with its neighbours as well as other major nations. Sometimes, it walks a tightrope to balance

the interests of all, as in the case of the present Ukraine–Russia conflict. Thus, the aim of every nation is to maintain friendly relations with others without sacrificing its interests.

Likewise, friendship is important for individuals too. Friends are called Vitamin-F, an important ingredient for happy living. People with many friends are generally happier. Thiruvalluvar has offered many pearls of wisdom on good friendship.

This Kural defines the duty of a true friend. Friends meet often and spend their time happily, merrily. Merrymaking is an important element of friendship, enjoyed by all friends. But this is not enough. A true friend has a duty. It is to prevent his friend from getting into bad habits. He should point out his mistakes, even in a harsh tone, and prevent him from committing any wrong. It appears that he should take some responsibility for the proper behaviour of his friend. Hence, it is his duty to intervene and correct him in time. A tall order indeed!

The word *mikuthikkan* used in this couplet requires some explanation. It means 'anything done in excess'. The intervention is called for when a friend does anything in excess in any aspect of life, such as eating, spending, or partying, among other things. Without a doubt, wrongdoings are included in this. In all such cases, a true friend should intervene. Suppose your friend spends beyond his means—you should intervene and correct him. It is not enough to merely point out his mistakes, you should also reprimand him with a view to correcting him. When soft words fail, harsh words are necessary. The purpose is to save him from the excess, which necessitates your repeated interventions till he mends his ways.

Another word, *mersenru*, means that you should 'intervene on your own' even at the incipient signs of excess to prevent it from becoming serious. A true friend should not ignore such a sign, thinking it is not his business. To intervene and correct a friend at the right time is the hallmark of good friendship. Spotting the excess, advising, castigating and monitoring till change happens are the duties of a good friend.

But what happens normally? We know the importance of friendship and do value good friendship. We even celebrate Friendship Day every year. Friends meet often and enjoy the company of each other, but hardly anyone intervenes in case of excess. Some even encourage it, but many just participate and do not attempt to intervene. Fearing that intervention could affect the friendship, most hesitate to point out even gently. For this reason, their friend gets into serious trouble in due course.

A person known to me started his own business, which thrived. He liked the company of friends and collected a large circle of friends. He had a great time with frequent parties and get-togethers and a lot of merrymaking. This led to the neglect of his business, which took a turn for the worse. But he continued entertaining his friends, spending beyond his means. Many of them knew about his excess, but none intervened. Ultimately, his business failed, and he became bankrupt. Had there been at least one such true friend to correct him, he could have escaped bankruptcy. We should have at least one such true friend to save us from excesses. It goes without saying that we should trust and listen to a good friend.

'Without friends no one would choose to live, though he had all other goods,' said Greek philosopher and polymath Aristotle, because friendship promotes the sharing of thinking and reasoning. 'Without friends the world is but a wilderness,' remarked Francis Bacon, English philosopher, statesman and essayist, stressing the importance of friendship. Explaining the worth of a true friend, classical Greek tragedian Euripides said, 'One loyal friend is worth ten thousand relatives.' He was perhaps referring to the kind of friend portrayed in this couplet.

KEY TAKEAWAY

True friendship means preventing a friend from falling into any excess through timely intervention. Therefore, friends bold enough to correct us are our real friends.

43

Selecting a Good Friend

*குடிப்பிறந்து, தன்கண் பழிநாணு வானைக்
கொடுத்தும் கொளல்வேண்டும் நட்பு.* (குறள் 794)

Transliteration
Kutippiranthu, Thankan Pazhinhaanu Vaanaik
Kotuththum Kolalvendum Nhatpu.

Translation
Descent from a family of noble traits, shrinking with shame from a deed of disgrace,
Are qualities of friendship worth seeking at any price.

Meaning
Friendship of a person born into a family of noble traits and ashamed to do anything that will bring him discredit should be obtained at any cost. Such a person will be a great friend.

Kural Discussions
This Kural features in the chapter 'Choosing Friends' or 'Nhatpaaraaythal'. After explaining the responsibilities of a good friend, this chapter gives advice on how to select a good one. We often see people's lives getting spoiled by bad associations that lead them astray and get them into serious trouble. We often judge a person by his friends. One should, therefore, choose one's friends carefully after understanding their character.

This couplet advises how a friend should be chosen; one should look for two important aspects. The first: he should be born into a noble family known for its values and virtuous living.

The noble family does not refer to a family of higher caste. What it refers to is a family that lives in the righteous ways prescribed by Thiruvalluvar; it is a family respected by the community for its values and conduct. Persons born into this family will invariably be brought up in a virtuous way. You would have observed this among your friends.

The second aspect is that he should feel a sense of shame about doing anything wrong. The feeling of shame should not be out of fear that he may be found out, but should be intrinsic. He should naturally be averse to doing anything wrong. Not only that, he should also feel remorse for his unintentional mistakes.

The couplet advises that one should get the friendship of such a person at any cost. The words used is 'give him whatever he wants' and get his friendship. Why? For he is so valuable. Some commentators have interpreted this to mean 'give him any amount of wealth demanded by him to get his friendship.' But the couplet does not mention wealth or money. It merely says to give him whatever he wants to get his friendship.

Is it possible to buy the friendship of such a person? He certainly knows that selling friendship for money is wrong, hence this interpretation is incorrect. Then what can we give? We can only give him our friendship by demonstrating that we are worthy of his friendship, for he himself will choose his friends carefully. We should, therefore, improve our own character, behaviour, culture, etc., to get his friendship. The couplet means that we should offer him the friendship he considers worthy. Once we get his friendship, we will become even better thanks to his association. Getting a good friend is, therefore, not easy, but quite beneficial!

In general, we do not make any effort to choose our friends. Rarely do we give a thought to our friends' backgrounds. As a result, we often make wrong choices and suffer. I have seen friends starting a business together with great enthusiasm but without any scrutiny. One starts cheating, leading to differences among them, ultimately resulting in the failure of the business. Good friends will not only prevent us from doing wrong but also help us in times of need. On the other hand, bad friends will vanish when needed. We often end up with the second type because we hardly make any effort to choose our friends.

The advice of this couplet is that finding the first type is difficult but necessary. Reading all the couplets in this chapter will help us choose good friends for a happy, meaningful and long association. 'You are the company you keep' is a well-known saying. The Book of Proverbs in the Old Testament also says, 'He that walketh with wise men shall be wise: but a companion of fools shall be destroyed.' To surround oneself with wise men is not merely a sagacious thing; it might also make one wiser. Similarly, the company of people who are virtuous will keep us on the righteous path.

KEY TAKEAWAY

Cultivate friendship only after a thorough examination of the person's background.

44

Long-Standing Friends

பேதைமை ஒன்றோ பெருங்கிழமை என்றுணர்க,
நோதக்க நட்டார் செயின். (குறள் 805)

Transliteration
Pethaimai Onro Perungkizhamai Enrunarka,
Nhothakka Nhattaar Seyin.

Translation
Take the faults of a friend either
As mere ignorance or folly of great intimacy.

Meaning
If a friend does something hurtful, we should treat it as an act of ignorance or great intimacy and remain calm.

Kural Discussions
After advising how to choose a good friend, Thiruvalluvar goes on to advise how to retain them. Long-standing friends are special because they know us well and have been sharing our joys and sorrows. They serve as our pillars of strength during our moments of struggle. Hence, they deserve special treatment. We should, therefore, be more tolerant and should not act in haste while dealing with them. Since it is difficult to get good friends, we should not lose them in haste. Many such pieces of advice are given in this chapter, 'Long-Standing Friendship' or 'Pazhaimai'.

This Kural explains how we should handle our long-standing friends. If they do something harmful or say something hurtful, we should not take it to heart. We should just ignore it, thinking that they have done so unknowingly or out of ignorance. Another possibility is that they might have done it because of our intimacy, which gives them the liberty to do what they did. We should not get upset with their behaviour. To maintain a long-standing friendship, our approach should be one of forgiveness and of letting go of grievances. Thus, we should treat long-standing friends differently.

Such situations do arise in real life. Due to intimacy and familiarity, friends do take liberties and say something upsetting or do something harmful. I recall an incident in my friends' circle. One person had been trying to sell his property for quite some time but could not either because of market conditions or the high price he expected. All his friends were aware of this. One of them took the initiative to sell the property to help his friend. Since he was abroad, his friend found a buyer and even finalized the price on the presumption that he would not object. Due to his intimacy and familiarity with him, he acted in good faith. Meanwhile, his friend was independently negotiating with someone else and was about to conclude the deal at a higher price. When he came to know of his friend's efforts, he went ahead with his friend's deal, even at a loss. He did not even mention his loss. He knew how to handle an old friend; perhaps he had studied this couplet thoroughly.

Just as we do not suspect the motive of family members even if they make a mistake, we should treat our friends the same way. A stray act of indiscretion should not sour a good friendship. As French moralist Jean de La Bruyère said, 'Two persons cannot long be friends if they cannot forgive each other's little failings.'

The lesson to remember is that we should go the extra mile to retain our long-lasting friends. This is equally applicable to friendships among nations. That is perhaps why India is treating its long-standing friend Russia more generously in its conflict with Ukraine, although self-interest is the dominant factor in international relations.

KEY TAKEAWAY

Treat long-standing friends generously.

45

Avoid Evil Friends

உறின்நட்டு, அறின்ஒருஉம் ஒப்பிலார் கேண்மை,
பெறினும் இழப்பினும் என்? (குறள் 812)

Transliteration
Urinnhattu, Arinoroom Oppilaar Kenmai,
Perinum Izhappinum En?

Translation
What do you gain or lose by the friendship of men
Who when you thrive are friends, and when you fail, depart?

Meaning
What is the use of friendship with friends who will be with you when you thrive and leave when you are down? There is no use in keeping such friendships.

Kural Discussions
This Kural figures in the chapter 'Evil Friendship' or 'Thee Nhatpu'. While you should choose good friends, you should also avoid evil friends. This chapter describes who evil friends are and what kind of trouble they can cause, and also advises that they should be avoided at any cost. The theme of the chapter is that it is better not to have any friends than to have evil ones.

This couplet brings out an important trait of evil friends. Such friends will cling to you when you have money, position or power, but will not be seen when you lose them. They are called fair-weather friends. For them, friendship depends on the benefit they get out of it. The moment they see no benefit, they will be friends no more. The couplet raises a rhetorical question: how does it matter whether you have such friends or not? The reply is obvious. There is no point in having them as friends.

In the couplet, the word *oppilaar*, meaning 'persons without equals', needs special mention. Normally, it is used for learned or virtuous people, but here it is used for evil friends. Commentator Manakkudavar explains, 'Because no one can be meaner than such friends, Thiruvalluvar has used this word.'[18] It appears that Thiruvalluvar regards such behaviour as highly repugnant, and hence he sarcastically refers to them as 'oppilaar', suggesting that they have no equal in meanness. Our life experience tells us that this is true. But the fact that such was human behaviour even two millennia back is surprising. Perhaps it is a part of human evolutionary traits.

I knew a person with a thriving business. He was a highly sociable person with a wide circle of friends, and he took pride and joy in their company. His network of friends continued to grow along with his business. He continued to be generous with them, entertaining and helping them in every possible manner. When his business turned for the worse, his friends vanished one by one. When he was in distress, no one was there to help him or give him advice or even to listen to his woes. Unfortunately, he had not picked up one good friend, and all of them turned out to be the evil friends defined by this couplet.

I have observed such behaviour in my career. Whenever I held an important assignment, many individuals sprang up, claiming to be my friends. Since I had observed my colleagues getting spoiled by such fair-weather friends, I was quite wary. I dealt with them professionally, without treating them as friends. Once I was posted to a very insignificant assignment; immediately, most of these friends vanished. Fortunately, this assignment helped me identify my true friends. We should, therefore, be careful about such friends and avoid them. Since

---

[18]Varadarajan, Mu., *Thirukkural Thelivurai*, Paari Nilayam, Chennai, 2019.

most people are like this, I would not call them evil, but just persons to be avoided.

KEY TAKEAWAY

Friends who move with us for their benefit are not friends at all.

46

Avoid Ignorance and Self-Conceit

ஏவவுஞ் செய்கலான்; தான்தேறான்; அவ்வுயிர்
போஓம் அளவுமோர் நோய். (குறள் 848)

Transliteration
Eevavunj Seykalaan; Thaantheraan; Avvuyir
Pom Alavumor Nhoy.

Translation
Advice, he heeds not; of himself knows nothing wise;
This man's whole life is all a plague until he dies.

Meaning
This man does not listen to the advice of knowledgeable persons although it is meant for his own good. And he himself learns nothing and knows nothing, and, therefore, is incapable of doing anything worthwhile. Such a person is a plague to society till he dies.

Kural Discussions
So far, Thiruvalluvar has dealt with different aspects concerning the polity, namely rulers, ministers, government employees, defence, friendship, etc. Now he turns his attention to safeguarding the assets or interests of the government. In the next twelve chapters, he explains the harms that can befall governments and the safeguards against them. Scholar and commentator Manakkudavar classifies them under the subdivision 'Thunpaviyal', meaning 'subdivision dealing with difficulties'. The first chapter in this subdivision deals with 'Ignorance' or 'Pethamai'.

This Kural figures in the next chapter, 'Handling Ignorance and Self-Conceit' or 'Pullarivaanmai'. *Pullarivu* refers to traits like ignorance, immaturity and small-mindedness, while the person concerned considers himself great and wise. The word is not in use nowadays and, therefore, its full meaning is somewhat elusive. However, such people do exist, and we do encounter them occasionally. In this chapter, Thiruvalluvar explains their traits, the damage they cause to the polity, and ways to manage their 'pullarivu'. Surprisingly, he has identified them as a group causing great damage. I have observed its truth in my career. Of course, I did not know it was 'pullarivu'.

This couplet describes the traits of a *pullarivaalan*, a person with the curse of 'pullarivu' or a small mind. He has no knowledge of anything, nor is he capable of doing anything. Nor will he listen to any wise counsel even in his interest. Even if someone knowledgeable on the subject guides him, he will not listen or take his advice, for he genuinely believes he knows everything, and is fully confident in his knowledge, wisdom and competence. Such a person is an incurable disease (*nhoy*) in society till he dies, causing great damage. Damage to whom? To his relatives, friends, fellow workers and organization. All those in contact with him will be frustrated and suffer because of his mindset. As they are powerless to change him, they must endure him till his death. A harsh condemnation of 'pullarivaalan'. The condemnation goes even further. Thiruvalluvar uses the word *avvuyir*, meaning 'its life'. The person is not referred to as he or she but is addressed as an inanimate object, which reflects his contempt for him, because of the great damage such individuals can cause to the rule if they occupy positions of importance. We may recall that Thiruvalluvar has used similar harsh language for the illiterate.

I recall an experience with one such person. When I was the secretary of a department, the government posted a senior officer to assist me. I assigned him some crucial subjects so that he could concentrate on them while I could focus on other areas. Soon I found that he was unable to cope with the work; complaints of delays kept coming in. I met with him to find out the reasons. He had issues with the staff assisting him and also with a few others in the department. I did not, however, face any such problem. Anyway, I requested him to choose his team and avoid delays. Still, there was no change in his style. Complaints kept coming in while he continued to complain about everyone and everything. Again, I advised him to focus on his subjects instead of worrying about others. Still, no improvement was visible.

His workload was so light that he could handle it with ease. Even my well-intentioned counselling did not help. He was unwilling to listen, genuinely believing he was right and others were wrong. After a few months, I had no other option but to take away the sensitive subjects from him and handle them myself. He was, however, not bothered by that, for, in his own view, he was always right. I later learned that he remained like that till he retired from service. Now that I have read this Kural, I can identify him as a good example of 'pullarivaalan'. I have seen how much damage such persons can cause to the administration, unknowingly of course, as pointed out by Thiruvalluvar. Only those managing them need to know how to minimize the damage. You, too, would have had similar experiences.

KEY TAKEAWAY

Without any self-conceit, we should be willing to listen to knowledgeable persons and learn from them.

47

Avoid Discord

இன்பத்துள் இன்பம் பயக்கும், இகலென்னும்
துன்பத்துள் துன்பம் கெடின். (குறள் 854)

Transliteration
Inbaththul Inbam Payakkum, Ikalennum
Thunbaththul Thunbam Ketin.

Translation
Joy of joys abundant grows,
When discord that is woe of woes dies.

Meaning
Discord is the greatest woe among all woes. If a person can overcome it, he will enjoy the greatest joy of all joys.

Kural Discussions
The next chapter in this subdivision is 'Ikal', meaning 'Discord'. As discord will bring ruin to the rule, Thiruvalluvar has devoted a chapter to it, in which he describes its evils and spells out steps to avoid or eliminate it. Discord or difference of opinion is quite common in life, even among relatives and close friends. If it is absent or is low, the relationship will be smooth and enjoyable. Friends with similar thinking get along very well, enjoying each other's company. When discord arises, fissures develop, affecting their relationship. When it escalates into words or actions, it sours relationships and even leads to enmity. The term 'ikal' generally refers to differences of opinion, usually in the mind or in debates, without resulting in any outward action or conflict. Thiruvalluvar

is against such discord and advises how to handle it. Realizing that differences of opinion are a part of life, we should learn to accept and navigate through them. The central theme of this chapter is the importance of avoiding discord for a harmonious life.

The message of this Kural is simple but profound. It says that discord is the greatest of all woes, but if a person can overcome it effectively, he will enjoy the greatest happiness. The absence of discord among individuals, families and communities can lead to immense happiness for them. Managing it, however, is not easy. It requires effort, but before that, the simple realization that it leads to unhappiness and enmity is the first step. That is what this couplet highlights. If everyone avoids it, realizing its evils, society will live in great harmony. Leaders have an important role to play in reducing discords in societies. Regrettably, some deliberately sow seeds of discord, dividing societies for political gains.

We often encounter discord in our personal and professional lives but fail to handle it effectively, leading to unhappiness and distress. I often faced discord in my professional life, but on many occasions struggled to handle those situations well, essentially due to my lack of skill and experience. At times, my ego came in the way. Not having studied this couplet earlier was also a great handicap.

I recall one such incident of discord that brought untold suffering to the public, in addition to unhappiness to me and my colleagues. When I was the administrator of the Corporation of Madras, we had to manage an outbreak of cholera affecting thousands of citizens. Our advice to drink boiled water was ignored. Cholera spread fast and wide. Hospitals filled up quickly, and more beds were added but to no avail. We struggled to control mortality.

One effective preventive measure was to improve the quality of drinking water. But it was supplied by the water board, another independent organization. It refused to admit that drinking water was the cause and kept claiming nothing was wrong with the quality of the water. However, our public health professionals alleged that residual chlorine in water as required was absent. I reached out to the senior officials of the water board to amicably resolve the discord. But they were unrelenting and blamed the epidemic on garbage and poor environment, holding the corporation responsible. They continued to assert that the supplied water met the standards. We took all efforts to clean up the affected areas, but there was little impact on the epidemic, since chlorine was absent in the drinking water. This went on for a month, causing considerable sufferings to the people while straining hospital resources.

Finally, because of adverse reports in newspapers, the chief secretary of the state had to intervene. After listening to both organizations, he ordered the water board to ensure residual chlorine. Once that was done, the cholera epidemic abated. This discord brought me unhappiness and great pain. As the couplet says, it brought great woes to all! Had I managed to resolve it in time, all officials would have been happy, including the citizens.

When discord arises in the family or among friends, we should not allow it to escalate but try to avoid unnecessary debates and discussions. Never raising contentious issues among loved ones is one way to avoid them. When discord arises in the workplace, it needs to be handled deftly. Empathetic listening to others' points of view and accommodating them could eliminate or minimize discord. Persuasion and negotiation skills could also help. Realizing that discord causes great unhappiness, as the couplet says, we should nip it in the bud.

The modern world is heavily immersed in social media, with individuals spending countless hours trapped in its lure. Unfortunately, they are often a source of discord. Social media should be a place for a healthy exchange of views to share happiness and joy and to enhance bonding among friends and citizens. But it turns into a platform for airing individuals' strong opinions and biases, creating rifts and discords among friends and colleagues. Although everyone knows that such unnecessary discussions lead to bitterness, the debate carries on, ending in greater discord. We should keep this couplet in mind and desist from subjects causing discord. Also, we should ignore any contentious or unpalatable comments from others, accepting that such differences are quite common. If we do so, we will be immensely happy.

The more one thinks of discord, the more one is convinced that it brings immense woes to families, friends and organizations alike. If we could develop the skill to avoid it or manage it deftly, happiness will be the outcome, as the couplet predicts.

KEY TAKEAWAY

Realizing that differences of opinion are quite common, we should cultivate a spirit of give-and-take. This approach will improve our workplace performance and also contribute to our overall happiness.

48

Enmity Within is Dangerous

ஒன்றாமை ஒன்றியார் கட்படின், எஞ்ஞான்றும்
பொன்றாமை ஒன்றல் அரிது. (குறள் 886)

Transliteration
Onraamai Onriyaar Katpatin, Egngnaanrum
Ponraamai Onral Arithu.

Translation
If enmity arises within kinship,
It is ever hard to escape ruin.

Meaning
If enmity arises among those who are together, it is difficult to prevent the damage that comes out of it.

Kural Discussions
After discord, Thiruvalluvar has devoted three chapters to enmity, assessing the strength of enemies and enmity within, advising the ruler on the precautions to be taken. The first two chapters contain advice on the defence and foreign affairs of the country. The third deals with 'Enmity Within' or 'Utpakai', containing advice not only for the ruler but for others as well. It warns us about the possibility of our friends and relatives interacting with us with enmity at heart. We could easily identify enemies and take precautions, but not so with such people. They are, therefore, more dangerous and could cause us greater harm.

This Kural gives us a stern warning about the dangers of internal enmity. Friends and relatives move closely with us, and therefore, we trust them as our well-wishers. We never imagine them harbouring any ill feelings or working against us. The couplet says that such enmity will bring ruin that cannot be prevented. Since their enmity is in their hearts, we rarely see it. We continue to treat them as well-wishers, while they act against our interests and cause us great damage. The damage for a ruler is, of course, immense—he could lose his life or his kingdom. For others, it could be loss of wealth or great suffering. The message is that we should identify them early and take precautions, but the couplet acknowledges that doing so is difficult.

History is full of instances of ruin wrought by internal enmity. One such instance has been well captured by Shakespeare in *Julius Caesar*. Caesar, who brought many victories for the Roman Empire, was its undisputed leader, liked and admired by his people. But envious of his achievements and power, the Senate members conspired to bring him down. They roped a popular leader Brutus into their conspiracy to assassinate him. But Caesar considered him as his best friend. He also counted other Senate members among his friends, without suspecting their enmity.

The conspirators decided to assassinate him in the Senate meeting to be held on 15 March. Worried that Caesar might not attend the meeting due to ill omens, some, including Brutus, went to his house to accompany him to the meeting. Without any inkling of the conspiracy, Caesar welcomed them warmly and offered them wine as he would to his friends. Accompanied by them, he then marched to the Senate to meet his death.

During discussions in the Senate, the conspirators started stabbing him one after another. Finally, when his dear friend Brutus stabbed him, Caesar died saying, 'Et tu, Brute? Then fall Caesar.' Caesar, the most powerful ruler of the world, was killed not by his enemies but by his friends. This led to fights among factions, and in the end, Brutus and the other conspirators were killed. The rulers who succeeded were even more authoritarian. Therefore, Brutus's noble intention to make Rome a republic did not fructify. The internal enmity caused the death of many leaders of Rome, including Caesar, in addition to ushering in greater tyranny. Thus, it only brought ruin to all, as the couplet has predicted.

We come across similar events all the time. The ruin of many political parties can be traced to internal enmity, arising from factionalism. The downfall of governments is often due to dissensions within the ruling party, leading to defection. Newspapers are full of reports of such internal strife. Even professional organizations suffer because of internal rivalry. Discord among relatives or partners has led to the downfall of many companies. The ruler should, therefore, always keep in mind the dangers of internal enmity and guard against it.

KEY TAKEAWAY

Since internal enmity always brings ruin, leaders should guard against it.

49

Listen to Men of Lofty Ideals

ஏந்திய கொள்கையார் சீறின், இடைமுரிந்து
வேந்தனும் வேந்து கெடும். (குறள் 899)

Transliteration
Eenthiya Kolkaiyaar Seerin, Itaimurinhthu
Venthanum Venhthu Ketum.

Translation
When blazes forth the wrath of men of lofty ideals,
Kings fall and perish in the flame.

Meaning
When men of lofty ideals rise in anger, kings will lose their kingdom midway and perish in their anger.

Kural Discussions
In the subdivision dealing with preventing damage to a king's rule, the chapter 'Not Offending the Great' or 'Periyaaraip Pizhaiyaamai' advises the king that he should not wrong the great. It explains that the great include more powerful rulers, wings of government, and other learned and great people in society. Obviously, the ruler should not pick a fight with a more powerful king; also, he should not estrange a wing of the government, although the ruler is the head. Remember, present-day rulers, too, are careful with independent bodies such as the Supreme Court, Election Commission, and certain other powerful wings of the government. Finally, the great people of his country are the most relevant. Virtuous and selfless, they are interested in society and give advice

and opinions only in public interest. The ruler should not offend them but listen to their sound advice.

This Kural says that if the great people of his country rise in anger, the king will lose his kingdom midway through his rule and will ultimately perish. The great people referred to in the couplet are those with lofty ideals who not only preach values but also practise them. Why would such people rise against a king? Even if they do, why will he fall? Normally patient, they ignore minor faults of the king. Even if he ignores their advice, they remain patient and do not rise against him. It is possible that the ruler and his machinery belittle and harass them for their views. They may tolerate this to an extent, but when the ruler crosses a line and acts against public interest, they will rise in anger and take a stand. Since they command the respect of citizens, they, too, will rise against the ruler. What can a ruler, however powerful, do when citizens rise against him? He will be forced to lose his kingdom and perish. The couplet's message is that the ruler should listen to their sane advice without giving them a reason to rise against him in anger.

History is full of events testifying to the veracity of this couplet. The first such event that comes to mind is the French Revolution (1789-99). French citizens rose against their king, Louis XVI, because of his total indifference to their woes and brought down his reign. The rule of the people emerged with a declaration that all men are born equal. The French Revolution sowed the seeds of democracy in many countries, bringing an end to monarchy. The writings of great thinkers like Voltaire, Jean-Jacques Rousseau and Montesquieu inspired many great people to rise against the king boldly. Particular mention may be made of Maximilien Robespierre and Charles-Alexandre de Calonne for their leadership in the revolution. Many others joined; many were jailed and some even lost their lives. But their fight for the rights of the people finally succeeded, with the king losing his kingdom.

Similarly, the Russian Revolution of 1917 is also a testimony to the veracity of this couplet. Leaders like Lenin, inspired by the thinking of Karl Marx, were responsible for the Bolsheviks' uprising in Russia, leading to the fall of the king.

Even India could get freedom only because people rose against British rule, inspired by leaders such as Mahatma Gandhi, Jawaharlal Nehru, Sardar Patel, Subash Chandra Bose, etc. They all rose against British rule in 1942 with the 'Quit India' slogan. Many of them, including ordinary citizens, suffered much and went to jail for years. Finally, British rule in India came to an end.

An event in recent history is worth mentioning. When Prime Minister Indira Gandhi declared an Emergency in 1975, abrogating the rights of the people, many great men rose against the government under the leadership of Jayaprakash Narayan and suffered considerably till full-fledged democracy was restored.

Despite all this evidence, rulers often act in a manner that angers great people and ultimately suffer. The lessons of history beautifully captured in the seven words of this couplet should be studied and followed by all rulers.

KEY TAKEAWAY

A government that listens to great people will last long.

50

Evils of Gambling

சிறுமை பலசெய்து சீரழிக்கும் சூதின்
வறுமை தருவதொன்று இல். (குறள் 934)

Transliteration
Sirumai Palaseithu Seerazhikkum Soothin
Varumai Tharuvathonru Il.

Translation
Nothing else brings greater poverty than gambling
Which causes misery and brings ruin.

Meaning
Nothing else brings greater poverty than gambling, which brings innumerable woes to a man in addition to spoiling his reputation.

Kural Discussions
In the subdivision on preventing damage to a king's rule, Thiruvalluvar has allocated a chapter to 'Gambling' or 'Soothu' in which he highlights its ills and warns people against it. Games that were played as a pastime became avenues of gambling over time. Card games and horse racing are traditional forms of gambling. Popular games such as football and cricket have become arenas of gambling—even players indulge in it to make extra money. Many online gambling sites have now sprung up. Those who gamble hope to make easy money, but most invariably end up losing; only those organizing the game make money. In view of the huge human cost, Thiruvalluvar strongly condemns it.

This Kural issues a strong warning against gambling,

highlighting that it brings great misery to someone indulging in it, in addition to ruining his reputation. It will plunge him into poverty quickly. The advice is to desist from gambling, as otherwise total ruin will be the outcome. People start gambling in the hope of making quick money. When their bets go wrong, they spend more and even borrow and bet. Still they lose, but soon it becomes a habit and, in due course, an addiction. When borrowing is no longer possible, some resort to theft and misappropriation to pursue their addiction, in the false hope that they will one day win their dream money and get out of all their difficulties. Rarely does their dream come true—most of them end up in penury. Some even commit suicide. In addition, gamblers lose their reputation.

A well-known example of one who lost everything to gambling is Yudhishthira in Mahabharata. He pledged not only his wealth but also his country and brothers in the hope of winning. He lost everything. In a last-ditch effort to regain everything, he pledged his wife and lost. The terrible sufferings that followed are the great story of Mahabharata, a lesson for all of us to avoid gambling, among other ills.

A division of the population, however, supports gambling. Their argument is that it is just entertainment like any other game. Furthermore, it generates employment and revenues for governments. It is just like any other industry, contributing to a country's growth. For these reasons, gambling is legally permitted in many countries. Most of us have heard of the famous casinos of Las Vegas in the USA. Millions travel to this city just for gambling. Casinos are run in many other countries too.

Fortunately, our governments are not that liberal with gambling. In India, casinos are allowed only in Goa and Sikkim. The government of Tamil Nadu abolished horse racing and lottery sometime back. It has recently abolished online gambling too. Such policies are good for a developing country like ours, where many poor people gamble away their own money and then borrow from others, plunging themselves and their families into misery. Unfortunately, despite government policies and measures, gambling carries on clandestinely. Unless people themselves realize that gambling will only bring immense misery and not money, it will not vanish.

KEY TAKEAWAY

Since gambling always brings ruin, it should be avoided like the plague.

51

Eat Sensibly for Good Health

மாறுபாடு இல்லாத உண்டி மறுத்துண்ணின்,
ஊறுபாடு இல்லை உயிர்க்கு. (குறள் 945)

Transliteration
Maarupaadu Illaatha Undi Maruththunnin,
Uurupaadu Illai Uyirkku.

Translation
Taking agreeable food with self-denial,
Will keep diseases away and the body fit.

Meaning
Carefully limiting the intake of even food that agrees with you will ensure a happy and long life.

Kural Discussions
Thiruvalluvar turns his attention to citizens' health in this last chapter, 'Medicine' or 'Marunhthu', of this subdivision to protect the interests of the government. It describes ways to prevent diseases, the need to approach a physician in time, and the ways a physician should handle the disease. It highlights the importance of patients, physicians, nurses and medicines, which are still core components of healthcare.

This Kural deals with a vital aspect of disease prevention. We take all kinds of food, mostly for taste, while avoiding food that is not agreeable to us. Sometimes, we take too much of agreeable food because we are slaves to our tongue. This couplet advises us that we should not do so but eat even agreeable food within limits.

In fact, eat only agreeable food, that too within limits. Never eat like a glutton. You will then be free from disease and be able to lead a healthy life. This is the message of this couplet.

An implied advice is that you should not touch food that is not agreeable. Many of us not only overeat but also do not avoid non-agreeable food. For example, those with diabetes do not stay away from food rich in sugar and suffer further complications. Similarly, those with heart diseases do not avoid fatty foods. Thanks to the availability of plenty of drugs, people are careless with their diet despite doctors' advice. The message of the couplet is simple: a balanced diet is the foundation of good health. But we do not seem to listen. Obesity is on the rise, in addition to many lifestyle-related diseases for which poor diet or overeating is largely responsible.

Why has Thiruvalluvar not mentioned exercises to keep diseases away? Probably, the need for them did not exist in those days when everyone relied on manual labour for survival. For them, diet control would be the key to good health. Our ancient medicines, namely Siddha and Ayurveda, stress the importance of a proper diet.

The World Health Organization (WHO), an international body set up with the objective of creating a world in which everyone can live healthy, productive lives, regardless of who they are or where they live, has also emphasized the need for a healthy diet. According to WHO, a healthy diet helps prevent malnutrition in all its forms, as well as non-communicable diseases (NCDs), including diabetes, heart disease, stroke and cancer. It has also recommended a menu of healthy diets. An unhealthy diet and lack of physical activity are leading global risks to health.

Many research findings have established that a balanced diet helps prevent many diseases. In addition, it helps in weight reduction, improved memory, improved mood, sound sleep, strengthened muscles and bones, etc. In short, it helps us lead a long and healthy life. A balanced diet will keep the doctor away. WHO and modern research thus strongly support the message of this couplet.

Yet another finding recorded by Héctor García and Francesc Miralles in their book *Ikigai* (2017) also highlights the importance of proper diet. The longevity of people living in Okinawa Island in Japan is the highest in the world. A team of researchers landed there to find out the reasons. After a detailed study and innumerable interviews, they came to some useful conclusions. One conclusion is that the residents of this island stop eating the moment their stomach is around 80 per cent full, avoiding overeating and opting for a lesser amount than their maximum capacity. This is the habit of *maruththunnul*, namely denying food at the right time, mentioned in the couplet.

The wisdom enunciated by Thiruvalluvar two thousand years back is now supported by WHO and modern research. Let us follow it and lead a healthy life.

KEY TAKEAWAY

Eat mindfully for a healthy life.

52

Duties of a Physician

நோய்நாடி, நோய்முதல் நாடி, அதுதணிக்கும்
வாய்நாடி, வாய்ப்பச் செயல். (குறள் 948)

Transliteration
Nhoynhaati, Nhoymuthal Nhaati, Athuthanikkum
Vaaynhaati, Vaayppach Cheyal.

Translation
Diagnose the disease, ascertain its causes and means of cure,
Apply remedies with utmost precaution.

Meaning
Examine the nature of the disease, analyse the reasons for its incidence, evaluate ways of controlling it, and apply the appropriate remedy in such a manner that it does not cause any harm to the patient.

Kural Discussions
After describing ways of preventing diseases in the same chapter, 'Medicine' or 'Marunhthu', Thiruvalluvar, in this couplet, explains ways of treating a disease. It is in the nature of advice to a physician. Surprisingly, this is how a disease is managed even today, reflecting his visionary thinking. Let us not forget that during his time, many parts of the world attributed diseases to divine acts.

As mentioned, this Kural is in the nature of guidance to a physician. While examining a patient, a physician should first find out the nature of the disease, and then examine its causes. Next, he should find out its origin or root cause. He should then consider all options to reduce its intensity and cure the patient. Some illnesses do not need any treatment, and time will be the healer. Prescribing medicines will then be unnecessary. Sometimes medicines alone may not be enough, and the illness may require surgical intervention. The physician should consider all these alternatives and choose the one best suited to the patient. After that, he should administer the chosen remedy. To ensure that no harm is caused to the patient, he should keep a watch on his progress; he should thus constantly evaluate his judgement and make suitable corrections to ensure that his treatment does not cause any harm to the patient. The words *vaayppach cheyal* used in this couplet mean 'the treatment should suit the patient and should not cause him any harm.'

No allopathic treatment existed in Thiruvalluvar's time. Only nature cure or Siddha medicines based on herbs would have been practised. Those physicians probably followed the practice spelt out in this couplet, based on which Thiruvalluvar has given this advice. What has been stressed is to be systematic about the treatment, without causing any harm to the patient.

Surprisingly, even today, physicians follow only this method. Suppose the disease is caused by a virus; allopathy offers no cure, and hence, no medicine is prescribed. The virus is allowed to run its course. For other fevers, the cause is first analysed. It could be due to many reasons, and only after finding out the reason is the treatment started. Fortunately, many diagnostic tools and testing methods are available today. A simple fever could lead to a diagnosis of cancer that can be detected by a PET scan. Sometimes surgical intervention is called for. What is appropriate for the patient is the judgement call of the physician. Periodical monitoring of the progress is his duty too. If there is a mistake in this process, the patient suffers. This is now called medical negligence, and physicians are held accountable. But if they have taken reasonable precautions in their diagnosis and treatment, as spelt out in this couplet, the question of medical negligence will not arise. Therefore, the physician should use his best judgement in the interest of the patient.

Hippocrates is a famous physician who lived in the fourth century BC. Before his time, people believed that diseases were caused by the wrath of God. Hippocrates was the first to establish by his detailed observations of diseases and their effects that health is often influenced by diet, breakdown in bodily processes, and the environment. He found out the causes of a few diseases. No wonder he is considered the father of medicine, and doctors take oaths in his name even today. In his work *Of the Epidemics* (n.d.), Hippocrates says, 'The physician should [...] have two special objects in view with regard to disease, namely, to do good or to do no harm.'[19] Thiruvalluvar has enunciated the very same principle in this couplet. Hippocrates was a student of medicine and spent his lifetime on it. But without any medical training, Thiruvalluvar had come to the same conclusion, which is indeed surprising. Or were our medical systems so advanced in his time that he could have easily observed these facts himself?

One more interpretation of this couplet is worth mentioning. Instead of attaching the traditional meaning of disease to the word 'nhoy', we could give it the generic meaning 'problem'. If so, the couplet will apply to every problem we encounter in life. We should first find out the nature of the problem, namely, whether it is serious or whether it is minor and can be ignored. Then we should examine the reasons for the problem. Once its nature and root causes are established, many solutions can be thought of to address the problem. The best option should then be adopted to remedy the problem while taking care to see that the chosen remedy does not worsen the problem. This is what managers keep doing in their job. Rulers, too, should keep this in mind while handling economic and other problems affecting the nation. Even individuals would benefit by addressing their problems this way. All those who approach problems in the systematic manner spelt out in this couplet will be successful.

---

[19]Hippocrates, 'Of the Epidemics', *The Internet Classics Archive*, https://tinyurl.com/mvcu4cm4. Accessed 16 September 2024.

For this, leaders, managers and individuals should be skilled like physicians, though.

KEY TAKEAWAY

The duty of a physician is to find out the right way to cure a disease and adopt it without causing any harm to the patient.

53

Nobility

இற்பிறந்தார் கண்ணல்லது இல்லை, இயல்பாகச்
செப்பமும் நாணும் ஒருங்கு. (குறள் 951)

Transliteration
Ilpiranhthaar Kannallathu Illai, Iyalpaahach
Cheppamum Nhaanum Orungku.

Translation
Except in noble families, we rarely find
Instinctive sense of right and virtuous shame naturally combined.

Meaning
It is rare to find an instinctive sense of right or wrong and a sense of shame to commit any wrong naturally combined, except in those born into families of traditional honour and virtue.

Kural Discussions
Thiruvalluvar has given equal importance to citizens in his discussions on polity, unlike other philosophers who gave prominence to nations. After dealing with the right conduct of kings, ministers, government servants and the army, he now turns his attention to citizens, who are as important as the ruler for good governance. Thirteen chapters under the subdivision 'Citizenry' highlight their role, elaborating their responsibilities and proper public conduct. Many *Thirukkural* researchers have expressed great admiration for the prominence given to citizens by treating them as a distinct and integral part of the polity. According to Thiruvalluvar, a nation is not distinct from its citizens; rather,

it is shaped and defined by them. In his perspective, citizens encapsulate the essence of the nation.

The first chapter in this subdivision is 'Nobility' or 'Kutimai', which defines the traits of citizens born into a highborn family. A noble family does not refer to high caste or any social hierarchy. Rather, it is a label given based on the noble characteristics exhibited by its members through their conduct in society. No caste division is implied, for it did not exist in the ancient Tamil country.

Their first trait is *cheppam*, which means many things: honesty, purity, pride, fair-mindedness, high-mindedness. Ancient scholar Manakkudavar explains that it refers to purity of mind, word and action, an intrinsic desire to be pure and right.

The second trait is *nhaan* or 'shame', which refers to a sense of shame in doing wrong. We often come across individuals who shamelessly commit wrongs without any sense of guilt. However, those who possess nobility will feel ashamed to do anything wrong. Their intrinsic sense of righteousness prevents them from committing wrongs.

The couplet goes on to say that both these traits will be present naturally in persons of noble birth. Without explicitly stating so, it suggests that those lacking in these traits are not noble. The inference is that individuals possessing these noble traits are regarded as noble, while those without them are perceived as lowborn. Thiruvalluvar lived in a rural agricultural economy. A few well-respected families in villages would have exhibited these noble traits. Villagers would have known and respected them. This Kural must have been based on his observations of members belonging to such families.

Note that the concept of nobility here is not based on caste or social hierarchy or any title, but rather on the qualities and virtues demonstrated by individuals. His aspiration is that all citizens should cultivate these virtues to be regarded as noble and honourable individuals. Although Thiruvalluvar does not explicitly say so, his intention is clearly the propagation of nobility among citizens. This couplet explains how they can become so.

Such traits are rare nowadays, more so in public life. Blind pursuit of money without any concern for right or wrong is the order of the day. Corruption, embezzlement and malpractices for personal gains are common in the public space, that too committed with impunity. According to this couplet, those who indulge in such things are lowborn or inferior. Maybe this unpleasant message can give them a sense of shame, leading to some improvement. All citizens should imbibe the message of this couplet and cultivate these traits to become highborn or noble. Eventually, their families will also be recognized as noble.

KEY TAKEAWAY

Purity of mind, word and action and a sense of shame about doing wrong are virtues citizens should cultivate.

54
Honour

பெருக்கத்து வேண்டும் பணிதல்; சிறிய
சுருக்கத்து வேண்டும் உயர்வு. (குறள் 963)

Transliteration
Perukkaththu Vendum Panithal; Siriya
Surukkaththu Vendum Uyarvu.

Translation
Practise humility in prosperity and fame;
Uphold dignity and self-respect in decline.

Meaning
When one is in a position of wealth or power or fame, he should demonstrate great humility; he should conduct himself with honour and dignity, even when he loses that position.

Kural Discussions
Thiruvalluvar expects citizens to live with honour. Therefore, after nobility comes the chapter 'Honour' or 'Maanam', which stresses its importance. Many couplets assert that honour is more important than life; a person may rather die than lose his honour. What Thiruvalluvar refers to as honour is, however, different from what we normally understand as honour—a fitting response to a perceived wrong done to us. Scholar Mu. Varadharajan explains it beautifully, 'Real honour is a feeling of regret for one's mistakes. It is not something done to avenge the perceived insults of others. On the other hand, it is the extreme patience shown at such insults

without a feeling of anger or revenge.'[20]

The honour Thiruvalluvar wants citizens to cultivate is doing everything to defend one's values or principles. He wants them to lead a life of honour, upholding great values without any compromise even if it means sacrificing their lives. Thus, the honour he speaks of is not about personal insults or harms but about upholding values and principles for public good.

This Kural highlights two important aspects of human behaviour for living honourably. The first, behaving with great humility when in a good position, namely when wealthy or powerful. The second, conducting oneself with dignity and honour even after loss of wealth or position. One should not behave in an undignified manner even after one's fall. Humility on rise and dignity in fall is the advice of this couplet. What happens normally is just the opposite. People in wealth or power behave arrogantly and do not treat even their friends well. The same persons after a fall from their position act abjectly for personal gains. They have neither values nor honour. A person of honour will not act this way.

The story of the Greek philosopher Socrates, who lived in the fourth century BC, is a good illustration of honour. His aristocratic philosophy was an irritant to some, and therefore, he was charged before a court of 501 citizens. The charges were: he did not believe in God, and he had corrupted the youth so much that they were drunk with debate. In his defence, Socrates denied the charges; he said that he was a believer in God and was only teaching the youth the importance of free thinking and learning. He spoke in the court with great dignity and without any obsequiousness.

After hearing him, the court concluded that he was guilty and asked for his plea on the sentence. Even then, Socrates did not beg for leniency. He was not willing to forego his commitment to his principles. The court had the power to pardon him; he refused

---

[20]Ramalingam, Namkkal Kavignar, *Thirukkural*, T.D.V. Publishers, Chennai, 2021.

to plead for pardon. He was condemned to death by drinking hemlock.

Wanting to save him, his friends hatched a plan for his escape to another city. Socrates refused. Consoling his grieving friend, Crito, he said the laws of the city would then question him. '...Further in the court itself, it was open to you to propose the penalty of banishment, if you wished, and to do with the consent of the city what you now attempt to do without it.'[21] Further, he said that after proclaiming in the court that he did not fear death, an undignified escape to another city was shameful, and as a law-abiding citizen, he must wholeheartedly accept the punishment it gave him.

After bidding farewell to his friends, he drank hemlock and died. He stood for his principles and values and maintained his dignity without worrying about death. He died a long time ago, but his thoughts still live on. The great philosopher Plato recorded these details in his *Dialogues* (n.d.).

History is full of such incidents of people giving their lives for their honour and principles. Joan of Arc and Giordana Bruno, who lost their lives for their beliefs, deserve special mention. Throughout human history, countless individuals have steadfastly upheld their principles and values, greatly benefiting humanity, even in the face of untold suffering. Even ordinary people have often acted with honour and dignity, despite great suffering. If you look around, you will identify many. They do not find a place in history but will be held in high esteem by those who know them. It is, therefore, possible for every individual to live with honour and dignity.

KEY TAKEAWAY

Living without deviating from values and principles is real honour.

---

[21]H. Eric, Phillip Rouse, and W.H.D. Rouse Warmington, *Great Dialogues of Plato (A Mentor Classic)*, New American Library, 1956.

55
Social Justice

பிறப்பொக்கும் எல்லா உயிர்க்கும்; சிறப்பொவ்வா
செய்தொழில் வேற்றுமை யான். (குறள் 972)

Transliteration
Piruppokkum Ellaa Uyirkkum; Sirappovvaa
Seythozhil Verrumai Yaan.

Translation
All men that live are equal in birth; only vocation and skills
Make the difference deciding their worth.

Meaning
All men are equal by birth; but their worth differs due to the differences in their vocation and the way they perform in their jobs.

Kural Discussions
This Kural figures in the chapter 'Greatness' or 'Perumai'. Thiruvalluvar is quite ambitious—he wants ordinary citizens to achieve greatness and shine. Commentator Manakkudavar defines greatness as not doing mean things. This seems to be a narrow definition. Fortunately, Thiruvalluvar himself has said in another Kural, 'Great people achieve extremely difficult things.' The greatness he refers to is about doing things of renown, which can be attained only through knowledge, skill and hard work. This chapter, after explaining the importance of greatness, discusses the traits of those who achieve it and those who do not. The intention is that citizens should imbibe the traits required to attain greatness.

This couplet has two parts. The first part is a simple yet profound statement that all men are equal by birth. There is no difference among them because of birth, while the second part explains how the differences arise. Irrespective of caste, religion, language, region and even sex, all are born equal. But what is today's reality? Our society is, unfortunately, divided by caste, religion and language, caste being the dominant dividing force, like race in Western societies. Even now, people born into higher castes consider themselves superior, and those born into the backward castes are denied even basic rights despite laws in their support. Caste prejudices embedded in our society for centuries cannot be erased just by these laws, but only by a radical change in our mindset. Perhaps a complete understanding of this couplet may help. Many studies have pointed out that caste divisions act as a great impediment to our development. Still, we have done little to remedy the situation. We seem not to have listened to Thiruvalluvar's pronouncement two thousand years back that all men are born equal. Consequently, our attempts to make society equal are, at best, half-hearted.

How can men born equal differentiate themselves and become great? The second part answers this question. It says that the difference leading to greatness arises from our vocation. One's vocation depends on his education, knowledge and skills, which can be acquired only through hard work. Anyone can become an accomplished scientist, engineer, doctor, professor or anything else by his hard work, irrespective of his caste or religion. Despite the inequality and handicaps suffered by people from lower castes, many of them have achieved greatness, differentiating themselves.

A logical question is whether only those in important positions can be considered great. What about those doing minor jobs, who, in fact, constitute a larger part of the polity? Are they to be excluded from greatness? The word used in the couplet, *seythozhil*, can also mean 'the manner of doing a job'. With this interpretation, those in minor vocations too can achieve greatness by doing them sincerely and flawlessly. Whatever the vocation, one can make a difference by his performance. Well-known scholar Kalaingar M. Karunanidhi agrees with this interpretation. According to him, the second part of the couplet means that the difference arises from the performance in a job rather than the job per se. As John W. Gardner, former Secretary of Health, Education, and Welfare of the United States, said: 'The society which scorns excellence in plumbing because plumbing is a humble activity, and tolerates shoddiness in philosophy because it is an exalted activity, will have neither good plumbing nor good philosophy. Neither its pipes nor its theories will hold water.'[22]

The interpretation that greatness comes from jobs implies that those in high positions are invariably great. Is that correct? They might have got that position through shortcuts. They may neglect the job and perform poorly, or they may work for personal gains, ignoring the interest of the organization. How can such people be considered great? Yet another interpretation of the word 'seythozhil' is *seyseyal*, meaning 'the deeds we do'. Our deeds should be virtuous and pure; they should be as per the standards laid down. Greatness is not solely derived from holding a high position but also from the proper and ethical discharge of responsibilities within that role. Only then can the tag of greatness be attached. Thiruvalluvar himself has made this clear in another couplet in which he says that those in high positions are not great unless they are ethical (973).

From the above discussions, it is clear that men are born equal, and no difference arises by birth. Differences leading to greatness, however, arise because of the following reasons:

- Greatness arises from people's occupations.
- However, the jobs should be performed well and in virtuous ways without any blemish.
- Interest in and commitment to the job counts for greatness.
- In any job, sincerity, commitment and excellence count for greatness.
- Any job should be performed as per its norms.

---

[22]Gardner, John W., *Excellence*, W.W. Norton & Co Ltd, 1995.

Only differences based on the above-mentioned principles will bring greatness to citizens. Not birth.

Many scholars consider Thiruvalluvar's thought in this couplet as the foundation for social reform. His thinking that all men are equal by birth and the way to greatness is through excellence in their vocations, attained with integrity and honesty, is far-reaching. It also implies equality of opportunity for all, enabling them to upgrade their knowledge and skills, make a difference, and become great, bringing credit not only to individuals but also to society. This is in line with his exhortation for universal education in another chapter. Such great thoughts two thousand years back when equality was a far cry! This cry was raised later only during the French Revolution.

Let us conclude the discussions by quoting from a website that discusses kurals (www.kuralthiran.com). It beautifully summarizes the essence of this couplet: 'There is no glory or dishonour by birth. The graceful are great and the graceless are lowly; the virtuous are exalted and the unscrupulous are low; skilled professionals are superior, and the incompetent are inferior. Thus, greatness is the product of virtuous ways, good character, competence in job and not a product of birth.' What great thoughts!

KEY TAKEAWAY

All are equal by birth. One gains greatness only through knowledge, vocation, effort and character. Therefore, we should achieve greatness only this way, without falsely claiming that birth confers it.

56

Sagely Perfection

அன்பு,நாண், ஒப்புரவு, கண்ணோட்டம், வாய்மையொடு
ஐந்துசால்பு ஊன்றிய தூண். (குறள் 983)

Transliteration
Anbunhaan, Oppuravu, Kannottam, Vaaymaiyotu
Ainhthusaalbu Uunriya Thoon.

Translation
Love, shame to do wrong, charity, compassion, truthfulness
Are the five pillars of sagely perfection.

Meaning
Love for all, shame about doing any wrong, helping the needy, compassion and speaking the truth are the five pillars of sagely perfection.

Kural Discussions
This Kural figures in the chapter 'Saanraanmai', a difficult word to translate. It can be split into *saalutal* and *aanmai*: the first means 'fullness' and the second, 'capability to rule'. Therefore, the word *saanraanmai* literally means ruling fullness. Hence, the chapter heading refers to ruling noble attributes in fullness or 'Sagely Perfection'. This couplet, then, is about individuals excelling in all that is good in humans. It has nothing to do with position, wealth or title, but deals with noble traits. The chapter covers citizens with noble attributes, who use them for society's benefit. It discusses what these noble qualities are, and how citizens could imbibe them and embrace them for the benefit of mankind. As

ever, Thiruvalluvar's expectations are high. He expects all citizens to shine with such noble traits and achieve sagely perfection!

This couplet describes five attributes of sagely perfection as its pillars. The first attribute is love for all; love shown to all humans—not just to the immediate family—without expecting any benefit. Next is shame, a sense of shame about doing wrong. Thiruvalluvar has emphasized this trait in other couplets too. Then comes altruism, joyously helping others in need. Another couplet equates the wealth of such people to the water stored in a village tank that is used for the benefit of the entire community. The fourth trait is compassion or empathy for others' sufferings. The last attribute is truthfulness, always speaking the truth.

Thiruvalluvar has merely defined sagely perfection but does not say that citizens should aim for it, as always. But that is his intention. One does not need a position, degree or wealth to become perfect. Anyone can if they try. Mahatma Gandhi personified these noble qualities. We know this because we have read and heard about him. However, one need not be a leader to cultivate these traits. I have come across many ordinary people with great nobility. I know a friend who ran around helping Covid patients, unmindful of the danger to him, when many others hid themselves in their homes. Covid did not spare him. He was hospitalized for days and suffered a lot. Fortunately, he survived. After being discharged, he went back to the same public service, caring for Covid patients once again. He did this of his own volition, out of compassion and not for any publicity or personal glory. Many like him live among us, but we do not recognize them. We do not see them unless newspapers report about them. Thiruvalluvar expects citizens to be like him; that is his message.

Scholar T.P. Meenakshisundaram explains this concept beautifully. 'The purpose of a nation is to create an ocean of citizens of such great character. Valluvar's polity envisages it as the pride of the society and its politics, which reflects his unique thinking. Although many other philosophers dreamt of such great people, only Valluvar saw them as the shining light of politics in the society.'[23] To realize his dream, let us embrace his ideals and endeavour to create an ocean of citizens of such character.

KEY TAKEAWAY

A great citizen is one endowed with great virtues and leads an exemplary life. All citizens should strive to emulate him.

---

[23]Kuralthiran, https://tinyurl.com/n2tn9jk. Accessed on 14 September 2024.

57

True Courtesy

எண்பதத்தால் எய்தல் எளிதுஎன்ப யார்மாட்டும்,
பண்புடைமை என்னும் வழக்கு. (குறள் 991)

Transliteration
Enpathaththaal Eythal Elithuenpa Yaarmaattum,
Panputaimai Ennum Vazhakku.

Translation
Those who easy access give to all men, they say,
Courtesy comes to them with ease.

Meaning
If a person conducts himself in a manner that anyone can meet and talk to him easily, the virtue of courtesy comes to him with ease.

Kural Discussions
This Kural comes under the chapter 'Panpudaimai' meaning 'Courteousness', which stresses the need for citizens to be courteous. Even while striving for greatness, pride and sagely perfection, a citizen should learn to move with others courteously and with understanding. Thus, the focus of this chapter is how one should move amiably with others. Well-known scholar Namakkal Kavignar Ramalingam explains, '"Panputaimai" or courtesy refers to one's refinement or gentleness. It refers to easy approachability, willingness to listen to others' grievances or difficulties, finding a

solution or at the minimum, comforting them.'[24] Thiruvalluvar's advice is that all citizens should embrace humility, actively listen, and help others—invaluable guidance for a meaningful life.

This couplet explains an important *panpu* or characteristic of *panpudaimai*. One who wants to be courteous should always be accessible to everyone. No matter what position he holds, no matter how busy he is, he should be accessible and move with everyone with great humility and listen to what they have to say. If they vent their grievances, he should listen patiently and try to find a solution. If it is not possible, he should at least offer them words of comfort. People who live this way have courtesy. While courtesy is inborn for some, we can cultivate it by practising what this couplet advises: be accessible, listen empathetically and offer some comfort to those approaching us.

Although the advice is simple, it is difficult to follow, for we are always immersed in our own thoughts and problems, making it difficult for others to approach us. Even when they do, we have no patience to listen to them. Neither do we attempt to solve their problems, nor do we offer words of comfort. In general, we have no time or patience for others' difficulties. Fortunately, there are still a few individuals with this trait who provide a valuable service to society. A couplet in the Tamil Sangam classic *Puranaanooru* regards them as the very reason for the existence of the world itself!

Fortunately, I have come across many courteous people in my public and private life and also immensely benefited from their association. Most of our leaders possess this great quality; it comes to them naturally, probably because they move with people all the time and rise to become leaders.

I recall an incident that happened over 50 years ago, but was narrated by a friend recently. I am recording it here since it is an excellent example of the courtesy mentioned in this couplet. He was then (1973) a medical student in Chennai. He depended on government scholarships for his studies and stayed in the college

---

[24]Kavignar, Namkkal, *Thirukkural*, T.D.V. Publishers, Chennai, 2021.

hostel. Due to some reason, he did not get the scholarship for months. Therefore, he was unable to pay for the accommodation and food. Ten more students also faced the same problem. The hostel mess was closed for them because of non-payment of dues. Without savings, some had to work as manual labourers to survive.

Unable to find a local solution, they decided to meet Kalaignar M. Karunanidhi, then chief minister of Tamil Nadu. They approached his secretary for an appointment. Surprisingly, they got it swiftly—the next day at 6.30 a.m., at the chief minister's residence. When they went there with great anxiety, they were surprised to see the chief minister waiting for them. Making them comfortable, he enquired about their background. They were in for another surprise—the chief minister's wife brought them coffee. After these preliminaries, the chief minister asked about the purpose of their visit. Saddened to hear about their problem, he immediately telephoned the department secretary. Expressing anguish over the delay, he instructed him to release the scholarship immediately. He also advised the students to study well and come up in life. When they returned to the hostel, the mess was open to them. Aid money also came in immediately.

My friend recalled this experience after all these years with great happiness. He fondly remembered the courtesy shown by the chief minister. When I heard it, I was reminded of this Kural on courtesy. I am still amazed how a chief minister with a great many responsibilities could find time to meet them and resolve their problem! I have recorded this in some detail because it fits so well with the essence of this couplet. If a chief minister could show so much courtesy, it should be possible for ordinary individuals like us to be courteous to everyone.

KEY TAKEAWAY

We should cultivate the habit of being accessible to others, listening to their grievances and trying to be helpful. That is what is expected of a worthy citizen.

58

Citizens' Duty

ஆள்வினையும், ஆன்ற அறிவும் எனவிரண்டின்
நீள்வினையால் நீளும் குடி. (குறள் 1022)

Transliteration
Aalvinaiyum, Aanra Arivum Enavirandin
Nheelvinaiyaal Nheelum Kuti.

Translation
Untiring efforts and profound wisdom and knowledge
combined together
With perseverance enrich society's welfare.

Meaning
A community's progress depends on the hard work and unceasing efforts of citizens having great wisdom and knowledge.

Kural Discussions
This Kural figures in the chapter 'Kutiseyal Vagai' describing the responsibilities of citizens to advance the *kuti*, which includes the family, clan, community, country, etc. According to the great scholar Parimelazhagar, the chapter deals with those qualities expected of a citizen that will help him to improve his community and, in turn, his country. It also stresses his responsibility to make strenuous efforts for the betterment of his community. Therefore, the appropriate chapter heading is 'Advancing the Community'.

Only small village communities existed during Thiruvalluvar's times. The situation has now vastly changed, with communities spreading out into cities and nations. With phenomenal improvement in communication, nations have become closer, with greater interdependence. What happens in one country affects another and its people. The rapid spread of the coronavirus across the globe is an example. Scholar Mu. Varadarajan explains this idea, 'The whole world is shrinking and becoming ever closer as one family. Realizing that, it is better to interpret the word "kuti" to mean "nation"; the chapter heading will then mean "Advancing the Nation", conveying a more appropriate message to the present generation.'[25] This is totally acceptable, and therefore, we can take it that this chapter envisages citizens' duties towards the growth of their country and the rest of the world.

This couplet specifically mentions two human qualities required for the progress of the community: one is hard work, and the other, a fine combination of wisdom and knowledge.

The first quality is *aalvinai*, which literally means 'governing a task' or implementing a task perfectly to the satisfaction of all. It includes not just hard work, but also energy, motivation, zeal and enthusiasm in its execution. We often encounter people with this trait in our daily interactions and are impressed by their enthusiasm and dedication, even in their ordinary tasks.

The second is in-depth knowledge required to perform a task in addition to sharpness, intelligence and smartness. A citizen should be hard-working and smart. An example of this can be found among students. Some students who work hard but without sufficient intelligence do not do well in their studies. Others with intelligence but without hard work also do badly. Only those combining intelligence and hard work perform well. The couplet expects citizens to not only work hard with zeal and enthusiasm but also be smart and intelligent. Such people can complete many tasks in a short time—their efficiency is quite high.

The couplet does not stop at this. Rapid growth and progress can take place with the *nheelvinai* of citizens with these two

---

[25]Ramalingam, Namkkal Kavignar, *Thirukkural*, T.D.V. Publishers, Chennai, 2021.

qualities. The word refers to their abundant energy to keep doing more and more. After completing one task, they will look for another and execute it also with the same zeal. They are so vibrant that they are capable of working hard without any rest. They keep doing something or the other all the time.

The unremitting work of such citizens will bring prosperity to their families, cities and nations, and sometimes to the world too. We know that the tireless efforts of many scientists, researchers and inventors have immensely benefited humanity, resulting in remarkable human progress. They are the great citizens who have met the standards of this couplet. I can think of Thomas Alva Edison (1847-1931) as one such remarkable citizen to highlight the import of this couplet. A leading inventor of his time, he was known for his hard work and knowledge. He never stopped working; more than a thousand inventions are attributed to him. Among his major inventions are the electric bulb, the gramophone and the motion picture camera, which benefited the entire world. Due to his inventions, he and his family became wealthy; his town and country prospered. In addition, the entirety of humanity benefited, with vastly improved living standards.

Countries blessed with a large number of such citizens have obviously made rapid progress and are advanced in many areas. In particular, the United States and China can be mentioned. China is now trying to overtake the United States in many niche areas; one reason for its confidence could be the presence of citizens with these qualities in their country.

KEY TAKEAWAY

A nation's progress depends on its citizens who, with their profound knowledge and talent, tirelessly work for its upliftment.

59

Pride of Farmers

உழுவார் உலகத்தார்க்கு ஆணி; அஃது ஆற்றாது
எழுவாரை எல்லாம் பொறுத்து. (குறள் 1032)

Transliteration
Uzhuvaar Ulakaththaarkku Aaniahthu Aarraathu
Ezhuvaarai Ellaam Poruththu.

Translation
Farmers are the lynchpins of the world; they bear
Them who perform other works, too weak its toils to share.

Meaning
Since farmers support others incapable of the hard labour required for agriculture, they are the lynchpins of the world, which cannot, therefore, function without them.

Kural Discussions
This Kural figures in the chapter 'Agriculture' or 'Uzhavu'. Thiruvalluvar, who has provided separate chapters for kings, ministers, education, etc., has given one on agriculture, too, to bring out its importance and its vital role in a country. In this chapter, he has eulogized the role of farmers, who were vital in the agrarian economy of his time. That he has given equal importance to manual work reflects his egalitarian thinking, while many philosophers have given prominence only to intellectuals.

This couplet explains the vital role played by farmers through a simile. A temple car can move only if its fulcrum is intact and well-maintained. Without it, the wheels will come off, and the car will not be able to move. Farmers are like this fulcrum for the proper functioning of the world. Why so? For they support all others incapable of putting in the arduous labour involved in agriculture. Only if farmers toil can the rest of the population, whether the king or ministers or high officials, or anyone, get food on the table. This is true not only of Thiruvalluvar's time but even today. Unless food is available in plenty, hunger and malnutrition will stalk the people. They can make little progress. In another couplet, Thiruvalluvar himself has listed abundant food as a prerequisite for a good country, which is possible only through the hard and tireless efforts of farmers. Hence, they are the lynchpins of the world.

The couplet talks of others as *aarraathu ezhuvaarai*, which means 'those who are incapable of the hard labour and care demanded by agriculture'. These words imply that they are held in low esteem. Although they would like to pursue farming, they find themselves unable to handle its physical demands and instead opt for lighter occupations. In an agricultural society, farmers play a vital role in providing food and clothing to the community, while the contributions of other artisans are relatively minor. Therefore, farmers are rightly regarded as the stars of society. Another couplet says that all others are simply worshippers of farmers, because none can survive without them.

Even in the modern era, farming continues to be vital. Many countries are concerned about their self-sufficiency in food production. Despite considerable farm mechanization, manual labour continues to be necessary. Hence, farmers play an important role even today. Recently, I came across a book on human history that highlights the major role played by farming in human progress and development. Only after the emergence of farming could the human race realize its full potential and move towards a new human history. This happened just 10,000 years back in the history of our species of over 130,000 years. Till then, man was living as hunter-gatherer like any other animal. Farming led to his settling down in a place and paved the way for the emergence of civilizations and continuous progress. Thus, farming laid the foundation of human progress. No wonder Thiruvalluvar praised its importance two millennia ago.

Self-sufficiency in food production in our country has been possible only because of the hard work of farmers. Yet, they are not given the respect due to them. Unfortunately, glamourous sectors and jobs grab greater attention thanks to urban communities' ignorance about the vital role of farming. Despite significant progress in farming, many countries are still unable to feed their citizens; they do not produce enough, nor do they have the resources to import. Fortunately, India is self-sufficient in food production. Still, we rank 68th out of 113 countries in the Global Food Security Index (2021),[26] reflecting widespread hunger in the country. It also emphasizes the need for greater focus on agriculture. Considering that 60 per cent of our population is still dependent on agriculture, it is time the government gives greater importance to agriculture and farmers and helps them in every way possible.

KEY TAKEAWAY

Agriculture is the foundation of a country's growth.

---

[26]Economist Impact, *Global Food Security Index 2022*, https://tinyurl.com/mrhvudcu. Accessed on 27 November 2024.

60

Poverty's Miseries

நல்குரவு என்னும் இடும்பையுள் பல்குரைத்
துன்பங்கள் சென்று படும். (குறள் 1045)

Transliteration
Nhalkuravu Ennum Itumpaiyul Palkuraith
Thunpangkal Senru Patum.

Translation
From poverty, the grievous woe,
A tail of endless miseries grows.

Meaning
Poverty leads to innumerable sufferings.

Kural Discussions
After many nuggets of wisdom on how to become responsible and exemplary citizens, Thiruvalluvar talks about what they should guard against in the last four chapters—namely poverty, beggary, shame of beggary and meanness—of this subdivision. This Kural figures in the chapter 'Poverty' or 'Nhalkuravu'. Thiruvalluvar's was an agrarian society dependent on rainfall. When it failed, misery and poverty were the outcome. Moved by the cruelty wrought by poverty, he highlights the immense suffering of the poor in this chapter. Since he has already emphasized the importance of wealth creation in another chapter, he clearly does not want citizens to be indigent. However, he has brought out the miseries of poverty probably for governments and generous citizens to appreciate them and take measures to mitigate them. It is also a warning to

citizens and governments to work hard to overcome poverty.

This Kural just makes a statement that poverty is a great misery and is a source of many greater miseries. The word used, *palkuraith thunpangkal*, means many kinds of miseries. Those living in poverty do not get enough food to eat, and, therefore, suffer from hunger and malnutrition, which in turn affect their ability to work and earn. Also, they are easily prone to diseases due to poor diet. They are often forced to borrow for medical treatment, which lands them in a debt trap. Sometimes, they have to beg to survive. Thus, poverty leads to more poverty and more misery. It is called the cycle of poverty. In another couplet, Thiruvalluvar says that there is nothing that afflicts one like poverty; nothing else can be worse. He compares people suffering from poverty to those sleeping on fire! It is so miserable and painful.

It is clear that Thiruvalluvar, moved by the plight of the poor, has expressed his anguish in this chapter. He has, however, not given any particular solution or idea to mitigate it. But his ideas in many other chapters on good governance, universal education, hard work, achieving greatness, charity, etc., will definitely help mitigate poverty. Individuals with a high level of motivation and ability to work hard will not fall into poverty, but not all citizens possess these traits. Hence poverty persists. Thiruvalluvar expects both governments and citizens to realize its cruelty and take steps towards alleviating it.

Sadly, poverty still afflicts humanity, and millions live in poverty across the globe, despite many global initiatives for poverty eradication. A commonly used measure of poverty is that based on incomes and expenditures. A per capita income of less than $2.15 (₹180) per day is considered extreme poverty. On this measure, 8.4 per cent (64.8 crore) of the world's population suffered from extreme poverty in 2022.[27] To assess poverty in

---

[27]'Fact Sheet: An Adjustment to Global Poverty Lines', *World Bank Group*, 14 September 2022, https://tinyurl.com/yc22xufj. Accessed on 20 September 2024.

specific countries, the World Bank uses the country-specific per capita daily expenditure, taking into account their cost of living, which was between $3.65 and $6.85. In 2019, a staggering 23 per cent of the global population lived below $3.65 per day, while an even more alarming 47% (360 crore) could afford less than $6.85 per day.[28] All of them are classified as poor, suffering from hunger, starvation, lack of shelter and chronic illness.

Do not think that poverty is confined only to poor countries. It exists even in many rich countries. The World Bank also calculates the poverty rate—the percentage of the population living in poverty—of different countries. It is 16.8 per cent in the US, a rich country dominating world affairs, 15.60 per cent in France (in 2021 based on national poverty line); 12.92 per cent in India (2021, at USD 2.15 per day); and 82.30 per cent in South Sudan (2016, using national poverty line), the poorest country. China has reduced poverty to zero (in 2021, using USD 2.15 a day), reflecting a remarkable achievement.[29]

Quality education and healthcare with abundant employment opportunities are the planks for fighting poverty. The sooner countries realize this, the faster will be the progress in poverty eradication. Genuine government support for citizens' efforts to fight poverty, through their motivation, effort and ingenuity, will also help.

KEY TAKEAWAY

Citizens and governments should work together to eradicate poverty, keeping in mind the cruelties of poverty described by Thiruvalluvar.

---

[28]World Bank Group, *Poverty and Shared Prosperity 2022*, https://tinyurl.com/2x5c9uet. Accessed on 27 November 2024., while an even more alarming 47 per cent (360 crore) could afford less than $6.85 per day.
[29]World Bank Group, 'Country Profile', https://tinyurl.com/mvjuzf87. Accessed on 27 November 2024.

61

When Begging is Justified

இன்பம் ஒருவர்க்கு இரத்தல், இரந்தவை
துன்பம் உறாஅ வரின். (குறள் 1052)

Transliteration
Inbam Oruvarkku Iraththal, Iranthavai
Thunbam Uraaa Varin.

Translation
Even begging is pleasure, if what is sought,
Is got without humiliation.

Meaning
Even begging can be pleasant to one if he can get what is sought without humiliation.

Kural Discussions
The chapter that follows 'Poverty' or 'Nhalkuravu' is 'Beggary' or 'Iravu'. Surprisingly, Thiruvalluvar, who has eulogized hard work and high motivation, has allocated a chapter for mendicancy. Does he support it? In the chapter devoted to avoiding beggary, he makes it clear that he does not. Moved by the miseries of poverty, he has thought of a few circumstances that justify beggary. His underlying theme is that though beggary should be avoided, those resorting to it due to extreme poverty need to be treated with some consideration. Instead of looking down upon them, we should treat them humanely, considering their indigent circumstances.

This Kural has a simple message. Begging that needs to be avoided is resorted to by one suffering from extreme poverty. If he can get what he begs for without distress, misery or suffering, even begging can give some happiness. For whom? For both the beggar and the giver. For the giver gives without humiliating the taker, and the taker receives without insult or suffering. If such a situation exists, even begging can be pleasant.

Due to extreme poverty, one approaches another for help, hoping that he will help. He will naturally be happy if the giver, realizing his poverty and difficult situation, treats him kindly, comforts him and gives him the requested assistance. A giver who behaves this way is a man of good character with a large heart. To assist people in distress is his innate quality. On the contrary, if the assistance comes with insult, there is no happiness for either. One should not approach such a person for help—in fact, the latter should treat those seeking help due to poverty with kindness and assist them.

Reports of suicide of entire families due to poverty keep appearing in newspapers from time to time. People commit suicide for various reasons. According to the latest National Crime Records Bureau (NCRB) report, 1.7 lakh people committed suicide in India in 2022. The government has many programmes to eradicate poverty and create employment. Even so, this misery continues. It is not known whether these people refused to seek assistance out of pride or approached the wrong persons. However, most would have been pushed to this extreme step only for lack of timely help, for compassion and helpfulness seem to be qualities that are slowly disappearing.

This couplet's message is: there is nothing wrong in begging to relieve the miseries of extreme poverty, but ask the generous-minded, who are willing to give. To give to the needy is a hallmark of good citizenry.

KEY TAKEAWAY

Let us develop the mindset to help those in distress, keeping in mind that our timely help may prevent suicides.

62

Dread of Begging

தெண்ணீர் அடுபுற்கை ஆயினும், தாள்தந்தது
உண்ணலின், ஊங்கினியது இல். (குறள் 1065)

Transliteration
Thenneer Atupurkai Aayinum, Thaalthanhthathu
Unnalin, Uungkiniyathu Il.

Translation
Nothing is sweeter than gruel thin as water,
If earned by one's labour.

Meaning
Nothing gives one greater happiness than even gruel as thin as water, if only it is earned through one's labour.

Kural Discussions
This Kural figures in the chapter 'Dread of Begging' or 'Iravachcham', which condemns beggary as a disgrace. It advises people to avoid beggary at any cost. Why, then, does Thiruvalluvar justify beggary in the earlier chapter? He justifies it only under extreme poverty while highlighting the need to help people in great distress. This chapter makes it clear that he is strongly against it and wants citizens to earn and live within their income.

This couplet is about a poor person. He can get gruel essentially of water, without any nutrients in it, because he can afford just that from his income. Such abject poverty! Drinking it gives more happiness than anything else since it is cooked out of his earnings through his labour. He is not reliant on anyone else for his food. Although it is not rich or tasty, it is his. Therefore, it brings him great happiness. This is what the couplet says. He could beg and get tasty and nutritious food, but it will not give him this happiness. Hence, one should live within one's means without begging for benefits from others. Other couplets in this chapter also reflect the same theme.

Sadly, begging has become a profession now! Many work as full-time beggars in India. It has been estimated that there are over four lakh beggars (2021) in our country. Many of them have been happily engaged in this profession for years. Some earn up to ₹100,000 per month, an impressive salary.[30]

Keen to abolish beggary, our governments have implemented many measures over the years. Many beggar rehabilitation centres provide free shelter and food. But professional beggars do not like to use them. They like the freedom to beg as they please. No one doubts that begging is a disgraceful profession. But people living through beggary do not seem to think so. With the growing opportunity for education and employment, we can hope that one day our country will be rid of beggars.

KEY TAKEAWAY

Everyone should stand on their feet without begging for their needs.

---

[30]ANI, 'West Bengal ranks top with 81,224 beggars: Govt informs Rajya Sabha', 11 March 2021, https://tinyurl.com/2wuyhw4s. Accessed on 27 November 2024. TOI Lifestyle Desk, 'How some beggars in Lucknow earn 1 lakh monthly, out-earning mid-level professionals', https://tinyurl.com/4xsap8wc. Accessed on 27 November 2024.

63

Avoid Meanness

உடுப்பதூஉம் உண்பதூஉம் காணின், பிறர்மேல்
வடுக்காண வற்றாகும் கீழ். (குறள் 1079)

Transliteration
Utuppathoom Unpathoom Kaanin, Pirarmel
Vatukkaana Varraakum Keezh.

Translation
The base cannot tolerate to see others dress and eat,
But stoop to find fault and blame.

Meaning
Mean people are good at deliberately finding fault with others merely on seeing them eat and dress.

Kural Discussions
The last chapter in the 'Wealth' or 'Porul' division deals with 'Kayamai', a difficult word to translate; it roughly means 'baseness' or 'meanness' or 'all that is bad in humans'. The chapter deals with the traits of mean people. Since it deals with the worst human beings, it is kept at the end. Tamil scholar K.A.P. Viswanatham says that this word is unique to the Tamil language, like 'saanraanmai', and both are difficult to translate. He adds that *kayamai* refers to the lowest limit of meanness, whereas 'saanraanmai' refers to the highest limit of virtues. Both have separate chapters in *Thirukkural*.

Let us see what this Kural says. It explains a bad trait of mean persons. They cannot even tolerate anyone eating or dressing and will invariably find some faults with them and complain. It is not necessary that the faults or defects exist in them. They just find fault without reason. One might wonder whether this is not simply envy that afflicts most of us. A careful reading of the words used in the couplet reveals that it is not so; there is no need for others to dress well or eat lavishly to provoke a negative reaction. Just ordinary dress and normal food are good enough for the mean people to start blaming, for they are so mean. It is in their character to be mean and keep blaming others for no reason. Thiruvalluvar is so contemptuous of them that he does not even call them mean people but just mean, like an inanimate object. He has used this form of address in other couplets as well to bring out his sense of disgust.

A quick reading of other couplets in this chapter will help us better understand the traits of such people. They are the meanest of the mean and the lowest of the low; they are unconcerned about anything; they do what they like; they have no culture, yet feel proud; they only pretend to be good; they always talk ill of others; they are great misers; they never do any good easily; they are ever willing to sell themselves; they never speak their heart. In short, they are like humans, but not humans. Better to stay away from such people in life.

He has highlighted meanness in this last chapter because he despises mean people as abject human beings. All their bad qualities have been described in some detail so that citizens steer clear of such behaviour. Also, the moment they spot these in others, they should stay away from them. This, in short, is his advice in this chapter.

KEY TAKEAWAY

Realizing the evils of meanness, citizens should never be mean and steer clear of individuals showing mean-spiritedness.

Aram

1
Praise of God

கற்றதனால் ஆய பயனென்கொல் வாலறிவன்
நற்றாள் தொழாஅர் எனின்? (குறள் 2)

Transliteration
Karrathanaal Aaya Payanenkol Vaalarivan
Nharraal Thozhaar Enin?

Translation
Of what avail is learning, if one fails to adore
The divine feet of Him of Perfect Wisdom?

Meaning
What is the use of learning if one does not worship the divine feet of the All-Knowing One?

Kural Discussions
The first four chapters of *Thirukkural* falling under the division titled 'Aram', meaning 'Virtue', are in the nature of its prologue or epitome. This Kural figures in the first chapter, 'Praise of God' or 'Kadavul Vaazhththu', in which Thiruvalluvar highlights the importance of worshipping God. He does not, however, mention the name of any God or deity in any of these couplets. He portrays God as a Supreme Being and addresses Him only in general terms such as Primal Deity, All-Knowing One, One with a Flowery Mind, One Above Likes and Dislikes, One Without Desires, One Beyond Compare, and a Sea of Virtues. Thus God has been portrayed in a manner acceptable to all faiths, so much so that many religions claim *Thirukkural* as theirs. For Thiruvalluvar, all religions are

equally acceptable. His principles for virtuous living transcend religious boundaries, encompassing the essence of humanity. His views on human life, ethics, morality, politics, wealth, governance and enjoyment were universally acceptable then; they are accepted today, and shall be accepted forever to the extent that *Thirukkural* is venerated as the Tamil Veda, an enduring source of wisdom.

This couplet raises a rhetorical question, 'What is the use of learning if one does not worship the divine feet of God?' The answer is clear: There is no use. It is thus a couplet in praise of God, highlighting the importance of worship. God is addressed here as *Vaalarivan*. Scholars have given different interpretations of this word: pure knowledge, limitless knowledge, priceless knowledge and wisdom. Scholar Mu. Varadarajan explains that this refers to 'God in the form of pure knowledge', which fits the term perfectly.[31] That God is the abode of all and pure knowledge, transcending boundaries, is universally accepted. We should therefore worship One of Perfect Wisdom.

The rhetorical question is directed towards educated or learned individuals. One might wonder why the uneducated are left out. The reason may be that educated people often tend to assume omniscience, thanks to the rapid pace of discoveries and inventions in the world. This presumption can lead to arrogance, with some even denying the existence of God. Hence, the question is directed towards them. It is surprising that even during Thiruvalluvar's time, there were learned individuals questioning the existence of God. Or did he give this advice to the learned of today in anticipation of later advancements?

The underlying principle is that the knowledge possessed by any human being is limited, whereas God is omniscient. According to a well-known Tamil proverb, 'What a man knows is as little as a handful of earth, and what he does not know is as big as the whole earth.' This is undeniably true, as revealed by successive discoveries,

---

[31]Ramalingam, Namkkal Kavignar, *Thirukkural*, T.D.V. Publishers, Chennai, 2021.

one theory disproving another accepted previously. Despite all the scientific discoveries we take pride in, our knowledge is still limited. And only the All-Knowing God is the epitome of all knowledge. This principle is well explained by scholar Namakkal Kavignar Ramalingam, 'Education is for our learning. No matter how well we are educated, there is still a lot more to be learned. When we try to explore where the limit of knowledge ends, we see it is beyond our reach. Thus, an ocean of knowledge lies beyond our limits. This "Perfect Knowledge" beyond our understanding is what we call "Vaalarivan" and "Bhagavan". What is the use of our education if we do not admit that our knowledge is insignificant as compared to the perfect knowledge of God! If we agree, we should humble ourselves before God.'[32]

What about others without education? When even educated individuals are required to worship Him, it goes without saying others should too. Thiruvalluvar suggests His divine feet for worship since it is difficult to worship formless knowledge, and it is easier for all to visualize God's feet for worship.

English polymath Isaac Newton beautifully explained the notion of God as though he were explaining the very term 'Vaalarivan': 'As a blind man has no idea of colours, so have we no idea of the manner by which the All-Wise God perceives and understands all things.' The All-Knowing God's knowledge, methods, efficacy, etc., are beyond our limited knowledge. Therefore, everyone, learned or not, should realize that our knowledge is nothing compared to His, and we should always remain humble and pray to Him.

KEY TAKEAWAY

True wisdom goes beyond mere knowledge and encompasses a deep reverence for the divine.

---

[32]Parimelazhagar, *Thirukkural Moolamum Uraiyum*, Aruna Publishers, Chennai, 2016.

2

Praise of Rain

நீர்இன்று அமையாது உலகெனின் யார்யார்க்கும்,
வான்இன்று அமையாது ஒழுக்கு. (குறள் 20)

Transliteration
Nheerinru Amaiyaathu Ulakenin Yaaryaarkkum,
Vaaninru Amaiyaathu Ozhukku.

Translation
Without water life cannot sustain;
Nor can virtue without rain.

Meaning
Life without water will be impossible for any individual, however highly placed he may be; similarly, ethical and virtuous life is not possible without rain.

Kural Discussions
The fact that 'Praise of Rain' or 'Vaansirappu' has been placed after 'Praise of God' or 'Kadavul Vaazhththu' emphasizes the significance Thiruvalluvar attaches to rain. It highlights its vital role in a country's prosperity, especially for one dependent on an agrarian economy. In many couplets in other chapters, too, he has highlighted the glory of rain. In one, he specifically mentions its magnanimity of contributing enormously to human welfare and happiness without expecting anything in return. It is surprising that even two thousand years back when climate change was not a concern, regular rain was considered important for prosperity.

This Kural highlights the importance of water and rain. Life without water will be unliveable for anyone, however highly placed he may be. Even individuals in high positions, such as kings and ministers, will suffer in case of water shortage. Therefore, water is the foundation of a good life. The second part of the Kural says that society's virtuous life will be eroded without rain. While inadequate water affects life, inadequate rain affects a society's ethics.

We are well aware of the importance of water. It led to the development of plants and organisms and, eventually, humans. Humans first settled in places rich in natural water resources, enabling them to take up agriculture. This led to the beginning of civilization and many subsequent developments. Even now, water is essential for agriculture and industries and is vital for human progress and healthy living. Thus, it is evident that there is no life without water.

The availability of water is closely linked to rain. Failure of rains results in water scarcity, causing misery for all. But how is morality affected by the shortage of rains? Even in a country with abundant natural water resources, these will dry up with the failure of rains, causing drought. Man-made water resources like dams, ponds, wells, etc., will also dry up. Food production will suffer, resulting in scarcity. People will fight for food. Starving people caught up in their daily struggle for food due to drought and famine do not have time to think about virtue. Many vices like theft, embezzlement, hoarding and selfishness start sprouting in society, even among good people, destroying its culture. That is why Thiruvalluvar says that virtue will be lost when rain is lost.

We have seen this often in Tamil Nadu. When rains fail, water shortage in Kaveri River causes disputes between Tamil Nadu and Karnataka, affecting the law-and-order situation in both states. Similarly, even within Tamil Nadu, water disputes surface between districts, leading to farmers' agitations. Daily clashes for even drinking water become common. We keep looking at the sky for signs of rain to get relief. Thus, the absence of rains leads to water and food shortages, resulting in disputes over water and food that impact our well-being and, eventually, discipline.

Despite many advancements, the world still suffers from water scarcity. The United Nations has taken several measures to address it. Since 1993, 22 March has been declared as World Water Day, and many conservation measures have been implemented. Nevertheless, the United Nations Water Development report 2024 estimates that half of the world's population currently experiences severe water scarcity for at least part of the year. One quarter of the world's population face 'extremely high' levels of water stress, using over 80 per cent of their annual renewable freshwater supply. By 2050, an additional 1 billion people are expected to live with extremely high water stress.[33]

The United Nations has warned that unless adequate measures are taken to prevent environmental degradation, people will suffer without water. To prevent this situation, the period from 2018 to 2028 has been declared as the 'International Decade for Action on Water for Sustainable Development'. Many measures are being taken to conserve water.

Despite years of concerted worldwide efforts, 2.2 billion people still do not have access to safe drinking water.[34] The motto of the United Nations today, 'There is no life without water', is an echo of what Thiruvalluvar said two thousand years back!

KEY TAKEAWAY

Realizing that water shortage could even affect the ethics of society in addition to its living standards, everyone should use water sparingly and take all possible measures to save it. Water

---

[33]UNESCO Digital Library, *The United Nations World Water Development Report 2024: Water for prosperity and peace*, https://tinyurl.com/npk2kwyy. Accessed on 27 November 2024. Kuzma, Samantha, Liz Saccoccia, and Marlena Chertock, '25 Countries, Housing One-Quarter of the Population, Face Extremely High Water Stress', World Resources Institute, 16 August 2023, https://tinyurl.com/4c97z7h7. Accessed on 27 November 2024.
[34]'UN: 2.2 Billion People Have No Access to Clean Water', *DW*, 22 March 2024, https://tinyurl.com/y2wffa6n. Accessed on 17 October 2024.

conservation, safeguarding water bodies, protecting underground water resources, and taking measures for environmental protection to ensure good rains are also necessary.

3

Praise of Great Men

செயற்கரிய செய்வார் பெரியர்; சிறியர்
செயற்கரிய செய்கலா தார். (குறள் 26)

Transliteration
Seyarkariya Seyvaar Periyar; Siriyar
Seyarkariya Seykalaa Thaar.

Translation
Things hard in doing will great man do;
Things hard in doing the small eschew.

Meaning
Great people will do rare deeds that are extremely hard, while small people are incapable of any such thing.

Kural Discussions
This chapter, titled 'Nheeththaar Perumai' in praise of great men, figures next to the one on the greatness of rain. *Nheeththaar* means 'renouncers', *perumai* means 'greatness'. Therefore, the title means greatness of those who renounce everything or live as ascetics, or 'Greatness of Renouncers'. Like God and rain, they constantly help others in their journey of life. Medieval commentators are of the view that Thiruvalluvar refers to saints, but modern commentators differ. Thiruvalluvar addresses these men with many distinctive epithets such as selfless, virtuous, men of great character, disciplined, etc. He has not used the word 'saint' anywhere. Furthermore, he has discussed sainthood in a separate subdivision. Modern commentators are, therefore, of the view that this Kural

is about selfless public-spirited individuals who are dedicated to the common good, with abundant love and compassion for all beings. This seems acceptable considering the epithets used by Thiruvalluvar for 'nheeththaar'.

This couplet states that truly great people do extraordinary things for their country and for society. With great love and compassion, they selflessly serve others, relinquishing their personal interests and desires, and continue to perform deeds that benefit others, regardless of age or illness. The Buddha, who renounced his royal life in search of a solution to the suffering of sentient beings, is a prime example of the greatness referred to in this Kural. Others such as Mahatma Gandhi, K. Kamaraj, former chief minister of Tamil Nadu, and Mother Teresa also fall under this category, as they worked selflessly for the common good till the end of their lives. However, many people are not willing to give up their personal pleasures and comforts, making them incapable of achieving anything great. This is because they live solely for themselves and their own happiness.

When it is said that great people do great things, it is understood that the small are incapable of that. Why repeat it? It seems that repetition serves to highlight the contrast between great and small individuals, emphasizing the greatness of selfless individuals and the insignificance of those who prioritize their own interests.

Another explanation has been offered by scholar K.A.P. Viswanatham. Palm leaves used in the days of Thiruvalluvar were susceptible to termite attack. Viswanatham postulates that the second *seyarkariya* (meaning 'difficult to perform') should be *seyarkuriya*, and the mistake must have crept in either due to damage by termite or in the process of reproducing the verse. 'Seyarkuriya' means 'those that need to be done'. If this argument were acceptable, the couplet would mean, 'Great individuals do great things while the small neglect even things that ought to be done.' Thiruvalluvar is frugal in his use of words and packs them with in-depth meaning. Therefore, he is unlikely to repeat words.

Hence, we may accept Viswantham's interpretation that brings out the contrast between the great and small individuals more sharply and clearly. Incidentally, we cannot but be struck by how much the change of a single letter can alter the meaning of a word.

Great are those who renounce everything for the sake of the common good and achieve great things, whereas small people do not even do what they ought to. We should associate ourselves with the great and avoid the company of the small.

KEY TAKEAWAY

Without joining the crowd of selfish small people, we should selflessly strive for greatness, working for or supporting the common good like the great people we admire.

4
Purity of Mind

மனத்துக்கண் மாசிலன் ஆதல் அனைத்தறன்;
ஆகுல நீர பிற. (குறள் 34)

Transliteration
Manaththukkan Maasilan Aathal Anaiththaran;
Aahula Nheera Pira.

Translation
Purity of mind is righteousness personified;
All else, worthless, mere pomp of idle sound.

Meaning
True virtue is nothing but keeping your mind absolutely pure; everything else is only fanfare.

Kural Discussions
This Kural figures in the chapter 'Emphasis on Virtue' or 'Aran Valiyuruththal', the last in the introductory subdivision. It highlights the importance of virtue, its basic elements and great benefits, which are elaborated in detail in subsequent chapters under the 'Virtue' division. As Thiruvalluvar believes that good must be done for its own sake, virtue is all-pervading in *Thirukkural*; he lays its foundation in this chapter, a preamble to what follows.

This couplet states that purity of mind is all that is required for virtuous living. All else is mere pomp and sound without any real worth. The message is that anyone wanting to follow the virtuous path must be spotless in mind!

Can purity of mind alone be considered virtuous? Should it not be accompanied by virtuous deeds such as speaking kindly or helping others? Virtue consists of three components—pure mind, good words and noble deeds. Without the latter two, there is no benefit to an individual or society. What, then, is the use of just purity of mind? Leading commentators have discussed this issue elaborately and clarified that a pure mind will definitely lead to kind words and good deeds since they all spring from the mind. Furthermore, they point out that any virtuous act without good intention, say, for publicity or propaganda, cannot be considered virtuous. Hence, a pure mind is the foundation of virtue, as claimed by this couplet.

A reasonable doubt arises on whether purity of mind is ever possible since the mind is the most difficult to control. It oscillates from the present to the past and the future in seconds. One moment it is in India, and the next, it flies to the US. Theoretical physicist Albert Einstein established that the speed of light cannot be exceeded, but this does not apply to the human mind. One moment, it can think of earth, and the very next moment, it can wander off to a star light years away. Similarly, good and bad thoughts keep flooding us constantly, unless we are one of those yogis who have mastered their mind.

Furthermore, it is possible to keep speech and action pure and good even without a pure mind. Thiruvalluvar has, however, set the bar high for virtue. For him, every virtuous act must be done with a pure mind, a high standard not easily attainable by ordinary individuals. That does not mean we should not try. We should keep trying and strive towards it with constant effort and practice. Realizing that good words and deeds without a pure mind are not true virtues, we should always aim for purity of mind.

He goes on to say that everything else is empty noise. Many charitable activities are undertaken for the sake of publicity or fanfare or to mitigate guilt, but they cannot be considered virtuous as they lack purity of mind. As they do offer benefits to people, why object to them? Thiruvalluvar does not object but merely points out that they are not true virtues. For him, the motive behind the action is what determines its virtuous nature. Doing good deeds with an ulterior motive is not a virtue, as also doing something with the expectation of a reward.

All should bear in mind the concept that purity of mind is the foundation of virtue. Although difficult, everyone can achieve it with perseverance. To be virtuous requires no money, no position, no power, and nothing except a pure mind. Anyone, whether rich or poor, educated or uneducated, can be equally virtuous!

All of us must, therefore, strive for a pure mind and do whatever we do with good intentions.

KEY TAKEAWAY

Since purity of mind is a true virtue, we must strive for it. Although difficult, it is not impossible to attain. By constantly driving away bad thoughts through ceaseless efforts and conscious practice, our minds will become purer by the day.

5

Traits to Be Shunned

அழுக்காறு, அவா,வெகுளி, இன்னாச்சொல் நான்கும்
இழுக்கா இயன்றது அறம். (குறள் 35)

Transliteration
Azhukkaaru, Avaa,vekuli, Innaachchol Nhaankum
Izhukkaa Iyanrathu Aram.

Translation
Envy, greed, anger, harsh words—
To shun these four is virtue.

Meaning
Jealousy, greed, anger, and using harsh or hurtful words are four traits that are incompatible with virtue.

Kural Discussions
This Kural figuring next in the same chapter 'Emphasis on Virtue' or 'Aran Valiyuruththal' defines four human traits that are incompatible with virtue. Since they pollute the mind, they must be avoided by all, especially those striving for purity of mind. We should study the previous and this couplet together to understand the concept of purity of mind and virtuous living.

Let us examine the four traits that should be avoided for a virtuous life: envy, desire, anger and harsh or hurtful words.

The first is envy. Envy is our innate quality that we should somehow overcome. We are envious of the achievements or fortunes of even our friends and relatives, sometimes to the extent of spoiling relationships and friendships. Although we know envy is undesirable, it seems ingrained in us.

Next is desire, which is the cause of much suffering. The desire referred to here is the greed that drives us to aspire for even what is not rightfully ours.

The third is anger. We are all familiar with the destructive effects of excessive anger. Excessive anger can damage relationships and have negative effects on our health and well-being.

The fourth is using harsh words. We often use harsh or hurtful language, sometimes unknowingly, without realizing the harm it can cause to others and to ourselves as well—often, they make us feel miserable later.

The couplet says that these four traits do not go with a virtuous life. Those who wish to lead an ethical life must, therefore, avoid them.

Many great leaders too have spoken against these traits. The Buddha said, 'He who envies others does not obtain peace of mind.' The Dalai Lama has often spoken against envy and anger as the destroyer of our happiness. In another couplet, Thiruvalluvar himself calls envy a sinner. Similarly, Confucius warns against anger: 'When anger rises, think of the consequences.' Greek philosophers Plato and Aristotle said that greed is at the root of personal immorality. Many other scholars, philosophers and religious thinkers have often spoken against these vices. Those who wish to attain purity of mind should, therefore, put them aside through persistent effort.

One may wonder why only four vices have been mentioned when there are so many. Thiruvalluvar has not said that others do not matter for virtuous living but has only prioritized these four in this introductory chapter. However, a careful study will reveal that they are the underlying causes of most vices. Therefore, those who want to walk the path of virtue, and those who seek to keep the mind undefiled, should avoid them entirely. Thiruvalluvar later devotes many chapters to explaining in detail the evils wrought by these and other vices.

KEY TAKEAWAY

Let us walk an ethical path with a pure mind by avoiding traits that are incompatible with it, such as envy, greed, anger and harsh words.

6

Ideal Married Life

அன்பும் அறனும் உடைத்தாயின், இல்வாழ்க்கை
பண்பும் பயனும் அது. (குறள் 45)

Transliteration
Anbum Aranum Udaiththaayin, Ilvaazhkkai
Panpum Payanum Athu.

Translation
If love and virtue in the household reign,
That is the life of perfect grace and gain.

Meaning
If married life is imbued with abundant love not only for its members but also for all relatives, friends and for humanity as a whole, and at the same time marked by virtuousness with willingness to help others, it is a perfect life of grace and gain.

Kural Discussions
After the introductory chapters, Thiruvalluvar discusses the characteristics of a good married life in the subdivision 'Illaraviyal' or 'Married Life' in the 'Virtue' division. The next subdivision focuses on asceticism. That he discusses married life first highlights the importance he attaches to it. He considers it superior to sainthood and asserts that one who leads a virtuous married life is comparable to heavenly beings. In this chapter 'Married Life' or 'Ilvaazhkkai', he explains lucidly the duties and responsibilities of a married couple.

This is a wonderful Kural in this chapter on how married

couples should lead their lives. It figures prominently in marriage invitations in Tamil but does not attract much attention or reflection. It is doubtful whether at least the couples getting married study it carefully as it concerns them intimately. But they take it as routine and begin their life without any understanding of the tenets of this couplet and often end up with misunderstandings and mistrust. Studying it and absorbing its full meaning before the start of their journey will be beneficial. Not that other couplets in this chapter are less important. Therefore, studying all of them is essential for establishing a strong foundation for married life.

This couplet stresses two elements vital for an ideal married life. The first is love, which refers to the affection shown to other human beings in general without any expectations. It is not merely the blossoming love between husband and wife and love for their offspring, but includes the love for all relations, including those marriage brings. It also encompasses love for friends, relatives, neighbours and all other human beings. This applies equally to both husband and wife. Marriage should thus be placed on the path of love from the beginning for a successful married life.

The second is virtue. Many scholars call it dharma. Some say it refers to not harming anyone and helping everyone. But Thiruvalluvar himself has explained the essentials of virtue in Kural 34 as eschewing the evils of envy, greed, anger and harsh words. In addition, helping others as much as possible is included.

If these two, love and virtue, are present, married life then becomes its grace and gain, and nothing more is needed. A life of love becomes its grace, and a life of virtue becomes its gain. In essence, if husband and wife live with love and virtues, as explained above, it is the ideal married life.

The current situation is rather disheartening. Love is pushed to the backseat; money and careers drive families. Differences between the two families, particularly between mother-in-law and daughter-in-law, often crop up just after marriage. Even worse are those between husband and wife, that too soon after the marriage, perhaps due to wrong priorities. Love is missing from the beginning. They quarrel over petty things and their perceived rights without the spirit of give and take, essentially because of an inadequate appreciation of the vital role of love stressed in this Kural. With love, mistakes are ignored, but without it, even right will appear wrong. That is the sad truth. That is why Thiruvalluvar says that the seed of love should be planted early in life for it to become a plant, and grow into a tree (of love), yielding fruits of love not only to the family but to humanity as well. Such a married life shines in love with virtuous conduct as its logical outcome, for where there is love, there will be virtue.

Some sceptics immersed in modern culture may harbour doubts about the feasibility of such an ideal life. If they look around, they can easily see that the foundation of all successful marriages is true love. Recently, I came across a couple living as per the tenets of this couplet. Love and affection between them and their families was so abundant that her in-laws praised her openly as an angel and a gift of God. Not that the couple do not have misunderstandings, but these arise primarily out of concern for each other's welfare rather than ego or individual desires. I could see them living joyously and happily, genuinely admiring each other even after 40 years of marriage. They also willingly and smilingly help all around them. If you look around, you too will come across many such couples, and learn from them how to lead a graceful and gainful life.

However, the present situation in our country is worrisome. Divorce rate is on the increase. Although it is just 1.1 per cent compared to about 50 per cent in developed countries like the USA, it has been going up over the years, which is a matter of concern.[35] To arrest this trend, married people must understand the importance of true love and virtue to live happily. Love shown to all is the foundation of life. And if virtue is added, then there

---

[35]'Divorce rate in India', *Advocate Khoj*, https://tinyurl.com/yc5m4x9d. Accessed on 27 November 2024.

cannot be a more useful life. Learn to lead a life of love and virtue for a happy and sustained married life.

KEY TAKEAWAY

All newlyweds should commit themselves to a life of love and virtue for an ideal married life. If every couple lives by this advice, our society will become virtuous and useful. Thus, the outcome of an ideal married life is a society of character and utility.

7
Role of a Life Partner

மனைத்தக்க மாண்புடையள் ஆகித்தற் கொண்டான்
வளத்தக்காள் வாழ்க்கைத் துணை. (குறள் 51)

Transliteration
Manaiththakka Maanputaiyal Aahiththar Kontaan
Valaththakkaal Vaazhkkaith Thunai.

Translation
A virtuous wife who lives within her husband's means
Is a partner in life.

Meaning
She who has the virtues necessary for the head of a family and manages it within her husband's means, is his worthy life partner.

Kural Discussions
After stressing the importance of married life, Thiruvalluvar turns his attention to various aspects concerning it. This chapter, 'Blessings of a Life Partner' or 'Vaazhkkaith Thunainhalam', that follows 'Married Life' or 'Ilvaazhkkai', discusses the immense benefits a wife brings to a family and highlights the virtues she must possess to manage the household efficiently. In other words, it brings out the vital role of a life partner for a successful and happy household.

This Kural talks about two qualities a wife should possess. First, she should be endowed with virtues necessary to run a happy family. Commentators have variously explained what they are. Here, the virtues referred to are her intrinsic qualities of love, kindness, and the care that will guarantee happiness. A wife's love creates a warm and affectionate atmosphere. Her kindness and care extend not only to her immediate family but also to relatives, friends, and the larger community. These virtues make her the foundation of the household, fostering a loving and harmonious environment.

Second, she must limit her household expenditure to her husband's income. Unfortunately, this aspect of household management is not given much importance. Some women might have been brought up in a wealthy family where money was not a constraint. But after marriage, they should keep an eye on expenditure, limiting it to the family income. Without the ability to manage finances, many families suffer, keep borrowing and end up in huge debt. Also, sometimes it pushes the husband, the earning member, into wrong ways and serious trouble. Thus, the wife holds two important portfolios, namely home and finance!

There is some criticism that Thiruvalluvar has assigned women a secondary role, focusing on their responsibilities rather than their rights. One reason is that the word *tharkontaan* figures in this couplet. It literally means 'wife possessed by husband', which is interpreted to mean that she is a slave to him. This is wrong. Scholar Thiru V. Kalyanasundaram explains beautifully: 'What the word means is "one who possessed her by his love"; one who keeps her at his heart all the time, to the exclusion of all other women.' The possession here thus refers to the heart where she remains cherished exclusively. Any wife is bound to be immensely happy if her husband thinks of her all the time!

Another criticism is that wives are given much higher responsibilities than husbands. A wife must possess all the good qualities needed to manage the household well, but no such requirement is laid down for the husband. We should remember Thiruvalluvar has stressed virtuous ways for a husband too in the previous chapter. In many chapters, he has castigated him in the strongest terms for any wrongdoing: he must not drink; he must not think of another woman; he must earn money but only in virtuous ways; he must be considerate to all, and more. On the other hand, he acknowledges the vital role of a wife in this couplet. That her role is pivotal for a successful married life is his message. Is it not true? When you look around, you will see its truth. In his days, women were subjected to such mistreatment that Greek philosopher Aristotle consigned them to the status of a slave. On the other hand, Thiruvalluvar gave them much importance and even regarded them as the queen of the house and life partner. Women are not inferior but have a major role in the management of the household.

Let us not forget that it was only after a long struggle that women got their rights even in Western societies. They got the right to vote only in 1925 in England, and the right to property only in 1956 in our country. But Thiruvalluvar raised their level to a life partner two thousand years back. 'Calling her a life partner means that the wife is an equal partner in husband's virtuous life, successful material life and sustained life of pleasure. Let me know who has given so much equal rights to women!' exclaims scholar T.P. Meenakshisundaram.[36] Those who criticize Thiruvalluvar must ponder over this.

It is, therefore, clear that Thiruvalluvar's comments are relevant to this century as well. It cannot, however, be denied that the responsibilities of women have increased in modern times, because they often have to juggle both work and household duties.

Even so, if the wife demonstrates virtue and thrift as this Kural says, love will prosper; petty quarrels will diminish; family life will become richer. For family happiness depends largely on the wife—not that the husband need not contribute. He does have a role, but Thiruvalluvar has given this vital role to the wife, because a virtuous and thrifty housewife can guide her husband too on the right path—an advice women should reflect on.

I am reminded of my friend's wife who was blessed with the virtues mentioned in this Kural. Her family was large with

---

[36]Kuralthiran, https://tinyurl.com/n2tn9jk. Accessed on 14 September 2024.

five children, but income was low. However, she always kept a watchful eye on the expenditure, keeping it within the income. Finding ways to cut unnecessary expenditure, she managed to save despite the low income; that helped in the higher education of her children without any borrowing. She even cut out going to cinemas as a luxury. She took good care of her family with love and affection and brought up her children to be good citizens. With her frugal financial management, all children could be well educated to become prominent members of society. It was a proud and successful family known for its hard work and virtuous ways essentially because of the wife's paramount role.

Another incidental benefit was that all her children carried with them her virtues and the quality of thrift, thereby benefiting the next generation. You can observe many such successful families, thanks to the virtue and thrift practised by the home-maker. You can also see many families, even those with abundant income, getting ruined when the wife lacks these traits.

KEY TAKEAWAY

A wife who possesses virtues and practises thrift is an invaluable life partner, serving as the foundation for great happiness and joy in married life.

8
Joy of Children

*குழல்இனிது, யாழ்இனிது என்ப,தம் மக்கள்
மழலைச்சொல் கேளா தவர்.* (குறள் 66)

Transliteration
Kuzhalinithu, Yaazhinithu Enpatham Makkal
Mazhalaissol Kelaa Thavar.

Translation
The flute and lute are sweet they say,
Who have not heard their babies' babbles.

Meaning
Only those who have not heard their babies' innocent babbles will say that the music of a flute or lute is sweeter. No music can match the sweetness of their children's babbles.

Kural Discussions
Thiruvalluvar has dedicated an entire chapter, 'Wealth of Children' or 'Makkatperu', to emphasize the importance of children to both married life and society as a whole. In this chapter, Thiruvalluvar eloquently explains the joy children bring, the responsibilities of parents, and the reciprocal duty of children towards their parents.

One of the immense benefits of married life is children who are more valuable than any wealth. The world once totally depended on human labour, when many diseases, natural disasters and devastating wars raged, keeping the population in check. During that time, childbirth was celebrated as a great boon and considered a duty, since it was essential for human survival. With our ability to control diseases and reduce droughts and famines over time, the need to control population arose in order to conserve the earth's resources. With births coming down rapidly, the situation has now changed in many countries, which are taking steps to reverse the decline. Childbirth is thus becoming important once again.

Be that as it may, an individual needs offspring for his life's fulfilment; that is why every birth is celebrated with great joy in all communities. Therefore, Thiruvalluvar has dedicated a full chapter to children, the greatest wealth of married life.

This Kural talks of the immense pleasure children bring to their parents. What is the pleasure? Their sweet babbles. It goes on to say that this pleasure is greater than that which one gets from the most melodious musical instruments, such as the lute or the flute. The lute, once a popular musical instrument in ancient Tamil Nadu, was renowned for its captivating music that could mesmerize even animals. All of us know the sweetness of music from the flute. This couplet asserts that this music is nothing compared to children's innocent babbles.

However, not everyone feels this way. Only parents do so. Only they, after hearing their children's sweet babbles, recognize them as sweeter than any sweet melody. But those who have not yet experienced parenthood do not always consider these sweet. Some are even surprised at why parents are so entranced by children's babbles. These people may, however, wax eloquent about the oneness they enjoy with nature when they hear a gurgling brook! For them, a tiny tot's babbles are mere meaningless prattle as they lack a bonding with the little soul behind that noise. How beautifully Thiruvalluvar describes what all parents have enjoyed since time immemorial!

In this modern age, some couples consider children a burden and a hindrance to their life of pleasure. They give priority to material possessions, position and personal comfort. They should study Thiruvalluvar's views and realize they have a responsibility to give birth to children and bring them up as good citizens. Although it is a huge responsibility, they should recognize the inherent pleasures of raising talented offspring. According to scholar Thiru V. Kalyanasundaram, Thiruvalluvar emphasizes in this chapter the importance of children to foster strong families and to ensure the sustainability of the human race as ordained by nature. It is the duty of all those entering married life to recognize that children are wealth and bestow that wealth on the family, the country and the world. That is the law of nature.

KEY TAKEAWAY

The sweetest music pales in comparison to the delightful babble of one's own children, offering profound joy in domestic life.

9
Parents' Duties

தந்தை மகற்காற்றும் நன்றி அவையத்து
முந்தி இருப்பச் செயல். (குறள் 67)

Transliteration
Thanthai Maharkaarrum Nhanri Avaiyaththu
Munhthi Iruppas Seyal.

Translation
A father's duty to his son is to make him
Fill the highest seat in the councils of the world.

Meaning
The duty of a father towards his children is to give them the best education and the required motivation to stand out in the assembly of the learned.

Kural Discussions
This is another Kural in the chapter 'Wealth of Children' or 'Makkatperu', explaining the duty of a father towards his son. His primary duty is to motivate him to do well in all walks of life and give him a good education to enable him to stand out in an assembly. The nature of the assembly is not specified, but many commentators have said that it is an assembly of the learned. The couplet, therefore, means that a father's responsibility is to do everything needed for his son to stand out in an assembly of the learned. A great and worthy duty for a father indeed.

The couplet uses the term 'son'. Does it imply the exclusion of daughters? The general interpretation is that it refers to the son in line with the then-prevailing status of women. Nonetheless, some commentators hold a different view that it encompasses both genders. Before the present-day gender-neutral writing, 'man' included 'woman', and 'he' included 'she'. Well-known *Thirukkural* scholar Namakkal Kavignar Ramalingam proposes that unless 'women' is explicitly mentioned, the couplet refers to both sexes. This interpretation is totally acceptable in the present-day context, when mothers work harder for the upliftment of their children. Therefore, it is correct to conclude that 'father' and 'son' refer to both sexes.

The couplet emphasizes parents' duty to ensure that their children stand at the forefront in an *avai*, meaning 'stage' or 'assembly'. This assembly refers to a gathering of the educated or learned as, in Thiruvalluvar's time, only such kind of an assembly would have existed. Ancient Tamil literature often mentions Sangam—an assembly of poets. This implies that giving good education to children is a priority. That parents should strive hard to give them the best education is the inference.

However, the couplet uses the generic term 'assembly' without specifying any particular assembly. The term includes various types of assemblies, such as those for sports, entertainment, arts, music, etc. The excellence of children, therefore, need not be confined to just education but can extend to many areas of interest. Nowadays, there are numerous platforms available for the youth to showcase their talent and excel. The duty of parents must be to encourage them in their area of interest and support them to excel. Many parents prioritize the education and grades of their children. But they should realize that their duty is to identify their children's interests and motivate them in that area, and not push them hard for grades.

Another emphasis in this couplet is worth mentioning. It is not enough if children enter the assembly; they must be in the forefront. This means that they should excel in the subject and stand out. A doctor should become an outstanding doctor, a lawyer an outstanding lawyer, a musician a renowned musician.

It is the duty of parents to help their offspring attain this level of excellence!

This is an arduous duty indeed! Some parents may argue that the success of their children depends on their own motivation. But this couplet says it is their 'duty', implying that they are responsible for that also. Note the word *nhanri* used in the couplet, which means 'gratitude'. It implies that parents should do this as an act of gratitude. Gratitude for what? For all the pleasures they get from their children, which are explained in this chapter. Therefore, rather than calling it a duty, Thiruvalluvar considers it an act of gratitude for the enjoyment they get from their offspring.

Reading this couplet reminds me of a family well-known to me. The father had no permanent job and, therefore, no regular income. So, the mother had to supplement the income by tailoring. They did not have enough income even for their essential needs. Still, keen to educate their children well, they put them in ordinary schools that they could afford but kept motivating them to come up in life through hard work. The children were hardworking, stood first in all classes, and came out with flying colours in their school education. Despite their financial difficulties, the parents put them in colleges by borrowing to supplement the modest amounts of scholarship the children got because of their merit. Today, two of them are renowned doctors, and one holds the position of a senior manager. Whenever I read this couplet, I am reminded of these parents who discharged their parents' debt admirably. They gave their sons and daughters the encouragement and facilities needed for their studies despite their hardships, by working tirelessly for their success.

All parents should remember this couplet and give their children the necessary encouragement and facilities to stand out in their field of interest. It is their duty and a debt returned to their children.

KEY TAKEAWAY

It is the duty of parents to help their children stand out in their fields of interest by motivating them and giving them an enabling environment for success.

10
Children's Duty

மகன்தந்தைக்கு ஆற்றும் உதவி, இவன்தந்தை
என்நோற்றான் கொல்எனுஞ் சொல். (குறள் 70)

Transliteration
Mahanthanthaikku Aarrum Udhavi, Ivanthannhthai
Ennhorraan Kolenung Sol.

Translation
Son's duty to father is to make others wonder
What penance got such a son to him.

Meaning
The duty of a son to his father is to make others wonder, 'What penance did this boy's father do to beget such a son?'

Kural Discussions
This is another Kural in the same chapter highlighting a son's duty; it follows the one on a father's duty. A son's duty is that he must do so well in life that others who see his achievements conclude that his father must have done a great penance to beget a son like him. He should get that much appreciation. That is possible only if he achieves something remarkable. A person of ordinary achievement will not even be noticed. To earn admiration, he should establish himself as a renowned doctor, scientist or leader in any field. It requires great zeal and enthusiasm to achieve something noticeable. Also a good character. For, whatever his achievement, there will be no admiration without it. Thus, a son's duty is to shine in life by his hard work and virtuous character to evoke the

admiration of people around him. A worthwhile goal for him, but not easy!

Is it the duty of a son only to a father who has given him the education and encouragement needed to succeed? No, it is the duty of every son, regardless of what his father has done. This couplet and the previous one need to be read together. One states the duty of the father; another, the duty of a son. Both are done without expecting any benefit. Therefore, a son's duty is not contingent on a father discharging his duty.

In the previous couplet, a father's duty is described as an obligation arising out of gratitude, but a son's duty is described here as help, although both are normally interpreted as duty. Scholars have extensively examined the nuanced differences between these two words. Scholar Thiru V. Kalyanasundaram has given a simple explanation, 'Both acts are not in the nature of business and are without any expectation. Father's act of gratitude results in son's help, that also without any expectation.'[37]

Thus, succeeding in life in a way that evokes admiration is the help a son can give to his father. How happy would a father be if his son led a life admired by all! How good would it be if our youngsters embraced this concept and brought great happiness and credit to their parents? The youth of today must remember they will be parents of tomorrow.

As discussed in the previous couplet, this applies to both son and daughter on the principle that the word 'son' includes daughter.

Dr C. Palanivelu, founder of Gem Hospitals, is a living example of this couplet. He is today the most renowned keyhole surgeon in Southeast Asia. Patients wait for months for treatment. Such is his talent. He travels around the world lecturing and teaching his unique methods.

His family background was quite ordinary. His father was

---

[37] Anbu, V. Irai, *Ancient Yet Modern Management Concepts in Thirukkural*, Allied Publishers Pvt. Ltd, Chennai, 2011.

a small farmer with dry lands dependent on rain. The family had such little income that he had to discontinue his education and migrate to Malaysia at a young age, where he worked as a plantation labourer. When he came back to Tamil Nadu at the age of 15, he was not admitted to school due to some archaic rules. Finally, after running from pillar to post, he managed to join a school and finished schooling at the late age of 21. He then joined medical college and did so well that he became a leading gastrointestinal surgeon. He is a two-time recipient of the prestigious Dr B.C. Roy Award for Physicians. What a great honour he has brought to his parents! His life is a model for other youth to emulate and bring pride to their parents.

KEY TAKEAWAY

The duty of children is to make their parents feel proud of them by earning universal acclaim.

11

Power of Love

புறத்துறுப்பு எல்லாம் எவன்செய்யும், யாக்கை
அகத்துறுப்பு அன்பி லவர்க்கு? (குறள் 79)

Transliteration
Purththuruppu Ellaam Evanseyyum, Yaakkai
Ahaththuruppu Anbi Lavarkku?

Translation
Of what avail are the body's external parts,
If there is not love within the heart?

Meaning
What is the use of external body parts if the important internal part of love is missing?

Kural Discussions
This Kural figures in the chapter 'Wealth of Love' or 'Anbudaimai', which explains the vital role love plays in human happiness and virtuous living. Already, in the chapter 'Married Life' or 'Ilvaazhkkai', Thiruvalluvar has explained that it is the foundation of a good married life. While it is no doubt important for marital harmony, all individuals will immensely benefit by leading a life of love.

Let us see what this couplet says about love. It raises a rhetorical question about the utility of external organs when the essential internal organ of love is missing. Normally, we are carried away by the external beauty of a person and judge him by his looks. This couplet, however, says that beautiful external organs such as eyes, nose, hair, body, etc., are of no use, if the person does not have love—love for all—at heart. Love is treated as an internal organ since we cannot easily see it. What is behind a beautiful face may be a loveless heart. The message is that we should give importance to love and always show love to others and surround ourselves with people with abundant love.

External parts are certainly useful because we speak, hear, see, eat and enjoy with them. Why, then, is it said that they are useless? Without the presence of love, other parts will lose meaning and purpose. With love, the mouth will always say sweet things, the eyes will shower kindness, and the face will shower sweetness. Thus, love is the force driving the external organs from inside. Scholar Thiru V. Kalyanasundaram describes this admirably, 'Like when the roots of a tree are cut off, all parts of the tree perish, so love is the source of everything.'[38] German scholar Max Muller has also expressed the same opinion: 'A flower cannot bloom without sunlight, and a man cannot live without love.' One likens love to the root of a tree and the other to sunlight. How true!

As love is the foundation of marriage, those entering married life should ponder over the in-depth meaning of this couplet and look for partners with abundant love rather than rely on external beauty. Although the internal part of love may be difficult to perceive, investing effort and time to assess its presence is worthwhile for a happy married life. Youths often make the mistake of relying on external beauty and regretting it later.

The message of this Kural extends beyond married individuals and is applicable to all divisions of society. Youngsters, students, teachers, parents and children alike can embrace the concept of love and lead a life of love for lasting happiness.

Over centuries, Thiruvalluvar and many learned men have emphasized the significance of love. Keeping this in mind, let us choose to walk the path of love, for it will imbue all our actions

---

[38]Anbu, V. Irai, *Ancient Yet Modern Management Concepts in Thirukkural*, Allied Publishers Pvt. Ltd, Chennai, 2011.

with deep meaning and bring immense benefits to society as a whole.

KEY TAKEAWAY

For a virtuous life, always choose true love over external beauty.

12

Always Speak Sweetly

இனிய உளவாக, இன்னாத கூறல்,
கனிஇருப்பக் காய்கவர்ந் தற்று. (குறள் 100)

Transliteration
Iniya Ulavaaha, Innaatha Kooral,
KaniIruppak Kaaykavarnh Tharru.

Translation
With abundant pleasant words, bitter words to use,
Is leaving sweet ripe fruits, the sour unripe to choose.

Meaning
When sweet words are aplenty, speaking harsh or unpleasant words is like picking a sour or unripe fruit from a basket full of sweet fruits by a deliberate choice and eating it.

Kural Discussions
This Kural figures in the chapter 'Kindness in Speech' or 'Iniyavai Kooral', stressing the importance of using pleasant or sweet words in speech. In Kural 35, Thiruvalluvar emphasized the importance of avoiding bitter words in a virtuous life. Here in this chapter, he further elaborates its importance. His definition of *inchol* or sweet speech is meaningful: it must be full of love, kindness, truthfulness and without any ulterior motive.

This couplet explains the importance of sweet or kind words through a powerful simile. While sweet words are available in plenty, we often fail to use them, instead using harsh or bitter words. This is like choosing and eating bitter or tasteless raw fruit from a basket containing many tasty, ripe fruits. It thus compares the abundance of sweet words to a basket full of ripe and delicious fruits, and describes the using of harsh or bitter words akin to selecting an unripe fruit from the basket. It makes the listener unhappy, affecting the relationship over time. The message is clear: always opt for sweet words and refrain from hurting others with harsh language.

How happy do we become when someone speaks a few sweet words to us! A good word has the power to change one's state of mind. Convey a word of appreciation to someone about his good deed and observe how happy he becomes. He may even float with immense joy the entire day, depending on the intensity of our appreciation. If it is from his superior, his joy will be even more. He may even share it with family and friends. A sweet word has such a magical effect, but we do not seem to notice.

I would like to narrate an incident that has been giving me great joy for 50 years. I was then working as the collector in Madurai district. I was entrusted with the important task of conducting the Third World Tamil Conference held in Madurai for ten days. M.G. Ramachandran (M.G.R.), the then chief minister of Tamil Nadu, all ministers and high officials stayed in Madurai and participated in the conference events. Many Tamil scholars from all over the world attended the conference. I was immersed in taking care of them and in many conference-related activities, with little time to wait for the chief minister. On the sixth day, the chief minister sent for me. I was worried that something had gone wrong despite my careful planning and execution. Many important people close to him were participating in the conference events, and anyone could have complained. My apprehension was completely unfounded.

I still remember well what he said when he received me warmly. 'Years back, I was given the responsibility to take care of the funeral arrangements of our great leader Arignar Anna. Despite my meticulous attention to the arrangements, many leaders were murmuring about the inadequacies. A few even complained to me personally,' he said with some anguish. This he narrated in some detail with the names of the leaders who had complained. All along, I did not understand why he was telling me all this that had happened ten years back. The reason came to light when he concluded, 'This conference is like a thousand marriages. When people could complain even at a funeral while in grief, I am happy that I received no complaint from anyone; on the contrary, only appreciation. Well done.' These kind words of appreciation, spoken by a popular leader, continue to resonate in my ears, leaving an unforgettable impression that will last a lifetime. Such is the power of sweet words!

However, if we look inward and examine whether we are using sweet words liberally, the answer is likely to be no. We are generally stingy with praise, while some hardly use sweet words. Why this stinginess? It seems ingrained in us. Although we are cautious with words while interacting with strangers, it is unfortunate that we often use harsh language in our interactions with friends and relatives. Psychologists should investigate the reasons for this behaviour. Maybe familiarity breeds contempt.

The key lesson is to always choose sweet words in our interactions, as they bring immense happiness not only to others but also to ourselves. Conversely, using harsh words leads to unhappiness, damages relationships, and creates bitterness. Even if we are unable to provide physical or financial help to someone, we can still help through the power of kind words. Let us, therefore, make a commitment to use sweet words generously, which requires willpower and training our minds. When we catch ourselves using harsh words with loved ones, let us reflect on the reasons behind it and work towards addressing them. With persistent effort, we can bring about perceptible change and be known for our pleasantness.

KEY TAKEAWAY

We must always speak sweet words and avoid harsh or unpleasant words.

13
Gratitude

நன்றி மறப்பது நன்றன்று; நன்றல்லது
அன்றே மறப்பது நன்று. (குறள் 108)

Transliteration
Nhanri Marappathu Nhanranru; Nhanrallathu
Anre Marappathu Nhanru.

Translation
Forgetting the good is not good, but it is good
To forget at once what is no good.

Meaning
To ever forget the good deeds of others is not proper, but the wrong done by them should be forgotten the same day.

Kural Discussions
The chapter 'Gratitude' or 'Seynhnhanriyarithal' deals with showing gratitude for the good done to us by others. Since showing gratitude is necessary for a virtuous life, it figures in the 'Virtue' division. It stresses the virtues of gratitude with the advice to be always grateful for whatever help you get from others, with a special mention that one should not forget even the smallest help received at times of need.

The first part of this Kural is that it is not good to forget the help and benefits we receive from others. This is a fairly simple message acceptable to all of us. How long should we remember these? Till the end of our lives.

An even more important message is conveyed in the next five

words of the couplet: if someone does not do us any good, or even does something bad, it is better to forget it the same day or immediately. We can easily forget those who refused us help, but it is difficult to forget someone who did bad to us. Although it is difficult, we should train our minds to do so, for forgetting evils and those who have committed them takes away our sadness and bitterness. The feeling of animosity against them and the urge to do something in return will also disappear, which will bring us happiness. Therefore, it is better to forget the wrongs done to us as we will be the ultimate beneficiaries in the long run.

However, what often happens is just the opposite. Good deeds are forgotten soon, but bad deeds are remembered till the end. When we refuse to let go of our resentment, we may even seek opportunities for revenge. Even if a person has done good on many occasions, but could not do so once because of some reasons beyond his control, even then we start nurturing some grudge against him, forgetting all his past good deeds. This common tendency is precisely why the couplet stresses the importance of promptly forgetting wrongs while cherishing acts of kindness indefinitely. Following this advice will not only help us in virtuous living but also help us lead a happy life without ill feelings towards any individual.

KEY TAKEAWAY

A virtuous life demands being ever grateful for the benefits received while forgetting the evils immediately.

14

Virtue of Impartiality

*தகுதி எனவொன்று நன்றே, பகுதியால்
பாற்பட்டு ஒழுகப் பெறின்.* (குறள் 111)

Transliteration
Thahuthi Enavonru Nhanre, Pahuthiyaal
Paarpattu Ozhukap Perin.

Translation
Impartiality is indeed a virtue,
If all can be treated impartially.

Meaning
If one could treat all individuals, whether friends or not, whether liked or not, equally, it is a great virtue called impartiality, bringing great benefits.

Kural Discussions
Since Thiruvalluvar considers impartiality a component of virtue, he has devoted a chapter 'Natuvu Nilaimai' or 'Impartiality' to it in which he explains its importance. He wants us to lead a life of justice, honesty and integrity without leaving room for any likes or dislikes. Impartiality must be practised both at home and at the workplace.

This Kural just says that if one could treat everyone impartially, it would be a great virtue, bringing great benefits to the individual and to society. The conditional statement implies that doing so is quite difficult. If we like someone, we overlook his faults; on the contrary, if we do not like someone, even his right actions will appear wrong. Those who disagree may look inward and analyse their thoughts and actions; they will quickly discover that they do suffer from such biases. Our words and actions are generally biased, based on our likes and dislikes. Great effort and training are, therefore, required to eliminate these biases.

Even within a family, likes and dislikes lead to biases. A father may not treat all children equally; he may like one more than the other, at least at heart, which sometimes becomes perceptible from his preferential treatment. The same is true of a mother too. Not that they do not love the other children, but such a bias is perhaps ingrained in us. The same is true even among brothers and sisters. Perhaps because of this inherent bias, even within families, the couplet implies that impartiality is difficult and if only it could be achieved, it would yield great benefits. The problem is that we are often blind to our own prejudices.

Obviously, the bias is more likely to be in a work environment where we develop likes and dislikes based on race, caste, religion, language, and region, among other things. The couplet's message is that if this could be avoided, the benefits would be invaluable. Without a doubt, society will immensely benefit if public officials are impartial, particularly those in the judiciary and other law enforcement agencies. Although equality of treatment is guaranteed under the law, its implementation is often affected by the inner bias and partiality of the individuals implementing the law. Showing partiality for whatever reason will definitely harm the administration, affecting public welfare, while causing bitterness even in one's private life. Therefore, impartial behaviour is essential in both private and public life.

Those who wish to live virtuously should strive to be impartial, keeping aside their biases arising out of region, caste, religion, etc. Impartiality is essential in public life for orderly and just governance.

KEY TAKEAWAY

We should always be impartial in our thoughts and actions, completely ignoring our likes and dislikes.

15

Humility with Values

நிலையின் திரியாது அடங்கியான் தோற்றம்,
மலையினும் மாணப் பெரிது. (குறள் 124)

Transliteration
Nhilaiyin Thiriyaathu Adangkiyaan Thorram,
Malaiyinum Maanap Perithu.

Translation
A man committed to noble principles, yet without self-conceit,
Towers larger than a mountain.

Meaning
The fame of a man who does not waver from his commitment to ethical values and yet acts with great humility, will last longer than that of a mountain.

Kural Discussions
Thiruvalluvar considers humility as an important virtue and has devoted a chapter to it, in which he explains its importance, the name and fame it brings, and the ways to show humility in words and actions. It is a good guide for those who want to lead a life of modesty.

This Kural in the chapter 'Self-Control' or 'Adakkam Udaimai' talks of the reputation a man earns from his humility. In addition to humility, he demonstrates steadfastness to his principles and values. He will not deviate from them under any circumstance. The fame of such a man surpasses that of a mountain and endures eternally. This is what the couplet says.

For a lasting reputation, virtuous conduct is also necessary in addition to humility—mere humility or mere righteousness is not enough. People with high moral standards and great virtues normally tend to be proud and show off their superiority. But Thiruvalluvar expects them to be humble—only then will their name last. On the other hand, if they allow arrogance to overshadow their virtues, they will soon be forgotten.

Thiruvalluvar has used a mountain as a metaphor for fame. Some may question the fairness of comparing a person to an inanimate mountain. But it is a fact that a mountain amazes us whenever we look at it. Not only that, it also remains unaffected by rain, thunder, wind, or even earthquakes. At the same time, it makes no claim about how big and quiet it is.

Hence, it is perfect that Thiruvalluvar compares a humble person with a mountain. His message is clear: the fame, name and reputation of such individuals, surpassing even that of a mountain, will endure just as the mountain itself endures.

Faced with life's tribulations and pressures, ordinary individuals often find it challenging to consistently adhere to their principles. They may waver and deviate from the virtuous path, unlike the unwavering nature of the mountain. Even more difficult is to be modest. We find these qualities in our great leader Mahatma Gandhi, Father of the Nation. The same can be said of A.P.J. Abdul Kalam, former president of India. Their lives were marked by great modesty and simplicity, with total commitment to their values and principles till the end. And their reputation still endures, like that of a mountain.

It is difficult to follow the advice of Thiruvalluvar. Yet, can we not at least make an attempt to lead a life of virtue and humility? We need not aim for a mountain's fame, but can we not hope for a hillock's? Let us try.

KEY TAKEAWAY

A man should display great humility even while adhering to noble values for his name to last.

16

Controlling Your Tongue

யாகாவார் ஆயினும் நாகாக்க; காவாக்கால்
சோகாப்பர் சொல்லிழுக்குப் பட்டு. (குறள் 127)

Transliteration
Yaahavaar Aayinum Nhaakaakka; Kaavaakkaal
Sohaappar Sollizhukkup Pattu.

Translation
Whatever else you fail to guard, rein in your tongue,
Else, slip of the tongue brings you grief.

Meaning
Even if a person does not guard any of the many things he should, he should at least guard his tongue; if not, he will come to grief because of what he said.

Kural Discussions
This is another wonderful Kural in the same chapter, 'Self-Control' or 'Adakkam Udaimai', which refers to the control of our five senses. Poet and commentator Parimelazhagar defines it as the control of mind, speech and action to stay away from evil ways. Noted scholar Mu. Varadarajan explains it beautifully: 'If you want to live virtuously in thought, speech and action, you should have the power to keep your mind, speech, and body under your control. Only a life led with such self-control is a profound life.'[39]

---

[39]Ramalingam, Namkkal Kavignar, *Thirukkural*, T.D.V. Publishers, Chennai, 2021.

This Kural has an advice and a warning unlike many others: whatever else you fail to control, control your tongue. It means that you should always speak carefully and never loosely. The warning is that failure to do so would cause you great grief because of what you have said unthinkingly. While most religions emphasize controlling various senses for a righteous life, Thiruvalluvar, being a practical philosopher, gives importance to restraint in speech because we often falter in our ability to control our words.

We often experience the truth of this message in our daily lives. We blurt out something in anger or without thinking, little realizing its consequences. Our words can hurt others, spoiling friendships and relationships. The damage can sometimes be permanent. Once we realize our mistake, we do regret our speech. But spilt words cannot be taken back. What is said remains said. We have no other option but to suffer the damage arising from our words uttered in haste. I myself had once suffered immensely by saying something to my boss without thinking. It is not appropriate for me to elaborate on the details here. I have often regretted speaking to my wife without thinking, but fortunately her abundant love and forgiving nature saved me from many miseries. Frequently recalling this couplet, I keep trying to be careful with my words—I wonder whether I will ever succeed!

I am reminded of the Buddha's statement: 'The tongue is like a sharp knife, kills without drawing blood.' How true! Thiruvalluvar himself has said in another couplet that an injury by fire will heal but not one by the tongue. 'Nature hath given men one tongue but two ears, that we may hear from others twice as much as we speak,' said ancient Greek philosopher Epictetus. Let us remember this ancient wisdom and speak less and listen more to lead a happy and virtuous life.

KEY TAKEAWAY

Always think carefully before you speak.

17

Benefits of Ethical Conduct

நன்றிக்கு வித்தாகும் நல்லொழுக்கம்; தீயொழுக்கம்
என்றும் இடும்பை தரும். (குறள் 138)

Transliteration
Nhanrikku Viththaakum Nhallozhukkam; Theeyozhukkum
Enrum Itumpai Tharum.

Translation
Good conduct is the seed of blessings,
Bad conduct causes endless pain and suffering.

Meaning
Ethical conduct is the seed of all blessings, but bad conduct will always bring endless misery.

Kural Discussions
Thiruvalluvar, an idealist, has dealt with ethical conduct in the chapter 'Purity of Conduct' or 'Ozhukkam Udaimai', in which he stresses its value and importance. He emphasizes it as the foundation of a virtuous life. In one couplet, he even asserts that ethical conduct is even more important than one's life!

The first part of this Kural says that ethical conduct is the seed of many benefits. The use of the word 'seed' is quite significant. A seed becomes a plant and soon a tree, bearing fruits. Not only that, it also gives shade and many nourishing nutrients to Mother Earth and the environment. We enjoy its fruits and all the associated benefits, which come out of just a seed. Similarly, all benefits to an individual come from his good conduct, the seed. Note yet another significance of the word. The benefit of a seed remains unseen till it starts yielding fruits—so is the case with good conduct, since its benefits may not be seen immediately but only in the long run. Society respects only men of position and money but not men of character. Sometimes, they are even ridiculed and deemed worthless. The couplet assures that they will surely reap the rewards, although these may remain hidden for some time. Ultimately, fame, happiness, wealth and position will come to them.

The second part says unethical conduct will certainly bring endless pain and misery immediately and continuously. This is a warning imploring us to live ethically, eschewing unethical conduct.

This message serves as an encouragement for us to uphold high ethical and moral principles, assuring us that benefits will be reaped in due course. It serves as a reminder not to lose hope, even when rewards are not immediately apparent. This message is particularly relevant in present times when moral and ethical values have deteriorated in both private and public life. We should, therefore, embrace ethical conduct for the benefit of both society and the individual.

KEY TAKEAWAY

Always live ethically, for the benefits, though invisible initially, will finally come.

18

Rewards of Patience

*அகழ்வாரைத் தாங்கும் நிலம்போலத் தம்மை
இகழ்வார்ப் பொறுத்தல் தலை.* (குறள் 151)

Transliteration
Ahazhvaaraith Thangkum Nhilampolath Thammai
Ihazhvaarp Poruththal Thalai.

Translation
As mother earth bears with its diggers,
To bear revilers is the chief virtue.

Meaning
It is a great virtue to tolerate someone who speaks abusively and contemptuously, like the patient earth that tolerates its diggers.

Kural Discussions
In a separate chapter, 'Patience' or 'Poraiyudaimai', Thiruvalluvar explains its virtues and greatness. Extreme patience should not be treated as a weakness or cowardice, as some consider. In reality, it is a great strength. In one couplet, he eulogizes it as the mother of all strengths. Indeed, true patience requires great strength and willpower, particularly when in dire straits. But it always leads to success and happiness. However, it requires a special mindset, which can be acquired only by constant training and practice.

This Kural explains the sort of patience required through a simile. One's patience must be like that of Mother Earth, which endures even those who dig it up. Not only that, it suffers them silently and patiently and does them no harm. Moreover, it gives them innumerable benefits: space to live, water to drink and irrigate, and food to eat. It thus gives all that is essential for human survival despite the harm humans do.

Thiruvalluvar must have chosen this metaphor after seeing the digging of wells. But nowadays, we dig a lot more, we dig deep mines to extract coal, oil and many other minerals for our needs. We cause a lot more damage by our many environmentally unfriendly acts. Still, the earth bears all this patiently without causing us any harm, while supplying us with all our needs for modern living.

The couplet concludes that an individual's patience should be such, and if so, it is a great virtue! The metaphor implies much more—not merely extreme patience but a willingness to do good to those doing wrong. Yet another couplet recommends doing good to those who wrong us. Medieval commentators have commented that the word *ihazhvaar* in the couplet includes abusive action in addition to abusive speech.

Although extreme patience is a great asset, it does not come naturally to ordinary individuals. However, its benefits are undeniable, as it enhances relationships and fosters enduring happiness. In the workplace, patience lays the foundation for success. On the other hand, losing patience makes us angry, affecting our health and relationships.

A Tamil proverb says, 'Those with extreme patience will rule the world.' Realizing the importance of this, the great Roman playwright Plautus said: 'Patience is the best remedy for every trouble.' Yet, practising patience, particularly in the face of extreme provocation, remains a daunting task. Greek philosopher Aristotle aptly noted, 'Patience is bitter, but its fruit is sweet,' acknowledging the difficulty in cultivating this virtue. Nevertheless, the rewards of patience are immeasurable, making it a virtue worth pursuing and nurturing.

This couplet perfectly conveys the timeless advice of many great thinkers at different times, with a wonderful and easy-to-remember metaphor. If only we could always remain patient, we would benefit a lot.

KEY TAKEAWAY

Always remember the patience of Mother Earth to remain patient even under extreme provocation.

19
Envy Kills

அழுக்காறு உடையார்க்கு அதுசாலும், ஒன்னார்
வழுக்கியும் கேடீன் பது. (குறள் 165)

Transliteration
Azhukkaaru Utaiyaarkku Athusaalum, Onnaar
Vazhukkiyum Keteen Pathu.

Translation
To the envious, their envy itself is enough
To bring ruin, even if their enemies fail.

Meaning
Envious people need no other enemy to bring them down; their envy alone is enough. Even if their enemies fail, it will definitely bring them ruin.

Kural Discussions
Thiruvalluvar has earlier pointed out in Kural 35 that envy is absolutely incompatible with virtuous living. To re-emphasize this, he has dedicated a separate chapter 'Not Envying' or 'Azhukkaaraamai' in which he vividly describes the perils of envy. Individuals devoid of love in their heart always suffer from envy. Constantly consumed by jealousy about others' good fortunes, they are perpetually trapped in discontent. On the other hand, those who embrace love and affection do not succumb to envy. Throughout his rendition, Thiruvalluvar has stressed the profound importance of love and affection in our lives.

This Kural, in this chapter, makes an unqualified assertion

that envious people need no external enemies for their downfall, and their envy itself is enough to ruin them. Even if their foes fail in their attempts, their envy will succeed in bringing them down, it says. It is a more formidable enemy than real external enemies. The message underscores the inherent danger of harbouring envy in one's mind and emphasizes the importance of guarding against it.

However, it seems envy is man's inherent quality. I read somewhere that envy is, in fact, a form of admiration, but this perhaps refers to the momentary envy we experience when we hear about the good fortunes of others, rather than harbouring it forever. Surprisingly, envy is seen even among close relatives, at times even among siblings, despite their love and affection for each other. Failing to control it leads to much bitterness, and sometimes even enmity, with disastrous consequences. The same is true among friends. In addition to affecting relationships and friendships, it also leads to inner unhappiness as we tend to compare ourselves with others and feel discontented. Remember, we do not know their sufferings, which could be worse than ours.

The best way, therefore, is to spot envy the moment it raises its ugly head and address it immediately. By acknowledging and confronting our feelings of envy, we can prevent them from festering and causing harm to ourselves and others. Instead of letting envy consume us, we should cultivate a sense of contentment in our own journey. Embracing the uniqueness of each individual path and avoiding constant comparison will lead to a more fulfilling and happy life.

The Dalai Lama considers envy as a great enemy of happiness. Greek philosopher Socrates referred to envy as the 'ulcer of the soul'. The Buddha also echoed Thiruvalluvar's sentiments, preaching that there is no peace of mind for those who are jealous. Mahatma Gandhi went a step further, condemning it outright: 'Bury jealousies underground or cremate them wherever you like.'

Let us imbibe the valuable message of this couplet, often

stressed by many great men over centuries, and control envy to lead a happy and virtuous life.

KEY TAKEAWAY

Realizing the harm envy causes, avoid it like the plague.

20

Avoid Slander

ஏதிலார் குற்றம்போல் தங்குற்றங் காண்கிற்பின்
தீதுண்டோ மன்னும் உயிர்க்கு? (குறள் 190)

Transliteration
Eethilaaar Kutrampol Thangkutram Kaankirpin
Theethundo Mannum Uyirkku?

Translation
If each his own, as others' faults would scan,
Would any evil fall on living man?

Meaning
If everyone could see his own faults while speaking about others' faults, would any evil befall the people of the world?

Kural Discussions
The chapter 'Puramkooraamai' or 'Avoid Slander' speaks about the evils of slander. *Puram* means 'back' and *kooraamai* means 'not speaking'. Therefore, it means not speaking about someone behind his back. In this chapter, Thiruvalluvar describes its evils, why and how it should be avoided, and why doing so is essential for ethical living.

Speaking ill of someone behind his back is our common disease. We call it gossip or carrying tales. We can easily observe that it is widespread in the workplace, both public and private, and in almost all conversations. We are aware of the presence of chronic gossipers in organizations who carry tales to bosses. We generally avoid them or run away from them because their gossip could harm us. They indulge in this because of enmity, dislike, or just out of habit or for enjoyment. That it was present even during Thiruvalluvar's time for him to devote a chapter to it is indeed surprising.

This Kural merely says that if we could observe our own faults while we criticize others' faults, it would bring great benefit to all. If we attempt that, we will pause before criticizing others and may desist from criticizing them. It is also possible that we may correct ourselves, realizing our faults. If everyone thus observes his faults and corrects himself, individuals and society will benefit.

The word used in this couplet, 'kutram', is interpreted as slander since it falls under this chapter. But it is a generic word that includes bad habits, faults, mistakes, and even crimes. That it refers to all sorts of faults appears more befitting, since the benefits to the world will then be indeed immense.

When thinking about the evils of slander, *Othello* by Shakespeare comes to mind. Iago, who nurses a grudge against the hero Othello, corrupts his mind little by little by speaking ill of his wife, Desdemona. He manipulates Othello into believing that his wife is unfaithful, inflaming Othello's jealousy. Believing the slander, Othello murders Desdemona, but he soon realizes his mistake and kills himself. All this misery is because he believed the slander he heard. Many Indian films have been made on a similar theme. Often, reports of serious crimes committed because of slander keep appearing in newspapers, but we still tend to waste time on gossip. Social media is another speedy and easy way to spread slander and falsehood, which we seem to relish.

As British mathematician, logician, philosopher and intellectual Bertrand Russell had said, 'No one gossips about other people's secret virtues.' We tend to talk about the shortcomings or vices of others behind their backs, little realizing that what we say may get carried to the person who was the subject of the gossip. Many friendships have been broken, and new enmities created because of slander.

There is a familiar saying in English: 'If you point a finger at someone, remember three fingers are pointing back at you.' We tend to focus on the flaws of others while being blind to our imperfections.

The New Testament carries a similar message: 'Judge not, that ye be not judged [...] And why beholdest thou the mote that is in thy brother's eye, but considerest not the beam that is in thine own eye?' (Matthew 7:1–3)

That is the message of this couplet as well: look inwards when you criticize others for their faults to see whether you yourself suffer from any. This will stop you from criticizing anyone and also help you correct your mistakes, bringing great benefit to all.

KEY TAKEAWAY

If we recognize our own faults, we will refrain from criticizing others.

21
Avoid Vain Speech

சொல்லுக சொல்லிற் பயனுடைய; சொல்லற்க
சொல்லிற் பயனிலாச் சொல். (குறள் 200)

Transliteration
Solluha Sollir Payanutaiya; Sollarka
Sollir Payanilaas Sol.

Translation
Speak, if you must, words that bear good fruit;
Speak not words that are useless.

Meaning
If you must speak, always speak fruitful words, and do not ever speak words that are not of any use.

Kural Discussions
Thiruvalluvar has devoted a chapter to 'Avoiding Vain Speech' or 'Payanila Sollaamai' in which he emphasizes that our speech should always be useful; he offers many suggestions to avoid pointless conversations. According to him, refraining from frivolous talk will lead to improved communication skills.

This Kural delivers a simple and easy-to-understand message. Whenever you speak, your words should have a purpose, and you should avoid uttering anything unnecessary. The beauty of the words used in the couplet is lost in translation. It also implies speaking only if you must—the word *sollir* means that. If you do not have anything useful to say, do not speak; just remain silent. Often, we underestimate the power of silence as a means of communication and continue to speak needlessly. Even if you wish to say something, pause and think whether there is anything useful to say. In sum, open your mouth only after pausing for a minute to consider whether you have anything useful to say; otherwise, remain silent. Some people mistake loquaciousness for precociousness, feeling impelled to have their two cents in on every topic, ignorant of this wise saying: 'Better to remain silent and be thought a fool than to speak and to remove all doubt.'

Thiruvalluvar's message is quite relevant in today's world when many of our daily interactions are meaningless. Many 24x7 news channels constantly broadcast purposeless debates that often devolve into shouting matches. These channels seem more focused on promoting personal viewpoints than sharing truths and useful information. Many of these debates are merely vehicles to push biased perspectives, with intellectual discussions becoming rare. Regrettably, people spend countless hours watching these debates or themselves engaging in such discussions.

The same trend is observed on social media, where mostly worthless viewpoints motivated by personal biases and prejudices are exchanged. All this underscores the need for more purposeful conversations and discussions.

Even workplaces are affected by gossip during office hours due to the neglect of work. Useless speech and idle gossip have become the great entertainers of our society. This trend not only hampers productivity but also sows seeds of resentment and bitterness. It is high time we imbibe the message of this couplet and stop wasting time on gossip and wasteful chats.

A learned man once said, 'The purpose of a conversation is to inform, educate and entertain.' Thiruvalluvar has, however, merely said that we should speak only useful words, without defining what they are. The decision is left to us, although it is clear these words should benefit the speaker and the listener. We may speak when we can provide a new insight, or when our words help the listeners in some way. Words to be avoided are dealt with in many other chapters—words that will hurt or slander others or cause discord, which will all amount to useless speech.

KEY TAKEAWAY

All of us should lead our lives without wasting time on useless talk, and by speaking purposefully, that too only when necessary.

22

Dread of Evil Deeds

*தீயவை செய்தார் கெடுதல், நிழல்தன்னை
வீயாது அடியுறைந் தற்று.* (குறள் 208)

Transliteration
Theeyavai Seythaar Ketuthal, Nhizhalthannai
Veeyaathu Atiyurainh Tharru.

Translation
Man's shadow follows his steps wherever he goes;
Like that, destruction follows one who commits bad deeds.

Meaning
As one's shadow always clings to his feet all the time, so does the evil arising out of his evil deeds. Without ever departing from him, it will always cling to him in the sense that he can never escape the consequences of his evil deeds.

Kural Discussions
This Kural comes under the chapter 'Dread of Evil Deeds' or 'Theevinaiyachcham'. An important component of virtuous living is refraining from evil deeds or deeds that harm others. In this chapter, Thiruvalluvar explains the repercussions of evil deeds, offers insights into their avoidance, and stresses the cultivation of a sense of shame for committing wrongs. The message is that a fundamental principle of ethical living is to do no harm to anyone.

This Kural says that those who commit evil deeds or cause harm to others will definitely get commensurate punishment. Although they may not get it immediately, they will definitely suffer in due course. This concept has been explained through a simile. The evil that befalls a man is like a shadow that never leaves his feet. It may be long or short, but it is always attached to his feet. Similarly, the consequences of his wrongdoings will never leave him, but follow him and catch up with him one day. No matter what he does—whether he prays, does grand poojas, or performs rituals—the effects of his wrongs will follow him like a shadow. Just as the shadow cannot be shaken off, the troubles and bad outcomes an evildoer faces cannot be avoided. So, avoid harming others.

We see many evildoers escaping from the clutches of the law with money and influence. We also see many living happily, without facing any bad consequences of their evil deeds. When we see this, we are lulled into believing that evil deeds carry no consequences or we can somehow escape their consequences. But Thiruvalluvar warns us: 'Don't be fooled by these things! Just as your shadow remains with you, evil deeds will not spare you.' Such a warning is even more necessary today when people are increasingly inclined to commit wrongs for personal gains.

Thiruvalluvar is a believer in fate—he has devoted a separate chapter to this topic. He believes that pleasure and pain are the consequences of fate. Linking fate to the outcome of one's actions, scholar Mu. Varadarajan elaborates, 'Fate that gives us the right to live virtuously has stipulated that ethical living will lead to good outcomes, while its neglect will result in bad outcomes. Its prescription is that if you live ethically, you will get huge benefits, but if you deviate from it, appropriate harm will befall. Therefore, an individual has a choice to live virtuously or otherwise but does not have any control over its consequences.'[40] The choice is, therefore, left to the individual, which is the concept of free will.

The assertion that the consequences of wrongdoings will follow like a shadow reminds me of a colleague in service.

---

[40]Ramalingam, Namkkal Kavignar, *Thirukkural*, T.D.V. Publishers, Chennai, 2021.

He joined the service with public service as his primary goal but lost track midway. One reason was the administrative environment then—corruption had become widespread and was the norm. Furthermore, he advanced a flawed argument to justify it. He was delivering some benefit that justified extracting a part for himself. He had a good time for a while, amassing wealth. When he was found out, he got entangled in many legal cases and suffered. He lost his savings, prestige and friends. He was denied his pension. Even after his demise, his wife could not get the family pension because of his transgressions. The shadow of his misdeeds haunted the family even after his death! As Shakespeare put it in *Julius Caesar*, 'The evil that men do lives after them; the good is oft interred with their bones.'

Therefore, no matter how much influence and money one has, refraining from wrongdoing is imperative, keeping in mind that there is no escape from its consequences.

KEY TAKEAWAY

Remember, evildoers will get their punishment sooner or later. Therefore, desist from doing any harm to others.

23

Service-Minded Individuals

ஊருணி நீர்நிறைந் தற்றே உலகவாம்
பேரறி வாளன் திரு. (குறள் 215)

Transliteration
Ooruni Nhiirnhirainh Tharre Ulakavaam
Perari Vaalan Thiru.

Translation
Wealth of men of true wisdom is like
The brimming water that fills the lake.

Meaning
The wealth of a philanthropist who lives for the common good is like the brimming water in a village pond that benefits all.

Kural Discussions
This Kural figures in the chapter 'Duty to Society' or 'Oppuravarithal', stressing the need for individuals to give back to society. Charity and doing good to others, not just to friends and relatives, are emphasized. Doing good to society does not require money, because even giving time or expertise to others is enough. Another important aspect emphasized by Thiruvalluvar is that such services should be like that of rain that gives us sustenance without expecting anything in return.

This couplet explains through an analogy how the wealth of service-minded people would benefit society. It benefits them like a village pond brimming with water that is used by all villagers for drinking and cooking. They do take care to see that the water is usable by prohibiting bathing and washing. All villagers use it without restriction—the pond is brimming with water. Likewise, the wealth of the *perarivaalan* or service-minded individual will be of use to all villagers. He is so generous that his wealth is shared by all! He is more concerned with the welfare of the community than about himself.

Why does the couplet refer to a pond full to the brim? If a pond is parched and completely dry, it will be of no use. If it has only a little water, its use will be restricted. On the other hand, when it is full and even overflowing with water, there is a sense of abundance; even the very sight of it will gladden people's hearts. This is the feeling a man who is generous will create in society.

In another Kural, Thiruvalluvar says that if wealth is in the hands of a munificent man, it is like a tree laden with fruits in the middle of the village—benefiting everyone. The corollary, presumably, is that if it is a selfish man who has wealth, it is like a tree in a private farm—of no use to anyone other than the owner.

The couplet's message is that one's wealth should be shared liberally without constraints. An ideal concept. A similar concept was advocated by Mahatma Gandhi, who was of the view that rich people should manage their wealth as 'trustees' for the benefit of the poor. These days, when many individuals profiteer, even at the cost of the poor, a few who follow such a lofty ideal still exist. We can only hope that their number will go up by imbibing Thiruvalluvar's advice on giving.

It is not easy for an individual to give away the bulk of his wealth in this manner. Bill Gates and Warren Buffet are well-known wealthy individuals who gave away most of their enormous wealth to charity. In Tamil Nadu, Alagappa Chettiar could count among such people. Barring a few like them, we cannot think of many others involved in the kind of philanthropy envisaged in this couplet. Since most are hesitant to give away their entire wealth, what can be the solution? Individuals can consider giving away a part of their wealth or income to the needy.

Bill Clinton, former president of the United States, wrote a book, *Giving: How Each of Us Can Change the World* (2007), in which he has suggested the concept of giving a part of our income, say just 5 per cent, to charity. Those who do not earn enough could contribute by giving their time or knowledge. Giving guidance and advice to those who struggle and stumble itself is a great service. If we cannot emulate the service-minded individual of great wisdom depicted in this couplet, can we not at least share a part of our income, or give time and expertise to charity or to those in need? Small contributions by many will be of great help to the needy; the contributors, too, will derive great happiness from their acts of kindness.

KEY TAKEAWAY

All of us should try to emulate the service-minded individual depicted in this couplet.

24

Pleasure of Giving

ஈத்துவக்கும் இன்பம் அறியார்கொல் தாமுடைமை
வைத்திழக்கும் வன்க ணவர்? (குறள் 228)

Transliteration
Iiththuvakkum Inbam Ariyaarkol Thaamudaimai
Vaithizhakkum Vanka Navar?

Translation
Is the happiness from the delight of giving unknown
To the cruel who hoard their wealth and lose?

Meaning
Do those wicked people, who hoard their wealth till their end and finally lose it, know the delight of giving to others? Unfortunately, they do not know.

Kural Discussions
This Kural figures in the chapter 'Charity' or 'Eegai', which emphasizes the need to give to the poor and needy without expecting anything in return. These indigent people are so impoverished that they obviously cannot give back anything except perhaps their gratitude and good wishes. Reducing hunger has been greatly stressed in this chapter while highlighting the benefits of helping the needy. The message is that the wealthy should be generous in giving.

This Kural is about those who keep accumulating wealth for life without giving anything to anyone. Why are they like this? Unfortunately, they are not aware of the joy associated with giving or the happiness derived from charitable acts. That is why they keep on adding to their wealth and hoarding it throughout their lives. 'But they will eventually lose it,' says the couplet. This can happen in many ways. By lavish spending or wrong investment decisions, the wealth accumulated over time could vanish. In any case, no one can take his wealth with him when he dies. It is well known that wealth is impermanent.

This couplet expresses anguish that hoarders of wealth are not aware of the joy of giving and labels them as evil individuals. Realizing that they will one day lose their wealth, wealthy individuals should appreciate the pleasures of giving, and give away as much as possible. Both the giver and the receiver are happy in charity.

Recent research on happiness has revealed that lasting happiness is the outcome of giving not only for the rich but also for those with modest incomes. Even individuals with limited income derive great happiness while prioritizing spending on others. To give, great wealth or high income is not needed, just a generous mind. Let us all, therefore, develop the mindset of giving despite our needs, and thereby enhance our happiness while bringing some solace to the needy.

I am reminded of the American businessman and philanthropist Chuck Feeney. Despite earning billions of dollars, he led a simple and frugal life. He donated his entire eight-billion-dollar fortune anonymously; no one knew of his charity. When it became public, his comment was: 'I feel great joy when my money benefits others.' He earned it just for the joy of giving. It seems like he was familiar with this couplet!

This habit of giving is still not widespread in our country. Many wealthy individuals keep accumulating wealth for generations; unfortunately, they are yet to think of giving. The government has recently mandated that wealthy companies spend at least two per cent of their profit on socially responsible activities. Wealthy individuals should consider charity without taking the usual view that it is the government's responsibility to help the needy. With their greater efficiency, they can do more than the government to make India prosperous.

Hunger is still widespread in our country. As per the Global Hunger Index, India is lagging at the 111th position out of 125 countries in 2023.[41] While the number of billionaires is on the rise by the day, the number of those who cannot afford two meals a day is also on the rise. Although the government is taking many measures to eradicate poverty, wealthy individuals can also help through charity. That requires generosity and a charitable mind.

KEY TAKEAWAY

Let us not hoard impermanent wealth till the end, but share it with the poor and the needy, and enjoy the happiness of giving.

---

[41] Welthungerhilfe, 'Global Hunger Index', 2023, https://tinyurl.com/2s35whbj. Accessed on 17 October 2024.

25

Excel in Anything You Do

தோன்றின் புகழொடு தோன்றுக; அஃதிலார்
தோன்றலின் தோன்றாமை நன்று. (குறள் 236)

Transliteration
Thonrin Puhazhotu Thonruha; Ahthilaar
Thonralin Thonraamai Nhanru.

Translation
Achieve fame and glory in whatever field you enter;
Or else, better enter not.

Meaning
In whatever field one enters, one should earn fame. Those who do not possess the skill to shine in a field should not get into it.

Kural Discussions
After explaining ways to lead a virtuous life, Thiruvalluvar now turns his attention to 'Fame' or 'Puhazh', to which he has devoted a chapter. In this chapter, he has explained how fame is important to all of us and how to achieve it. One is recognized by one's good behaviour, good deeds and ethical ways. In a sense, fame is a natural outcome of ethical living, but such a virtuous path alone will not make one famous. Therefore, Thiruvalluvar advises us to pursue fame while elaborating on various ways to achieve it in this chapter.

Before discussing the meaning of this Kural, the confusion created by the word *thonrin* in this couplet needs some discussion. Old commentators had interpreted it to mean 'if born' and given the following meaning: 'If one is born in this world, one should be famous; otherwise, let one not be born at all.' This interpretation raises an obvious question. Fame and name can be earned only by achievements through hard work and ethical living. How is it then possible for anyone to be born with fame?

Modern commentators have, however, given a different interpretation. They have interpreted the word 'thonrin' as 'if one appears'—another meaning in Tamil. With this interpretation, the couplet would mean: 'if one appears or enters a field, one should shine and get a name in it; otherwise, one should not enter it at all.' This appears sensible. Accepting this meaning, the way to fame as per this couplet is: if one enters any field or trade or business, one should do it diligently with an objective to become the best in it and become famous. If one cannot do that, one should not enter that area at all but should choose some other in which one is confident of shining. A sensible and necessary piece of advice to everyone, particularly the youth of our country.

Unfortunately, what we see in the workplace is disheartening. Many youngsters exhibit little enthusiasm or spirit in their work. It is possible that they chose it out of compulsion; it could also be just to satisfy their parents or someone else. This is not correct. They should choose an area of interest and work diligently rather than sticking to a field they are not keen on. A similar approach should apply to the subject of study as well. Many complain that their choice was just to satisfy their parents despite their inherent dislike for it. Instead, children should choose subjects of their interest and excel in them. Parents, too, should allow them that freedom.

We normally associate fame with great leaders, scientists or artists because of the publicity they get. One does not have to be a great scientist, artist or politician to be famous. Everyone can be famous—even those in ordinary professions. For example, a plumber could be quite famous among those whom he serves for his excellent service. He will be sought after and appreciated by all, thanks to his good work. Similarly, a bank official or a manager can get appreciation for his sincere and helpful nature. Likewise, we see many talented doctors, teachers and engineers becoming famous just for their dedicated and competent service. None of them needs media coverage for fame, but they are certainly famous in their fields. Although leaders and scientists are recognized nationally or internationally, all others will get recognition and fame within their area. This is a time when people are acquiring fame and name through advertisements and by spending money. Even in such a situation, we can become famous by earning a name through our efforts to excel in whatever we do.

KEY TAKEAWAY

No matter what field you are in, no matter what business you are doing, you should be committed to it to earn a reputation for yourself. At the same time, it is better not to take up a vocation in which you are not interested.

26

Greatness of Compassion

*அல்லல் அருளாள்வார்க்கு இல்லை; வளிவழங்கு
மல்லல்மா ஞாலம் கரி.* (*குறள்* 245)

Transliteration
Allal Arulaalvaarkku Illai; Valivazhagnku
Mallalmaa Ngaalam Kari.

Translation
Woes are not for men of compassion;
The wind blowing the earth is witness.

Meaning
Men of compassion will never suffer any woes. The proof of this is the earth that is thriving because of the contribution of the wind.

Kural Discussions
This Kural figures in the chapter 'Compassion' or 'Aruludaimai' under the subdivision 'Asceticism' or 'Thuravaraviyal'. Although we understand compassion, ancient Tamil scholar Manakkudavar's definition is worth quoting: 'The feeling of suffering of any life as one's own is compassion.'[42] It is different from love, which is something shown to friends and relatives or known individuals. On the other hand, compassion is love for all living beings, not limited to human beings alone. Compassion represents the maturity of love.

This Kural says that individuals with compassion do not

---

[42]Varadarajan, Mu., *Thirukkural Thelivurai*, Paari Nilayam, Chennai, 2019.

experience any suffering, nor does any hardship affect them. The proof of this is the vast earth sustained and enriched by the wind. How could this be the proof for the suffering-free life of compassionate people? The earth is sustained by the wind throughout the ages, and no living being can survive without it. Despite our indulgence in many activities that pollute our environment, the compassionate wind continues to sustain us and the earth, unaffected by the harm it endures. Similarly, those who feel compassion for others will easily find solace in alleviating their sufferings, like the wind.

There is a fundamental reason why compassionate people do not suffer. They find profound solace because of their inner, innate feelings for others deep in their hearts. Their genuine concern for the suffering of others becomes so all-consuming that they tend to forget their own troubles. Their empathy and support for others fill their minds and hearts to such an extent that they hardly notice their own sufferings. Just like the compassionate wind remains untouched by our acts of pollution, their unwavering care for others shields them from personal distress.

The Buddha exemplifies the compassion mentioned in this couplet. Driven by a desire to find a solution to the sufferings of ordinary people, he renounced his kingdom and family and embraced the life of an ascetic. After immense personal struggles, he attained Enlightenment and founded the great religion Buddhism. This faith continues to sustain millions of people across the world like the wind.

Similarly, in more recent times, Mother Teresa stands as a beacon of great compassion, instilling hope in the hearts of thousands through her sincere and selfless work. Her boundless empathy and dedication touched the lives of countless individuals, making her an enduring symbol of compassion and love.

Ordinary individuals like us cannot emulate the compassion of these great people, but we can always perform our tasks with compassion for our own benefit. This approach can lead to reduced suffering and heightened happiness in our lives. As the Dalai Lama says, 'If you want others to be happy, practise compassion. If you want to be happy, practise compassion.' If we remember this and lead a life of compassion, our sufferings will definitely lessen.

I am reminded of an act of compassion benefiting a large number of poor people. As Madurai district collector, I was responsible for the implementation of the old-age pension scheme, which gives a monthly pension to indigent people. Unfortunately, due to limited funds, around 3,000 indigent people were left waiting for an extended period without receiving their pension. Every Monday, on the grievance day, these individuals would come to meet me, hoping for a resolution, but I was unable to do anything except give them empty words of hope. I wrote to the government several times for additional funds, but this was not approved for want of funds—the routine response of the bureaucracy, known for its rule-bound administration.

Finally, I mustered up the courage to mention this problem to M.G.R., the then chief minister of Tamil Nadu, during one of his visits to my district (as a matter of protocol, we were not supposed to take up financial matters directly with the chief minister). Mentioning the long waiting period, I requested for sanction of funds for an additional 3,000 indigent citizens for my district. The chief minister listened to my plea but remained silent. To my surprise, within two days, I received the orders for additional sanction. We cleared all pending applications, bringing great happiness to 3,000 poor people.

During the chief minister's next visit to my district, I thanked him. He responded cheerfully, 'I ordered the allocation of additional funds not only for your district but for all the districts.' I was surprised and happy. His decision reflected his profound compassion. Instead of merely addressing my request, he recognized the similar sufferings of the people in other districts and took prompt action. More than one lakh people benefited from his act of compassion. He also ordered that funds should never become a constraint for this scheme, ensuring that no applicant would be left waiting in the state.

An unexpected benefit for me was that senior bureaucrats could not pin the blame on me, as the chief minister's order was a general directive for the entire state, emanating from his compassionate nature. His act of compassion touched countless lives, exemplifying his commitment to the welfare of the people. I am fortunate to have witnessed such compassionate leadership and its far-reaching impact on the lives of the less privileged.

It is essential for all of us to cultivate a sense of compassion and willingness to help others. Money or position is not needed for this; all that is required is a compassionate heart. Often, just listening to others' sufferings is enough. A word of consolation is better. Unfortunately, we often fail to do this because of a lack of time or patience. Immersed in our own problems, we become oblivious to the suffering of others, making it impossible to offer any solace. Remember what the Buddha said: 'Our sorrows and wounds are healed only when we touch them with compassion.' Showing kindness to and spending time with others is ultimately for our happiness. Developing compassion does not necessitate grand gestures akin to the vastness of the wind. Instead, it begins with small acts of kindness that lead to a meaningful and fulfilling life.

KEY TAKEAWAY

In our fast-paced world, taking a moment to acknowledge the struggles of others and offering a kind word can create a ripple effect of positivity and healing. Let us choose compassion as a guiding principle, enhancing our lives and the lives of those around us.

27

Reason for Lack of Abundance

இலர்பலர் ஆகிய காரணம், நோற்பார்
சிலர், பலர் நோலா தவர். (குறள் 270)

Transliteration
Ilarpalar Aahiya Kaaranam, Nhorpaar
Silaar, palar Nholaa Thavar.

Translation
The many too many things lack. The cause is plain,
The penitents are few. The many shun such pain.

Meaning
The number of people lacking in things is large, because those who practise penance are few while those who do not are many.

Kural Discussions
This Kural figures in the chapter 'Penance' or 'Dhavam' under the subdivision 'Ascetism' or 'Thuravaraviyal', but is not meant only for ascetics and is applicable to all of us as we see.

Medieval commentators had interpreted the word *ilar* to mean 'individuals without wealth' and the word *nhorpaar* to mean 'those who practise penance'. Therefore, the meaning of the couplet is that people without wealth are many because only a few people engage in penance, whereas a lot more abstain from it. The connection between penance and wealth is not clear. Only those who renounce desires, particularly the desire for money, do penance, and therefore, penance for the creation of wealth is contradictory. Or does it imply that if many practise penance, overall prosperity will increase?

Somehow, it does not seem correct to link wealth to penance. The word 'ilar' is derived from the word *illaamai*, denoting 'a state of wants'. 'Ilar' could, therefore, refer to deficiency of many other essentials like education, knowledge, compassion, wisdom and social status, among others. Likewise, a broader interpretation of the word *nhonbu* or penance offers more clarity. Penance essentially means striving towards a goal while relinquishing ordinary comforts and pleasures. Ascetics pursue this for spiritual enlightenment or to become one with God. Consequently, 'nhonbu' could signify this single-minded devotion to achieve a specific objective.

With these generic interpretations of the words, the meaning of this couplet becomes clear: only because individuals with single-minded dedication to their goals, observed in penance, are scarce, many individuals are wanting in so many essential aspects of life.

Tamil scholar Kalaignar M. Karunanidhi's interpretation is worth quoting here. According to him, the couplet means: 'Many are without talents only because only a few have the willpower while countless others do not have it.'[43] While his interpretation focuses on talents, it may be broadened to wants in different domains of life. With this interpretation, the couplet would mean, 'Many are found wanting in many aspects of life only because they lack the willpower and the efforts analogous to penance.'

However, many commentators are still hesitant to accept this interpretation because Thiruvalluvar has devoted another chapter to efforts. Nevertheless, he draws a distinction here, highlighting that the effort he mentions entails unwavering dedication to a task or cause, akin to the devotion seen in penance. Moreover, it seems incorrect to link penance to general or individual wealth. Hence, the latter interpretation is the most appropriate. The same message is conveyed by poet and Shaivaite ascetic Kumaragurupara Desikar in his poem 'Nheethi Nheri Vilakkam':

---

[43]Karunanidhi, Kalaignar M., *Thirukkural*, Thirumagal Nilayam, Chennai, 2017.

Pay no heed to their pain; nor fret over hunger or sleep;
Confront hurdles with resolve; time spent
Embrace with serenity; calmly bear all insults;
Those focused on pursuit of their goal.

It is only because such focused people are not many that wants are still widespread.

This couplet essentially makes an observation about the existing situation of huge needs and wants in society, while subtly emphasizing the importance of unwavering, dedicated effort, akin to penance, to eliminate them.

KEY TAKEAWAY

The persistence of substantial needs and wants in society is due to the absence of focused effort and willpower akin to penance.

28

External Appearances are Unimportant

மழித்தலும் நீட்டலும் வேண்டா, உலகம்
பழித்தது ஒழித்து விடின். (குறள் 280)

Transliteration
Mazhiththalum Nheettalum Vendaa, Ulakam
Pazhiththathu Ozhiththu Vitin.

Translation
Tonsured head or matted hair are of no avail, if
What world condemns is not shunned.

Meaning
If the evils condemned by the people of the world are eschewed, there is no need to tonsure the head or grow matted hair.

Kural Discussions
This Kural figures in the chapter 'Improper Conduct' or 'Koodaa Ozhukkam' from the 'Asceticism' or 'Thuravaraviyal' division. It is clear that Thiruvalluvar wrote it with ascetics in mind, even though the advice extends to all with deception in the heart but an external appearance of goodness. From this, it seems that even during Thiruvalluvar's period, fake godmen were cheating innocent people. If people are willing to be cheated, there will always be cheaters!

The key emphasis in this Kural is that for a saint, external appearance holds no significance; what truly matters is the abandonment of unethical values that society condemns. Typically, ascetics shave their head or grow a beard. Some choose not to shave their head but prefer to grow their hair long and braid it. They wear saffron clothes. They also wear ornaments to look majestic. Every saint has a unique style. Most of them dress to impress their followers and get more followers. This couplet says all this is totally unnecessary; shunning what the world condemns is all that is required. In other words, they should strictly follow the moral code of society, focusing on inner purity.

People are so gullible that fake saints are thriving despite many laws against them. Unfortunately, people believe in tales of their miraculous feats and flock to them. People in distress go to them for solace, making them popular and powerful. Some of them flourish because of their money power or political patronage. As a result, those who must relinquish everything indulge in all activities from business to politics. When some of them are caught by the law, we come to know of their misdeeds. We should, therefore, avoid being carried away by the appearance and sweet words of saints.

Also, the message applies to other fraudsters not in saffron clothes. There are many who, despite not wearing saffron, project an air of virtue while harbouring deceit in their hearts. We should be careful with them too. It is wise to assess everyone carefully, based on their background and values, without being fooled by their external appearance or demeanour.

The same message applies to rituals as well. What is the use of performing rituals with evil thoughts in mind or after committing wrongs? It is futile to treat rituals as a remedy for wrongdoings; rather, we should refrain from wrongdoings. Therefore, it is vital to choose the path of virtue, keeping in mind that shunning all that the world condemns is most important.

KEY TAKEAWAY

Rather than focusing on external appearance, our emphasis should be on shunning all that is disapproved by society.

29

Light of Truthfulness

எல்லா விளக்கும் விளக்கல்ல; சான்றோர்க்குப்
பொய்யா விளக்கே விளக்கு. (குறள் 299)

Transliteration
Ellaa Vilakkum Vilakkalla; Saanrorkkup
Poyyaa Vilakke Vilakku.

Translation
All lamps are not lamps in wise man's sight,
The lamp of truth alone is the lamp.

Meaning
Not all lamps that eliminate external darkness truly qualify as lamps; only the one that dispels inner darkness, namely truthfulness, deserves the name 'lamp'.

Kural Discussions
Thiruvalluvar has devoted a chapter to 'Truthfulness' or 'Vaaymai' to emphasize its importance for a virtuous life. Although it figures in the 'Asceticism' or 'Thuravaraviyal' division, it is relevant to all, particularly for ascetics. Tamil scholar Mu. Varadarajan explains that a life with truthfulness in heart, in speech and in action is an ideal life that will harm none and help everyone.

The first part of this Kural asserts that all external lamps that give light cannot be considered lamps at all. How can that be so? We are so upset when electricity trips suddenly, plunging us into darkness. We are unable to bear darkness even for a few minutes. Consider, then, a world two thousand years ago, where darkness was the norm, making external lamps even more vital. Despite this, the couplet asserts that these external lamps are insignificant.

Why does it say so? Because the only worthy lamp is the *poyyaa* lamp, the word 'poyyaa' means 'not speaking untruth'. Hence, truthfulness is the real lamp of worth. Truthfulness is the lamp that is far more important than the external lamps that have become part of our modern life.

Anything that emits light is called a lamp and removes darkness from the external surroundings. But there is always some kind of light in the external world, except on a few days. Therefore, the external world is perhaps never dark because there will be some light at all times of the day due to the sun, the moon or the stars. But our inner self lacks the advantage of any such external light and, therefore, is naturally dark.

Thus, a guiding lamp is essential for our inner realm, which is nothing but the lamp of truthfulness that dispels our inner darkness. It steers us on the right path. A lamp that helps the eyes is a device that emits light, but the lamp that guides the soul is the lamp of truthfulness.

The couplet refers to *saanror*, meaning 'wise men'. Does this mean truthfulness is necessary only for the wise and not for others? Is it because no matter how wise and learned they are, truthfulness should be their guiding principle? Or is it to stress that if truthfulness is the guiding lamp even for the learned, it is even more important for others?

Tamil scholar Kalaignar M. Karunanidhi has given a different interpretation to the word 'saanror', which helps us better appreciate the reference to the wise and the learned: 'The lamp of truth that dispels the inside darkness is the real shining lamp that elevates one to a wise person, rather than the lamps that dispel the outside darkness.'[44] This interpretation aligns with the notion that truthfulness is not solely for the wise, but rather is the very quality that distinguishes an individual as wise or learned.

---

[44]Kuralthiran, https://tinyurl.com/n2tn9jk. Accessed on 14 September 2024.

In this context, truthfulness becomes the essential attribute that elevates a person's character and wisdom. This perspective further emphasizes the intrinsic importance of truthfulness for individuals of all backgrounds, as it serves as a defining trait of wisdom and ethical conduct.

What is truthfulness? Thiruvalluvar himself has explained profoundly what it is: it means not saying something against one's conscience and not speaking harsh words. Everyone can easily understand this. But do we follow this? Unfortunately, no. Many individuals readily resort to lies for personal gain.

The State Emblem of India proclaims 'Satyamev Jayate', meaning 'Truth Alone Triumphs.' Yet the prevalence of falsehood in speech and action raises questions about our commitment to this principle. In the land of Mahatma Gandhi, who lived by truth, it is regrettable that truth or truthfulness has little place. He proclaimed that there is no greater God than Truth. Similarly, Thiruvalluvar says truth is a unique lamp guiding us. Truthfulness is necessary for an individual and society. While it strengthens society, falsehood weakens it. Therefore, let the unique lamp of truthfulness guide us.

KEY TAKEAWAY

A society that does not value truthfulness will descend into darkness. Therefore, let us cultivate the habit of consistently speaking the truth.

30

Avoid Anger

தன்னைத்தான் காக்கின் சினங்காக்க; காவாக்கால்
தன்னையே கொல்லும் சினம். (குறள் 305)

Transliteration
Thannaiththaan Kaakkin Sinangkaakka; Kaavaakkaal
Thannaiye Kollum Sinam.

Translation
To guard yourself, keep wrath at bay
Unguarded, it will kill you.

Meaning
If a person wants to protect himself, he should guard himself against anger, and if he does not do so, his anger itself will destroy him.

Kural Discussions
This Kural figures in the chapter 'Restraining Anger' or 'Vehulaamai'. Thiruvalluvar has already said in another Kural (35) that anger has no place in a virtuous life. Expanding on the same aspect, he describes the suffering it causes and the ways to guard against it in this chapter.

This Kural gives a simple warning against anger. If a person does not guard against it, it will kill him. How can anger kill? Anger within families sometimes creates enmity, which, on occasion, ends in murder. Thus, it destroys the murdered and the murderer, who lands up in jail for life. We read in newspapers about mere arguments between strangers resulting in fatalities. Similarly, road rage too leads to deaths at times. All these actions stem from uncontrolled rage, driving ordinary individuals to commit crimes on the spur of the moment. Thus, there is enough evidence to show that anger has the potential to kill.

However, most of the time, it does not go this far. But those who get angry do suffer in some ways. We cannot afford to be angry with those who are stronger or more powerful than us. Usually, we suppress anger because it can cause us much harm. Therefore, we can and do show our anger only to those who are less powerful than us. Even this is harmful. Expressing anger within the family will sour relationships, affecting happiness. It can spoil the relationship between spouses, making life miserable. Likewise, we could lose friendships due to anger. If we get angry in the office, work will suffer.

American essayist, lecturer, philosopher, abolitionist and poet Ralph Waldo Emerson said, 'For every minute you remain angry, you lose sixty seconds of happiness.' Anger can also have detrimental effects on one's health, contributing to issues like elevated blood pressure and even depression. The harmful effects of anger on health are well documented. Thus, anger affects not only relationships and friendships but also health. Considering all these negative impacts of anger, we should take Thiruvalluvar's advice seriously and control our anger whenever it raises its ugly head. Thankfully, many books and courses on anger management are now available for us to guard against this evil. 'When angry, count to ten before you speak; if very angry, a hundred,' said Thomas Jefferson, American statesman and Founding Father. Modern psychologists approve of the prescription of counting to ten, adding that it will be better still to take a deep breath between each number.

Some may wonder how it is possible to completely eliminate anger as it is a normal human emotion. Psychologists say that anger is a natural human trait and is even justified on occasion. Thiruvalluvar himself has justified it under certain circumstances in another couplet, but he is definitely against excessive anger that is destructive.

Indeed, anger can be justified under certain circumstances. Instances involving the neglect of public duties that result in significant harm to society, or repeated mistakes that inflict harm, are situations that can justify anger. Although justified, anger should be within limits—this controlled form of anger is referred to as indignation. Indignation serves the purpose of addressing and rectifying the situation, while also providing an outlet for the internal tension that arises due to negligence. Yet, it is essential to draw a clear line between justified indignation and anger that can be harmful and destructive.

We somehow manage to control our anger when it comes to our superiors or those in positions of authority. Can we not show the same restraint towards our relatives and friends in order to maintain a harmonious relationship? The advice is: it is ideal to lead a life without anger but to eliminate destructive anger is a priority.

KEY TAKEAWAY

Avoid anger for cordial relationships and a healthy life.

31

Punishment for Wrongdoers

இன்னாசெய் தாரை ஒறுத்தல், அவர்நாண
நன்னயம் செய்து விடல். (குறள் 314)

Transliteration
Innaasey Thaarai Oruththal, Avarnhaana
Nhannayam Seythu Vidal.

Translation
The punishment for those who have done great harm,
Is to shame them with good deeds.

Meaning
The best punishment for a wrongdoer is to do some good to him so as to put him to shame, and then forget the good we did to him and also the wrong committed by him.

Kural Discussions
This Kural figures in the chapter 'Not Doing Harm' or 'Innaa Seyyaamai', which advises us on how an ethical life includes not causing any harm to others. This Kural is a well-known, oft-repeated couplet, easy to understand but difficult to follow. When someone causes us some harm or wrongs us, we feel upset and angry and want to retaliate. We are not at peace unless we find ways to do that. It is a natural human tendency. If the wrongdoer is known to us, our urge to retaliate is even greater.

This couplet recognizes this urge and advises us to punish the wrongdoer. The punishment, however, is not seeking revenge but doing a great good to the wrongdoer so as to make him feel ashamed of the wrong he committed. One could easily appreciate the benefit of this kind of punishment. His shame will, in due course, change his attitude towards us. He will become extra kind and will never think of harming us again. We will also be at peace with this benevolent punishment in which our wrongdoer is won over. Even sworn enemies can become friends.

After doing great good, the couplet uses the term 'vidal', which means 'leave'. Tamil scholar and commentator Parimelazhagar has given an excellent explanation for this. He says that the word implies forgetting the wrong done to us and the good done by us. Even the thought that he did something wrong and we did him a great good should not arise. Only then will there be a real improvement in the relationship between the two. Doing good in return for wrong itself is difficult, but to forget everything is even more difficult. However, it is obvious that it is the right way to proceed.

This couplet echoes Christ's Sermon of the Mount: 'If someone strikes you on one cheek, show him the other cheek.' This teaching inspired the famous Russian writer Leo Tolstoy to develop the concept of non-violent resistance against cruelty, which he elaborated on in his book *The Kingdom of God Is Within You* (1894). This work subsequently influenced Mahatma Gandhi's philosophy of non-violent resistance, which has evolved into a powerful political tool.

But Thiruvalluvar's advice has nothing to do with politics and is meant for an individual in order to lead an ethical life. His advice to respond to harm with good and then simply forget everything is timeless wisdom. Some of us may wonder whether this is possible. It is certainly doable with some practice. Do some good (not great good) to anyone who has harmed you and observe the positive change in his attitude. You will then be convinced that this is the right thing to do.

Is it possible to practise this advice with everyone? Will it always yield transformative behaviour in the other person? These are justified reservations. Those with good values will certainly change positively. But others may not. Even in such cases, it is better to proceed without expectations—after all, the intention is to let go and forget everything. If you follow this advice at least within the circle of your relatives and friends, relationships and friendships will deepen, leading to greater happiness.

KEY TAKEAWAY

The most fitting punishment for a wrongdoer is to do him good, thereby causing in him a sense of shame, which in turn will improve relationships and happiness.

32

Impermanence of Wealth

கூத்தாட்டு அவைக்குழாத்து அற்றே பெருஞ்செல்வம்
போக்கும் அதுவிளிந் தற்று. (குறள் 332)

Transliteration
Koothaattu Avaikkuzhaaththu Arre Perugnselvam
Pokkum Athuvilinh Tharru.

Translation
Wealth is just like the gathering of a theatre crowd;
Slowly comes but quickly disperses.

Meaning
Wealth accumulates slowly like the crowd that gathers in a theatre, but disappears quickly like the same crowd dispersing at the end of the show.

Kural Discussions
Thiruvalluvar has devoted a separate chapter to 'Impermanence' or 'Nhilaiyaamai' to highlight the transient nature of all things in this world. Youth, wealth, position, and fame are all fleeting. Yet, we live as if everything is lasting and permanent. Realizing the ephemeral nature of things in life is critical for ethical living; hence this chapter.

This Kural highlights the impermanence of material possessions using a vivid simile. Wealth is like the crowd gathering in a theatre. People go to the theatre for entertainment, where they gather slowly. If the show is at 6.00 p.m., people start gathering from 5.00 p.m. onwards but more rapidly near the start of the show, filling the hall. Wealth also accumulates like this, slowly at first but rapidly after some time. As a familiar saying goes, 'It is the first million that is difficult to make.'

Wealth also dissipates quickly, like the crowd after the show. The crowd that took more than an hour to gather and fill the hall disperses just minutes after the show, emptying the hall. Similarly, the wealth that took time to accumulate can vanish quickly. The impermanence of wealth is thus explained through an easy-to-understand metaphor so that all of us can remember it. However, we behave as though it will be everlasting, despite our seeing and hearing of wealth vanishing rapidly for many wealthy individuals.

The words used in the couplet could also refer to the actors in a play. They dress up and act like the characters they represent, but after the play is over, these characters simply vanish. All characters are impermanent. Some commentators have, therefore, compared wealth to the impermanent characters in a play. Whatever may be the interpretation, the message is that wealth is temporary.

Expanding on this couplet's significance, Tamil scholar K.A.P. Viswanatham says, 'Never assume that wealth will endure eternally. Recognize its impermanence. And, therefore, spend it on charity or give it to good causes. That is good for you.'[45]

The Buddha has preached that the desire for money could only increase our suffering. A wise man said, 'Your real wealth is not the money you have, but it is the respect you have after all is gone.' Despite such counsel, we often disregard this wisdom, both from Thiruvalluvar and other sages, and cling to material wealth. We should remember the simple simile of this couplet and reduce our attachment to wealth by giving away to good causes, for our fulfilment and happiness.

---

[45]Viswanatham, K.A.P., *Thirukkural Puthai Porul*, Paari Nilayam, Chennai, 1990.

KEY TAKEAWAY

Wealth is impermanent; only good deeds and character are permanent. Therefore, nurture them.

33

Impermanence of Life

நெருநல் உளனொருவன் இன்றில்லை என்னும்
பெருமை உடைத்திவ் வுலகு. (குறள் 336)

Transliteration
Nherunal Ulanoruvan Inrillai Ennum
Perumai Udaithiv Vulahu.

Translation
That one was alive yesterday, but not today,
Is a marvel of the world's way!

Meaning
This world's marvel is that one who was present yesterday is not there today (or has died).

Kural Discussions
This is another Kural in the same chapter 'Impermanence' or 'Nhilaiyaamai' that highlights the transient nature of life, whereas the previous one talks about the fleeting nature of wealth.

Many times, we have known of people we were talking to yesterday who are gone permanently from the world today. We also see friends and relatives passing away suddenly without any forewarning of illness. Even in cases where someone is undergoing treatment for an ailment, we are always optimistic that they will recover, without thinking of the possibility of their passing. When such unfortunate events occur, shock and distress envelop us profoundly.

Even when we hear the news of the death of leaders, we are shocked that a leader who was all-powerful yesterday is no more today. Having seen all these in life, we know well that life is temporary. All of us are, therefore, aware that men are mortal. That is the message of this Kural. Thus, it reemphasizes this well-known truth only to enable us to fully absorb it and lead the life of virtue that *Thirukkural* enunciates.

This impermanence is called a marvel of the world, or 'perumai'. How can it be so? Can death that brings so much grief to so many be considered a marvel? A moment's reflection makes the sense apparent. Imagine the consequences if all those who are born were to live forever. The earth would become unsustainable and eventually face destruction. Even with mortality, population explosion has been a matter of concern. Therefore, death is the law of nature. Hence it is called pride—impermanence is the pride or marvel.

Do we lead our life conscious of the impermanence of life? The answer, perhaps, is no. When someone known to us leaves the world, we are reminded of it for a fleeting moment, but the next moment, we revert to living as if permanence is assured. We avoid doing what needs to be done; we do things we should not; we indulge in many fruitless activities; we give in to petty pleasures; we ignore values and ethics. In view of this aspect of human nature, Thiruvalluvar has in this couplet reminded us of the fleeting nature of life to guide us to a meaningful life.

I am reminded of the renowned Quaker missionary Stephen Grellet's memorable lines on how to live a life: 'I expect to pass through this world but once. Any good, therefore, that I can do, or any kindness that I can show to any fellow creature, let me do it now. Let me not defer or neglect it, for I shall not pass this way again.'

This effectively captures Thiruvalluvar's teachings on virtuous living and the impermanence of life. The explanation of scholar Mu. Varadarajan offers deep insight into the meaning of this couplet: 'If you are aware of the nature of the world, particularly the impermanence of body, life, and wealth, our mind will then be free from distress or disturbance when faced with separation or changes. However, acknowledging impermanence of life should not evoke fear of life or a desire to flee from it. It is only to appreciate its true nature and lead a meaningful life with determination and courage.[46] Let us keep this in mind and face the vicissitudes of life with fortitude.

KEY TAKEAWAY

Appreciating the fleeting nature of life, let us walk the virtuous path laid by Thiruvalluvar.

---

[46]Ramalingam, Namkkal Kavignar, *Thirukkural*, T.D.V. Publishers, Chennai, 2021.

34

Reduce Attachments

யாதனின் யாதனின் நீங்கியான், நோதல்
அதனின் அதனின் இலன். (குறள் 341)

Transliteration
Yaathanin Yaathanin Nheengkiyaan, Nhothal
Athanin Athanin Ilan.

Translation
From whatever from whatever a man gets free,
From that whatever his griefs flee.

Meaning
If a person leaves his attachment to a person or an object or, for that matter, anything, he will be free from the sufferings that attachment brings him.

Kural Discussions
This Kural appears in the chapter 'Renunciation' or 'Thuravu', which highlights life's fundamental truth that all sufferings arise from attachments. Since renouncing all attachments is difficult, this couplet does not advocate it but merely says that one will be free from the sufferings of those attachments or desires that one renounces. The message is: reduce your attachments to reduce sufferings, particularly those arising out of them. The couplet thus makes a simple statement of fact, perhaps well-known but often overlooked, without offering any advice to reduce desires. That decision is simply left to the individual.

The truth of this is easily observable in our daily life. An excessive attachment to food causes obesity with its attended sufferings, which can be alleviated by curbing the craving for food. Those with diabetes suffer owing to their craving for sweets. Attachment to money or wealth brings many woes, affecting the physical and mental well-being of those entrapped by it. Besides these, there are many other attachments like those to religion, caste, region and language, which bring their associated grief. Even though we often recognize this correlation between desires and suffering, we often fail to reduce our desires or even attempt to do so. Sometimes attachment turns into addiction. Instead of us controlling desire, desire starts controlling us.

The Buddha preached that desire is the root cause for human suffering and, therefore, advised sentient beings to eliminate all desires. Thiruvalluvar's advice, however, is different. He has made a factual observation that the more one gets away from desires, the less will be the suffering. Thiruvalluvar does not advocate renouncing all desires outright. Instead, he leaves the decision on which attachments to relinquish to the individual. Perhaps he wants every individual to evaluate his sufferings and then address those that cause maximum pain. As it is difficult for us to renounce all desires, this pragmatic approach offers us a simpler way to handle our woes.

This couplet, though placed within the 'Asceticism' or 'Thuravaraviyal' subdivision, is relevant to everyone, not just ascetics. Human tendency, however, is not to diminish desires and attachments, but to keep adding to them, one bringing another with it. To counter this tendency, it is imperative to lessen this load of desires, thus rendering our life journey lighter, smoother and, consequently, happier. Ultimately, the choice rests with us. We should make the right choice, keeping in mind this brilliant piece of advice from Thiruvalluvar.

KEY TAKEAWAY

Gradually diminish desires and attachments, one by one, liberating yourself from the suffering they inevitably bring.

35

Finding the Truth

எப்பொருள் எத்தன்மைத் தாயினும், அப்பொருள்
மெய்ப்பொருள் காண்பது அறிவு. (*குறள் 355*)

Transliteration
Epporul Eththanmaith Thaayinum, Apporul
Meipporul Kaanpathu Arivu.

Translation
Whatever thing, of whatsoever kind it be,
True wisdom is to see its reality.

Meaning
Regardless of the nature or outward appearance of anything or any object, it is wise to investigate and find out its true essence without being taken in by its superficial nature or appearance.

Kural Discussions
This Kural figures in the chapter 'Finding the Truth' or 'Meyyunarthal', in which Thiruvalluvar emphasizes the need to find the truth of everything without accepting anything at face value. In our daily lives, we witness cycles of birth and death, as well as numerous ongoing changes. These experiences provoke contemplation about many things, including the meaning of existence. This chapter encourages us to delve into these matters and unravel the underlying truth.

Scholar Mu. Varadarajan explains the purpose of seeking truth this way: 'An individual, who wants to take a walk in a town with eyes blindfolded, will perceive obstructions where there are none;

but where there are, he will fall and suffer. In the same way, as long as there is ignorance and false knowledge about life, we imagine non-existent suffering, causing us much anxiety and fear. A good worry-free and fearless life, therefore, requires real wisdom and knowledge to drive away false knowledge.'[47]

This couplet asserts that real wisdom is to find out the true essence of everything, regardless of its apparent nature or outward appearance. One should not go by appearance alone but should possess the curiosity to question and analyse to uncover the truth about everything. This is the fundamental principle enunciated by many eminent philosophers for acquiring knowledge. It is a matter of great pride that Thiruvalluvar has advocated a questioning mind as the cornerstone of true wisdom.

Many commentators have interpreted the word *porul* to mean 'an object or matter'. Let us examine whether this is correct. In the Tamil lexicon, 'porul' assumes nine distinct meanings, of which two—'subject' and 'matter/object'—are particularly pertinent to this couplet. Furthermore, Thiruvalluvar has used the same word in Kural 423 in the sense of information, which advises that whatever information you hear from whomsoever, you should not accept it without verification. It can, therefore, be inferred that the term 'porul' in this couplet encompasses the meanings 'object', 'information', and 'subject'. Thus, the couplet's advice is that real wisdom is to question the nature of an object, the accuracy of information, or the essence of a subject.

By adopting this comprehensive interpretation of 'porul', a wide array of subjects, ranging from science and theology to politics and medicine, can be covered. The quintessence of this couplet lies in uncovering the fundamental truths that underlie every subject and matter, without assumptions based on their apparent exteriors. The directive is clear: question, scrutinize and unveil the authentic reality that resides beyond superficial

---

[47]Ramalingam, Namkkal Kavignar, *Thirukkural*, T.D.V. Publishers, Chennai, 2021.

impressions. This principle extends across a multitude of fields, and the significance of persistent inquiry and thorough investigation has been emphasized. Medieval commentator Parimelazhagar aptly explains that wisdom, as enunciated in this couplet, is 'to find out the permanent truth of all "porul" after discounting the imaginations of the people of the world.'[48] People may say many things based on their imagination, but wisdom demands distilling the truth of any subject or matter.

The history of scientific evolution presents a compelling example of the significance of questioning accepted beliefs. For centuries, it was believed that the sun and other planets orbited the Earth, for that was what the Bible said, as did the great Alexandrian astronomer Ptolemy. In the early 1500s, Polish mathematician Copernicus unveiled an alternative hypothesis, which asserted that all celestial bodies, including Earth, circumnavigated the sun. Since this contradicted the Western religious doctrine, he was charged with heresy, but before the inquiry was over, he died. However, his book was proscribed. Thus, his attempt to find the truth was curbed since he questioned a dominant belief of his time.

A century later, Florentine astronomer Galileo reiterated this theory with evidence collected through extensive observations of the solar system. He thus took great pains to find out the truth as enunciated by this couplet. He was also charged with heresy for defying the conventional wisdom and imprisoned. An inquisition was held against him in 1633. He was released from prison on his giving an undertaking not to discuss the matter further. But he remained under house arrest till his death. These two great scientists discovered the truth of the solar system, defying the accepted beliefs of the time. This groundbreaking discovery was the basis for many later discoveries and rapid scientific progress. Today, Galileo is widely acknowledged as the father of science.

Similarly, in India, too, many baseless claims are made. For example, it was asserted that airplanes existed in our mythological

---

[48]Pappaiah, Solomon, *Thirukkural*, Kavitha Publishers, Chennai, 2018.

past and also that plastic surgeries were performed then. As per this couplet, we should subject such statements to thorough scrutiny without simply accepting them; that is true wisdom.

After the fall of the Western Roman Empire, there was a period of about a thousand years marked by economic, intellectual and cultural decline. Then came the Renaissance, spearheaded by the famous British philosopher Francis Bacon (1561-1626), laying the foundation for the scientific method of finding out truth. This approach, still used by scientists around the world, eventually led to rational thinking, and the skill to draw the right conclusion from logic and data, leading to subsequent breakthroughs.

Thiruvalluvar's emphasis on rational thinking two millennia ago remains a source of pride and joy. For him, genuine wisdom involves questioning rather than passively accepting the world's assumptions. If our youth imbibe this concept of rational thinking, without taking things at face value, it will pave the way for innovative discoveries and scientific advancements in our nation, fostering growth and progress.

KEY TAKEAWAY

True wisdom lies in analyzing and uncovering the truth in any subject. To achieve this, a questioning and inquisitive mind should be cultivated.

36

Reducing Desires

வேண்டாமை அன்ன விழுச்செல்வம் ஈண்டில்லை;
யாண்டும் அஃதொப்பது இல். (குறள் 363)

Transliteration
Vendaamai Anna Vizhusselvam Iindillai;
Yaandum Ahthoppathu Il.

Translation
No other greater fortune is here or there
Than the fortune of having no desire.

Meaning
There is no greater fortune in this world than the desireless state; nowhere else is there such a fortune.

Kural Discussions
This Kural figures in the chapter 'Curbing Desires' or 'Avaa Aruththal', which talks of the elimination of desires and is essentially meant for saints. Since they have chosen the path of renunciation, they should strive to attain a desireless state to achieve enlightenment. However, there are valuable lessons for others too, which we will discuss.

This couplet talks about eliminating one's wants and desires. It just makes a statement that a desireless state is a great fortune for an individual, and again reiterates that it is a greater fortune than anything else in this world. To re-emphasize its importance, it again states that this is so anywhere else, referring to any place beyond the world. Simply put, a desireless state is a great fortune in our world and in any other world.

Man is born with desires. These desires serve as the driving force for personal growth and development. Without desires, man has no urge to improve. He works hard to gain position and status so as to live happily. A desireless state offers him little incentive to aim for anything. The desire for fame, name, money, happiness and well-being is the wheel moving the world. Therefore, desire is the driving force behind human progress.

Why, then, does this couplet extol the value of a desireless state? It clearly applies to monks because they have renounced worldly pleasures. Hence, the desireless state is their aim, and achieving it is certainly a fortune for them. Similarly, this concept holds relevance for the elderly, who, having fulfilled their life's responsibilities, can aim for a desireless state to attain tranquillity in their twilight years. In Hinduism, the final stage of life is that of a *sannyasin*, which aligns with this notion of seeking total detachment. Hence, it can be deduced that this Kural primarily pertains to monks and those in the final stage of their life journey.

What, then, is the lesson for others, whose driving force is the desire to improve? For them, the desireless state could refer to abstaining from greed, improper desire, evil desire, unworthy desire, etc. Greed is the seed of evil deeds and bad character. It is one of three poisons, the other two being ignorance and hatred, which are the causes of our sufferings, says the Buddha. Therefore, living without evil desires is essential for good health and happiness.

As we saw earlier, desire propels human progress, and it is impossible for ordinary people to live without it. Therefore, let us interpret the desires mentioned in this couplet as inappropriate and evil desires insofar as they apply to the common man. A life of the desireless state is the domain of saints and the elderly.

KEY TAKEAWAY

Let us get rid of evil desires and greed to lead a happy life.

37

Power of Fate

ஊழிற் பெருவலி யாவுள? மற்றொன்று
சூழினுந் தான்முந் துறும். (குறள் 380)

Transliteration
Oozhir Peruvali Yaavula? Marronru
Soozhinunh Thaanmunh Thurum.

Translation
What is stronger than destiny?
It will be a step ahead of us.

Meaning
What force is mightier than destiny? Regardless of our attempts to sidestep or elude its consequences through various methods, fate stays one step ahead of us.

Kural Discussions
Fate is something we are all familiar with. We call it by different names—destiny, divine will, nature, chance, etc. Frequently, events unfold in ways we struggle to comprehend. We anticipate a specific outcome, but what happens is something entirely different. This common experience is what we call fate. Some consider it the result of one's karma, the consequences of the deeds done in the past birth. Those who do not believe in karma view it as a law of nature. Without going into the root cause of fate, Thiruvalluvar has explained its immense power and its invisible influence over our lives. Although we experience it in our day-to-day lives, we fail to fully grasp the extent of its power

and struggle to reconcile ourselves to it.

Hence, Thiruvalluvar has devoted a chapter to 'Fate' or 'Oozh' in a separate subdivision under the same name—this subdivision has only this chapter. Some commentators are of the view that fate applies solely to matters of wealth and love, not to virtuous conduct, and therefore this chapter has been kept as the last in the 'Virtue' division—we cannot blame fate for our unethical conduct.

This Kural highlights the power of fate. It categorically says that no force is more powerful than fate and that even if you try to do something to change its course, it will always remain a step ahead. Thus, the message of the couplet is simple: beware of the power of fate. An implied message is that fate is difficult to overcome. In light of this perspective, a question might arise: What is the significance of effort and diligence, if everything is governed by fate? Can we then leave things to the hand of fate and relax? Let us examine this.

Destiny's play is beyond our comprehension and prediction. Accepting unexpected events as divine intervention, we move on. For instance, when a candidate fails to clear a competitive examination after exceptional preparation and hard work, he ascribes it to fate. On the contrary, those who are successful attribute it to their own intelligence and hard work, with only a few acknowledging the role of luck. Of two individuals who studied the same course, one ends up in a successful career and the other struggles to get a job. Fate is blamed for the misfortune of the latter. It appears that we readily attribute misfortunes to destiny, more or less accepting that fate is all-powerful.

Is that so? A careful reading of the couplet reveals a subtler message. It says that fate will be ahead of whatever we do, but not that it will win. It appears as though there is a continuous race between human effort and destiny in which the latter is ahead. But the final victory for fate has not been declared. If fate were to be the winner, human effort and motivation have no place. Individuals can remain idle and leave things to fate.

This could not have been Thiruvalluvar's thinking, who has

devoted a separate chapter to human effort. Kurals 619 and 620 throw a better light on his thinking about fate. In Kural 619, he says that effort can overturn even divine will, and in 620, he asserts that those who are committed can win over fate. Therefore, this couplet should not be seen as a surrender to fate's supremacy, but rather a reminder of the intricate interplay between human action and destiny.

Indeed, Thiruvalluvar's message is a nuanced one. While fate might initially seem overwhelming, his intention is not to advocate passivity or idleness. Instead, he proposes that attributing failures to fate can serve as a psychological strategy for managing setbacks, allowing us to confront life's trials with resilience. However, he does not endorse complacency. He does not imply that we should simply watch life unfold. Rather, he underscores the importance of sincere effort, commitment and resolve in shaping our destinies.

Thiruvalluvar's perspective on fate is not that of an inflexible force that dictates every outcome, but rather a factor that interacts with our actions and willpower. By recognizing its presence, we can handle life's uncertainties and challenges with equanimity, all the while actively pursuing our aspirations. This balanced approach combines an acknowledgement of fate's influence with the empowerment derived from individual exertion.

KEY TAKEAWAY

Fate is very strong, but that should not deter us from making efforts to succeed in any task. If we do not succeed even after serious efforts, let us reconcile to the power of fate.

Bibliography

Anbu, V. Irai, *Ancient Yet Modern Management Concepts in Thirukkural,* Allied Publishers Pvt. Ltd., Chennai, 2011.

Gardner, John W., *Excellence,* W.W. Norton & Co Ltd, 1995.

H., Eric, Phillip Rouse, and W.H.D. Rouse Warmington, *Great Dialogues of Plato (A Mentor Classic),* New American Library, 1956.

Hippocrates, 'Of the Epidemics', *The Internet Classics Archive,* https://tinyurl.com/mvcu4cm4. Accessed on 16 September 2024.

Jagannathan, Ki.Va., *Karpaha Malar,* Amutha Nilayam, Chennai, 2012.

Kalyanasundaram, Thiru. V., *Thirukkural Virivurai,* Poompuhar Publishers, Chennai, 1951.

Karunanidhi, Kalaignar M., *Kurlovium,* Bharathi Pathippagam, Chennai, 2010.

Karunanidhi, Kalaignar M., *Thirukkural,* Thirumagal Nilayam, Chennai, 2017.

Kuralthiran, https://tinyurl.com/n2tn9jk. Accessed on 14 September 2024.

Maavalan, A.A., Ed., *Essays and Tributes on Tirukkural (1886-1986 AD),* International Institute of Tamil Studies, Chennai, 2009.

Mankkudavar, *Thirukkural Moolamum Uraiyum,* Poompuhar Publishers, Chennai, 2015.

Munusamy, V., *Thirukkural Athikaara Vilakkam,* Vanathi Publishers, Chennai, 2021.

Pappaiah, Solomon, *Thirukkural,* Kavitha Publishers, Chennai, 2018.

Parimelazhagar, *Thirukkural Moolamum Uraiyum,* Aruna Publishers, Chennai, 2016.

Pillai, K. Kothandapani, et al., *The Sornammal Endowment Lectures,* Madras University, 1967.

Pillai, M.S. Purnalingam, *Critical Studies in Kural,* Asian Educational Services, New Delhi, 2004.

Ramalingam, Namkkal Kavignar, *Thirukkural,* T.D.V. Publishers, Chennai, 2021.

Sundaramurthy, E., *Kuralmutham,* Tamil Valarchi Iyakkaham, Chennai, 2000.

Swamy, V.C. Kulandai, *The Immortal Kural*, The International *Thirukkural* Conference, USA, 2005.

'Thirukkural Study Group', *Auroville Today*, September 2023, https://tinyurl.com/29at9rsj. Accessed 14 September 2024.

Varadarajan, Mu., *Thirukkural Thelivurai*, Paari Nilayam, Chennai, 2019.

Varadarajan, Mu., *Thiruvallvar Allathu Vaazhkai Vilakkam*, Paari Nilayam, Chennai, 2019.

Vasudevan, M., *Thirukkural*, e-book, 2015.

Viswanatham, K.A.P., *Thirukkural Katturaikal*, Pusthak Digital Media, n.d.

Viswanatham, K.A.P., *Thirukkural Puthai Porul*, Paari Nilayam, Chennai, 1990.

Translations of *Thirukkural*

Aiyar, V.V.S., *Thirukkural*, Mullai Publishers, Chennai, 2010.

Gandhi, Gopalkrishna, *The Tirukkural*, Aleph Book Company, New Delhi, 2015.

Narayanasamy, J., *Thirukkural*, Sura Books (Pvt) Ltd., Chennai, 2004.

Pillai, M.S. Purnalingam, *Thirukkural*, International Institute of Tamil Studies, Chennai, 2007.

Pope, G.U., W.H. Drew, and John Lazarus, *Thirukkural: English Translation and Commentary*, Gangai Puthaka Nilayam, Chennai, 2017.

Rajaram, M., *Thirukkural*, Rupa Publications, New Delhi, 2009.

www.ingramcontent.com/pod-product-compliance
Lightning Source LLC
Chambersburg PA
CBHW031755220426
43662CB00007B/414